MARY F. CLEUGH ON TEACHING CHILDREN WITH LEARNING DIFFERENCES

Volume 3

TEACHING THE 'SLOW' LEARNER IN THE SECONDARY SCHOOL

TEACHING THE 'SLOW' LEARNER IN THE SECONDARY SCHOOL

Edited by
M. F. CLEUGH

LONDON AND NEW YORK

First published in 1961 by Methuen & Co. Ltd.

This edition first published in 2021
by Routledge
4 Park Square, Milton Park, Abingdon, Oxon OX14 4RN
605 Third Avenue, New York, NY 10017

Routledge is an imprint of the Taylor & Francis Group, an informa business

© 1961 by Taylor & Francis.

This book is a re-issue originally published in 1961. The language used is a reflection of its era and no offence is meant by the Publishers to any reader by this re-publication.

All rights reserved. No part of this book may be reprinted or reproduced or utilised in any form or by any electronic, mechanical, or other means, now known or hereafter invented, including photocopying and recording, or in any information storage or retrieval system, without permission in writing from the publishers.

Trademark notice: Product or corporate names may be trademarks or registered trademarks, and are used only for identification and explanation without intent to infringe.

British Library Cataloguing in Publication Data
A catalogue record for this book is available from the British Library

ISBN: 978-1-03-200270-5 (Set)
ISBN: 978-1-00-317552-0 (Set) (ebk)
ISBN: 978-1-03-200471-6 (Volume 3) (hbk)
ISBN: 978-1-03-200473-0 (Volume 3) (pbk)
ISBN: 978-1-00-317430-1 (Volume 3) (ebk)

Publisher's Note
The publisher has gone to great lengths to ensure the quality of this reprint but points out that some imperfections in the original copies may be apparent.

Disclaimer
The publisher has made every effort to trace copyright holders and would welcome correspondence from those they have been unable to trace.

Teaching the Slow Learner
in the Secondary School

EDITED BY

M. F. CLEUGH

*Senior Lecturer, University of London
Institute of Education*

LONDON
METHUEN & CO LTD
36 ESSEX STREET · WC 2

First published 1961
© *1961 Methuen & Co Ltd*
Printed in Great Britain
by The Camelot Press Ltd
London & Southampton
Cat. No. 2/6380/10

CONTENTS

I	SOCIAL, MORAL AND RELIGIOUS EDUCATION. Mary K. Fleming	*page* 1
II	PHYSICAL EDUCATION AND HEALTH. E. A. Say	11
III	SPEECH AND ORAL WORK. L. H. Lyon	27
IV	READING AND ENGLISH. Josephine Stopa	33
V	ARITHMETIC. M. E. Richards	60
VI	ART. Joyce Myers	83
VII	MUSIC. William Brien	104
VIII	DRAMA. C. G. Golding	126
IX	HANDICRAFTS. R. E. Beinder	131
X	HOUSECRAFT. Hilary Devereux	143
XI	ENVIRONMENTAL STUDIES. W. C. Beagley	166
XII	SCHOOL JOURNEYS. E. G. W. Sterry	192
XIII	THE KEEPING OF RECORDS. Minna Smith	207
XIV	BACKWARD LADS IN APPROVED SCHOOLS. Ralph S. Taylor	214
XV	TEACHING BACKWARD ADULTS. D. H. J. Phillips	230
XVI	A UNIFIED CURRICULUM. J. M. Cooper	250
	INDEX	267

PREFACE

This is the third volume of a series written by experienced teachers holding the E.S.N. Diploma of London University, and the planning follows the same broad lines as in previous volumes, thus facilitating cross-reference. Those who are interested in the teaching of one particular subject may find it helpful to consult also corresponding chapters in the Primary School or Special School books. More importantly, it is hoped that specialist subject teachers will be tempted to read other chapters in this book than that which deals with 'their' subject, for there is a growing opinion, to which it is hoped this book will give impetus, that rigid specialist divisions are unsuitable for slow children. In the final chapter, the suitability of organizational patterns is discussed, but previously a picture of 'a unified curriculum' in action has been given in the Approved School chapter. Teachers in secondary modern and comprehensive schools may find much of interest in this account, widely different though the conditions are. In view of wide-spread concern about illiteracy in adults, a chapter on this has been included, though on a strict interpretation of the title it might seem to fall outside the scope of this book.

The opinions expressed in the chapters are those of the writers and are not to be taken as the official policy of any Authority which employs them.

Acknowledgments are made in the first volume of this work and will not be repeated here, but mention must be made of Mr M. Peterson, who undertook the arduous task of providing an index.

M. F. C.

Chapter I

SOCIAL, MORAL AND RELIGIOUS EDUCATION

'The aim of all education is to enable men and women to lead fuller, happier lives, in adjustment with their changing environment.'

That quotation from UNESCO's 'Fundamental Education' seems as good a definition as can be made of the aim of education, indicating as it does the two-sided aspect of living – the individual and the social. In order to lead our lives 'fully and happily' we need the encouragement and opportunity to develop the gifts that are within ourselves, and we need the friendship and companionship of others, to enable us to take our full share in the society in which we live. Few of us are so gifted naturally that we are completely self-sufficient and, the more limited our personal resources, the more we need others for our happiness. Indeed, since man is by nature gregarious, even really gifted people seem to find greater delight in the love and companionship of friends than they do in the exercise of their own talents.

Dull children have few talents to help them lead 'full' lives. The idea of everyone being naturally endowed with some gift is not borne out by the experience of those who work with the dull. Dull children are backward in everything. They might be better at manual skills than they are at academic subjects, but their ability is relative. They are still not as good as bright children. No skill comes easily, imagination is often limited, so backward children are more dependent on the friendship and acceptance of others than are the intelligent. To be accepted by the group in which we live and move is a fundamental human need, but we are accepted only in so far as our behaviour is acceptable. Intelligent children will adjust their behaviour as they see they are accepted or rejected as a result of it. Dull children often cannot reason why they are unacceptable, and find it difficult to adapt their behaviour anyway. Quite often they come from homes where the normal pattern of behaviour is well below the acceptable standard. They are doubly handicapped; they have little social training so have not acceptable social habits; they have little intelligence so will find learning to adapt their behaviour difficult, even if they realize the need for adapting it. So deep is the need for acceptance, however, that even the dullest will try hard for it, except those too timid to do so.

Most of them will seek for notice and acceptance. They might try the simple method of buying friendship by sharing their money and sweets. The joy of popularity won by this method has driven many children to steal. Sometimes they try to win admiration by flouting authority. Rudeness and open defiance often arouse a degree of admiration in class companions, and the inevitable punishment is often an added thrill. Lack of intelligence can bring resentment against authority and an attitude of defiance to it that might well last beyond school days and be transferred to all authority, including – and possibly especially – the police, symbol of authority in the adult world. Sometimes these children find a place with younger ones and, because of their age and size, become leaders of nuisance gangs which can and do land in the juvenile courts.

Not all dull and backward children are potential delinquents, but it is an accepted fact that many delinquents are dull and backward. Dullness, then, would seem to be a social and moral problem at least as much as, and probably more so than an academic one.

The teacher of any group of backward children is usually well aware of his or her special responsibility. This responsibility is greater, or rather more obvious, as the children get older. The infant and junior school teachers pass the children on, knowing there is still a period of training before they leave school. The teacher in the secondary school has no such consoling thought. He or she knows these children must soon leave the protecting atmosphere of school, to enter the often frightening atmosphere of the adult world. School is a place where children are all important. Everything done there is done with the children in mind. Some adult is always at hand to help, advise or take over. Children leave this atmosphere, specially conditioned for them, to enter one where they are quite unimportant,

SOCIAL, MORAL AND RELIGIOUS EDUCATION

and often nobody's responsibility. They are themselves responsible in the office, shop or factory for a job, and the help which until now they have accepted as their right is not forthcoming. Even intelligent children often find adjustment difficult; how much more so must the dull? It is then that their behaviour, their attitude to others, including those in authority, and their attitude to the job, will decide whether they will be accepted and therefore content.

A few years ago the famous Hawthorne investigation considered the causes of frequent changes in jobs among young people.[1] The chief cause was not a dislike of the job nor the inability to cope with it; it was the inability to 'get on' with workmates. This inability in extreme cases can cause youngsters to become drifters, wasters and social misfits. It would seem, then, that social adequacy and acceptance should be a more important aim than academic attainment for the teacher of dull children.

Social adequacy is dependent on behaviour, and behaviour surely is dependent on respect; self-respect, respect for companions, respect for authority and respect for the job, and the particular aim of the teacher in the secondary school, mindful of the adult future of these children, should be the building up of respect in all its aspects.

In such training the attitude of the class teacher is all important, and a large proportion of class teaching is desirable for the dull, even in a school where there is much specialist teaching. Miss Cooper will deal with this fully later, so here I will only say that dull children find it difficult to adapt themselves and need the feeling of security that 'belonging' to one teacher will give them. They need to be with a teacher, too, who is concerned with the child rather than the subject – one who can maintain a 'climate' where anti-social behaviour does not occur. It is also desirable that the classes should be small in number. In a small group an informal atmosphere is possible. It is easier to talk in a group of twenty than of forty, even for adults. Individual observation is possible in a small group, and a teacher must see these children as individuals if he or she is to understand and help them.

Given our group, how are we to achieve our aims?

For children to respect themselves, certain things are necessary. Of these the most important, surely, is the respect of the adult. We

[1] *Management and the Worker*, Roethlisberger and Dickson.

tend to be – or rather we try to be – what we are expected to be, and children can have no respect for themselves unless they see they are respected. For this reason, only teachers who are really aware of the importance of these children as individuals should try to tackle the job.

An understanding teacher will realize their need to achieve, especially in the fundamental skills. Reading and arithmetic are social needs and every effort should be made to achieve some degree of skill in them, always with the thought in mind that it is what it does to the child rather than the actual achievement that is important. The work should in the beginning be made simple enough for them to cope, and new steps should be introduced slowly in case new-found confidence is lost in failure. Constant praise in success and encouragement in failure should be the rule. The class teacher's attitude should be positive always – 'You've got two right', rather than, 'You've got four wrong'.

The responsibility of a little job can help give these children the feeling that they matter, and in a small group it is possible to find a job for every child and point the need in any group for the individual. As many of these children lack the feeling of responsibility, it is not enough just to give a job. The class teacher must keep a check on its being done. These children are lacking in foresight. Quite often things are done, or left undone, according to immediate needs or pleasures. Adult interest and approval will give importance to a job and an incentive to do it 'on time'.

Acceptable behaviour towards companions can only come with the opportunity of working and playing with them. In a group of backward children work should be arranged so that there is the maximum of co-operation. Practical arithmetic can be arranged in groups, so can reading. The group does not always have to be of several children; sometimes children will work better with 'partners' than with a group, and often a timid child cannot at first face a group even of four or five children.

Dramatic work is of great value in social training. In drama children must co-operate; they must control their own feelings and, if they enter into the spirit, they must actually subdue their own feelings and attempt to produce the feelings of another. This is a lesson not only in control but in sympathetic understanding. A very useful exercise is to let the children act out daily occurrences, pretending to be characters in their own lives. This not only gives them the opportunity to rid themselves of some resentment or fulfil some desire; it will also prove revealing to the teacher.

An idea I have found useful is to have some class activity going on to encourage co-operative work. It can form the basis of English and arithmetic work, and in the drawing, printing, painting, writing or modelling, every child can find some part to play. This piece of co-operative work is useful as it can become a 'show piece' to the rest of the school. It can only be worth showing if it is done well, and like all the work in the group should be simple enough and tackled slowly enough for a good standard to be achieved.

Recently our class activity was a row of shops, or rather shop fronts. We made miniature children's wear, adult wear, shoes, etc., and with cardboard frames and cellophane 'windows' made an attractive row of shop fronts along the classroom wall. A needlework mistress of the Evening Institute was so impressed that she wrote a note of thanks and appreciation to the children. This delighted them. Outside approval gives special satisfaction in a job well done, and gives added respect for it.

Though the work must be of a high standard, it must of course be the work of the children. It is so much easier and often so much quicker for the teacher to take over the harder parts, but these children, like all children, learn more from doing than from watching, and self-respect and pride in a job can only come from the joy of self-achievement.

One important point to notice is the need to give these children the best material available. Giving them good material is a measure of our respect for them, and in any case the better the material they use the better is the result likely to be, and the greater their joy in it.

Finally, since the class teacher does in effect represent authority to the children, their attitude to him or her – or rather the teacher's attitude to them – is likely to condition their attitude to future employers. We should then be ever on our guard against arousing any feelings of resentment or antagonism. From the first the children should be made aware that we are on their 'side'. We must show pride and pleasure in their progress rather than annoyance at their failure. Even more than the teacher of the intelligent we must be consistent in our dealings with them. Dull children find it difficult to adapt their behaviour to a changing mood and will become puzzled or resentful if words or actions which one day bring a smile next day provoke a rebuke, or if one child is laughed at for what in another child brings a scolding. These children are quick to notice apparent unfairness, and class teachers should be mindful that not only should they be fair but should seem to be so. It is worth while making sure always that the children understand the fairness of any decision; indeed, a share, where possible, in decisions of classroom happenings is a necessary step towards self-confidence.

The surest way to avoid misunderstanding is to try to know the children as individuals and to get them to know us. If we show a personal interest in all their doings, inside and outside school, and in return give them a knowledge of ourselves as people, they are more likely to trust us than if we adopt a teacher-pupil relationship only.

One sad aspect of my own work with these children is that so often there is an almost complete absence of religion in their lives. Religion can and should give a pattern of behaviour, moral and social, and those children who have it are well on the way to being acceptable socially. Too often, however, in my experience with these children, have I found that the illegitimate baby, mother's 'boy friend', the broken home, are part of the normal pattern of living for them and there is little we can do to help. Intelligent children can rise above an amoral atmosphere but dull children will always tend to take the easier way of behaving, and who can really blame them if they follow the pattern of living of those who are nearest to them?

Teachers who have definite beliefs of their own will, I think, even unconsciously, influence their children. I think they should do so consciously. On the one hand they will be supplementing the moral training of a good home, and on the other they can at least show another way of life to that normally seen by children from morally bad homes. Religion is the most important subject we teach, since the possession of a real faith can make the difference between mere existence and meaningful living and, surely, if we are hoping to give these children a belief in the importance of the individual, we can

SOCIAL, MORAL AND RELIGIOUS EDUCATION

use no greater argument than that of the Christian belief that we are made in the image of our Maker.

It can be best taught to any children by example, and since dull children will not have the ability or the interest to seek for the truth themselves, they are more likely to pattern their way of living on the example of those who seem to get most happiness from life.

For this reason I feel that the religious lesson for dull children should always be pleasant. A certain amount of drudgery is permissible in other subjects. The children are ready to accept the facts taught by arithmetic, in spite of the effort involved in the learning situation; they know that in English hard words have to be learnt and mistakes corrected. But religion is different. It can be accepted or rejected. Since for our children's sakes we want it accepted, we should promote and maintain a pleasant atmosphere where acceptance is likely.

Probably the happiest situation in the classroom is the story-telling one. It is friendly, it is informal and is the one, I think, to be used for the teaching of religion. Indeed, story-telling was the method used by Our Lord Jesus Christ himself.

It would be a pity for the children to miss the beauty of Bible language, but I think the reading should follow the telling. When the stories have been told the children can then listen to the words as they are read, look at pictures, talk about, write, draw and best of all dramatize, what they have heard and seen.

One group of my children made and dressed figures for a Christmas crib. We had many periods of real pleasure in making the figures, choosing materials for clothes, adapting oddments of 'jewellery' for the costumes of the Wise Men and we finally had the very real joy of seeing our work on exhibition in the school's entrance hall on the day of the Christmas Carol Service.

The vital thing, surely, is to make religion as important as arithmetic, and to try to make it matter more.

A fitting beginning for the school day is that of assembly for service. Sometimes the service is preceded or followed by a lecture on behaviour. It is a pity when this happens too often, as the dull mind cannot dissociate the one from the other.

In our school the Friday morning service is very popular. We listen to and share in the B.B.C. services which are usually admirably presented in dramatic form – one which is particularly pleasing for the dull. Some 'follow-up' of these services is desirable, of course, as seemingly obvious facts can be misinterpreted and misunderstood.

The pattern of the daily service cannot vary much – prayers, hymns, Bible readings are the essentials, but 'special' day services, as for Harvest Festival, United Nations' Day, beginning and end of term days, Easter and Christmas Carol Festivals, point to the importance of religion as a part of living rather than just a 'get-together' in the hall. One of these 'special' days in our school is the annual Leavers' Service for the children of the whole area which is held in a local church. It is one of the happiest and most inspiring. But even here, care should be taken that over-emphasis on perfection of production does not detract from the religious significance of the occasion, for whereas at its richest religion is a reason for life, even at its poorest it is a prop for behaviour, social and moral. It can never be confined to the religious lesson, of course. In a friendly, informal atmosphere discussions are often started by some child's question or remark, and these can be aided and guided by the teacher.

In the moral sphere as in the others, dull children are more dependent on us than are intelligent ones, and we should let no opportunity pass of 'pointing the moral' and, what is more important, of letting those children who can also point it. I remember a very lively drawing of a fruit stall in a market; a little boy was obviously stealing some fruit. The drawings of the groups were discussed and I asked the artist what the little boy was doing. 'Pinching bananas while the old man's serving the lady,' she said. The surprise I expressed did not compare with the horror of the other children. 'But he's got plenty, he won't miss any,' she argued. 'And how about if everybody pinched some? And suppose he's not the owner anyway, and he's got to pay? And suppose he's got a lot of little children to feed?' were just a few of the indignant questions she had to answer in what had become a very real situation. 'Pinching' was one of her own regular habits, but the little discussion made her think.

The moralizing should not become obvious. The dull mind is more easily persuaded by pleasant things, and just as acceptable social behaviour is best learned in a socially pleasant atmosphere,

SOCIAL, MORAL AND RELIGIOUS EDUCATION

so surely good moral standards can best be encouraged by those whose own moral standards have made them sympathetic to others and obviously happy in themselves.

Though these children can learn best in a small group under the guidance of a class teacher, they should at the secondary level be encouraged to take their share in the life of the school as a whole and recognize their importance as members of a larger group than that of the classroom. In our school the backward streams of children are encouraged to, and do, play a full part in our school life.

One delightful activity we have, and one that has proved its value in encouraging self-confidence, is that of half-yearly poetry reading sessions. Each year group meets for appreciation in the hall and volunteers from each form recite to the whole year group. Quite often the simple ballad or poem recited or mimed by D stream girls is more appreciated than difficult poems chosen by A stream girls, and the girls are very generous in their applause for the duller children who are obviously making real effort.

Our D stream girls join the school choir, even though it is an after-school activity, and on one occasion the two 'Leads' in a musical play were both D stream girls. The development in their poise was good to see.

Recently the games captain of the house that won the games tournament was also one of our 'dull and backward' stream, and she had the honour of going to the platform at assembly and receiving the cup from the head teacher.

The thrill of going to the platform was also experienced by one of the 1D girls. As a member of the 'Young Sowers' League' (we have a branch in the school) she had, by answering questions on the New Testament, earned a copy for herself, though I think she is the first D stream child to do so.

Another activity that has proved most popular and looks like becoming an annual event, is the end of year 'Dress Show' when some of the girls 'model' the clothes they have made in needlework periods. On these occasions pride in achievement has done much to make once timid girls really poised and confident.

Perhaps the most popular of our school activities – one reserved for the senior girls – is that of ballroom dancing. Our duller girls enjoy this just as much as do the brighter ones, and since it is an activity shared with boys from our companion school, it is most valuable in helping them to make easy contact.

Finally, where possible the children's horizon should be widened to include people outside the school, both by bringing them in and by going out to them. Talking about them is not enough for dull children. They need actual experience of a situation before they can fully understand and the more opportunities we can make for giving them practice in acceptable social behaviour the more chance they have of learning it.

Parents and friends are invited into schools for Christmas and Easter music festivals and sports days; children go out on visits. These occasions can be used to impress on the children the need for considerate behaviour.

One of the happiest of such occasions in our school is the Harvest Festival. The children bring gifts and also the names of friends and neighbours who are sick. After a service they help choose the gifts they are to take – fruit for sick children or groceries for the old – and I feel sure that our duller children get even more pleasure on these occasions than the brighter ones. The joy of giving is one of the great joys of life. I wonder if it is because when giving we are, for the time being, in the superior position of helper, and is it perhaps for that reason that dull children find very real joy and take particular interest in the choice of charities which benefit from our Christmas and Easter collections? Most of the time they are in the position of being helped.

Whatever the reason, they can in many situations learn that they have a contribution to make to society, and if they learn to do so willingly and with consideration for others, they are likely to win approval and, being approved, can become happy members of their group.

In this introductory chapter, I have ranged briefly over a wide field: subsequent contributors, from their several points of view, will amplify these remarks.

MARY K. FLEMING

Chapter II

PHYSICAL EDUCATION AND HEALTH

Although much work has been done in the fields of academic and social training for the backward child, very little has been done in the aspects of his education which deal with health and physical training. The importance of the 'physical' approach in the education of all children has long been recognized, but the need for the adaptation of physical training syllabi for the peculiar needs of the backward or dull child, has hardly been explored, despite the obvious fact that it is with his body the child will probably earn his daily bread. It is also more true of the dull child than of his more normal fellows that he has greater need to learn through the use of his body. A baby in the playpen making a pile of bricks, an infant at school learning to write, a junior learning to measure, are all learning through the use and manipulation of materials with controlled bodily motions. The senior child carries on this pattern of learning and although all children will need help in the different stages of adolescence the dull child with his unevenness of intellectual, physical, social and emotional progress will perhaps of all children in the secondary modern school need the greatest amount of help and encouragement to develop and control his body.

In addition to help in mastering and using his or her body (the remarks apply equally well to boys and girls), it will be necessary to assist the dull child in the care of his body and to inculcate those habits of health that will be most useful throughout the whole of his life, thus resulting in a more healthy adult who is not too much of a handicap in the community. Thus it will be seen that the dull child will have need of two kinds of education concerned with the health and welfare of his body, Health Education and Physical Training.

The first task of the school is the creation in the child's mind of a correct attitude of mind towards health and the realization that there is a real connexion between health studies and health habits. The whole effort of health teaching should be concentrated on training and study designed to equip the child with such habits and knowledge as will result in increased bodily and mental health.

It is unfortunate from the point of view of health education, that in many secondary modern schools because of specialization, subjects have been put into watertight compartments each taken by a specialist teacher. Science, P.E., organized games, biology, hygiene and indeed most subjects have been divorced the one from the other, and the tendency in schools is to insist upon some accumulation of facts, some acquiring of bodily skills or attainments, rather than the realization that all these subjects have the same end product; a child practising habits of health and cleanliness, with some understanding of the workings of his body.

For the backward child it is particularly important that health education instruction be presented in an extremely practical way. At times, no doubt, it will be necessary to introduce to older pupils scientific generalities about health and fitness, but this should only be a subsidiary part of the instruction and only worthy of attention if such information can be related to the child's experiences and needs.

It was once the custom in many schools for the teacher to examine the class for such things as clean hands or finger-nails, brushed hair or polished shoes, general tidiness or the possession of a handkerchief; but such examinations are not so common now. Such inspections did ensure a certain amount of effort by the child to present himself reasonably clean at school, and were, possibly, the foundation of habits carried on into after-school life. The treatment of those who fall short calls for tactful handling by the teacher, but most teachers go to the trouble of trying to understand their children and will know the best way to handle each child.

'Every teacher is a teacher of English' is a truism and so is 'every teacher is a teacher of health education'. A teacher's own personal appearance, general tidiness and habits all come under the microscope of a child's eyes and much that the teacher does is copied. Let the teacher see that only good and worth while habits are presented for duplication.

PHYSICAL EDUCATION AND HEALTH

A knowledge of a child's home circumstances is particularly valuable in this sphere of education. Dull children often have unfortunate home circumstances. For example, sleeping arrangements may be such that a child either has to wait to go to bed until late at night or is disturbed by the early exodus of parents or siblings, so that there is a consequent lack of sleep; the family management may be such that there is inadequate or unsuitable food; there may be considerable overcrowding; or the family may be in the care of an older sibling either temporarily or permanently. Such circumstances would have definite effects on the health of a child and the teacher should know of them and make due allowances for them, and extend all possible help and assistance to the child. Such knowledge should be used tactfully, sympathetically and confidentially and should be used to arouse in the child feelings of interest and co-operation.

The co-operation of the child is most important and the syllabus of study and training must always accept the qualification that it is not only the teacher's views that are important, but that the interests and desires of the class should point the way in which the series of lessons will develop. The teacher must be prepared to increase the scope or curtail his scheme of work at the reaction of the children and for the dull child especially should realize that activities should be real, practical and have some bearing on his everyday life. Many boys for example, belong to some youth organization wherein first-aid is studied, so that ultimately a badge can be earned. During the course of school life many opportunities occur for the introduction of some knowledge of first-aid in a practical and realistic fashion. Here, then, in a simple and obvious way, is a linking of the child's interests, needs and experience. Great care, however, must be taken to see that such a topic is not presented in a morbid or lurid fashion. Dull or backward children could by their incomplete grasp of the subject matter be frightened or worried, as was the child who following a lesson on the circulation of the blood complained that he could 'feel the blood dripping down inside of me' and reached a pitch where psychiatric attention was deemed necessary.

Many children now stay to a midday meal at school, and often find fault with what is served to them. Complaints are not always directed at the quantity but at the kind of food served. Such complaints could very easily be the source of a whole series of lessons concerned with the need for a balanced diet and perhaps the cook or meals supervisor could be called in to say a few words in her own defence. Such lessons will need to be quite simple and any records kept will be in the form of diagrams or illustration. There is here, of course, a link in the girls' school with the teacher of domestic science who has the immediate task of teaching some cookery skills but the more important ultimate aim of preparing a girl in some measure to be the head of a family and the provider of a balanced diet for her own husband and children. It could also be that a child of a badly managed family could be stimulated to interest and co-operation to a degree that he carries the teacher's comment into his own home for the good of the whole family.

Every teacher on a staff can be of assistance in the Health Education of the child both in the subject he teaches and in his general attitude and conduct. There is, for example, no point in Mr S. explaining the needs and benefits of ventilation and fresh air and insisting upon open windows, if the class goes to Mr F's room where the windows are firmly shut and requests for an open window are met with curt comments. All subjects lend themselves to some introduction of Health Education but it is to be understood that the introduction of such a topic should come naturally and not be laboured and should be aimed at being a reinforcement of other work rather than an entity in itself. History abounds in plagues and heroes who have fought with disease; geography could introduce footnotes on ways of life, food, housing, living conditions; religious instruction is filled with stories of all kinds dealing with the healing of the sick; even woodwork and metal work can introduce the need for care and cleanliness, safety precautions and the like.

All teachers can assist in the bodily welfare of the children in the school if they are continually on the look out for such outward signs of physical malaise as:

Undue fatigue, lassitude, paleness.
Afflictions of the skin, e.g. dermatitis, ringworm.
Defects of the eyes, nose, throat.
Defective hearing, discharging ears.
Deformities, e.g. spinal curvature, flat feet.

PHYSICAL EDUCATION AND HEALTH

Early symptoms of common infectious diseases, e.g. coughs, colds, sore throats, vomiting.

More unusual illnesses, e.g. 'growing pains' which may be rheumatism, or deteriorating handwriting which could be an early symptom of chorea (St Vitus's dance).

It can be a matter for surprise what a normally conscientious and observant teacher can miss seeing in his own class that a colleague will see at once. All children with defects of eye or ear will, of course, be given their most advantageous position in class, near the blackboard or the teacher, in a good light, and contact made with the appropriate medical authorities for advice and treatment. The wearing of glasses by those children who need them can be the source of bother to the conscientious teacher who makes every effort to see that spectacles as prescribed are worn, but the effort has to be made and tactful but very firm measures have to be used to overcome those excuses with which most teachers are already familiar.

Knowing something of a child's background should encourage a teacher to see that those children who qualify for them should have free meals and that the meals are taken. It is only too common for a family through pride or a false set of values to refuse to allow the children to have a free meal at school, preferring to feed them at their own, possibly lower level. There can, of course, be no compulsion, but a teacher or the Head teacher can make some tactful approach if the case warrants it. Milk, too, should be taken and drunk regularly.

At some time during the school life of an adolescent the problem of sex education must be considered. All opinions concerning this vexed subject will be conditioned by the particular teacher's moral, religious, social background and the answer to what to teach and when to teach will be an extremely individual thing.

Most teachers are agreed, however, that the parents are the best sources of information for questions concerning sex matters but unfortunately in the case of many of the backward children in our schools parents are quite incapable of answering questions because they are either too shy, too lacking in knowledge of the subject or too unaware of its importance. This leaves, if nothing else, a moral onus upon the teacher to act in lieu of parents.

The cardinal virtues in the approach to sex education include honesty, sincerity, and lack of embarrassment. Almost all teachers have the opportunity at some time for the honest answering of a genuine question. The term 'genuine question' is used to differentiate from those apparently innocuous questions which all experienced teachers can recognize as bait to get the teacher on a hook.

With backward adolescent boys the subject is often one of great interest and many will suppose that they know all about it having culled their knowledge from playground and street corner conversations, but one must aim to educate the quiet sensitive boy as well as the more rowdy extrovert. Sex lessons as such, should not be arranged, indeed, it is infinitely preferable that instruction should be private and individual, but if in the course of any lesson questions are asked the answer should be given as simply, honestly, completely and confidently as possible. Great care should be taken not to frighten or puzzle the child. Remember in this subject, too, the always present possibility of an incomplete understanding of an explanation. The keeping of livestock or the study of reproduction of flowers or plants will often provide concrete example upon which to build abstract explanations. Thus it is a good thing even in an urban secondary modern school to maintain a nature table or raise some livestock. What the children can see as perfectly natural and open is infinitely better than their furtive and secretive attempts to find out for themselves and familiarity with such knowledge will take away some of the excitement of ignorance.

There may be at some time hostility by parents or even head teachers to the answering of questions of this kind. In the event of such hostility one must be prepared to put a case and stick by it. Provided the teacher has observed normal codes of accepted behaviour in the instruction, there can be no harm in helping these children to a greater understanding of themselves and their differences to others and the need for the maintenance of socially acceptable conduct between the sexes.

Turning now to 'physical education' in the narrower sense, every teacher should know something of this since it is an integral and fundamental part of every child's education. Not every teacher should, however, be expected to take physical education lessons consistently and seriously as physical education is not only a source of great potential good – it can also be the source of much harm. It will

PHYSICAL EDUCATION AND HEALTH

be necessary to advise many teachers of physical education who deal with the backward children of their special needs and to secure their active co-operation and understanding. Such advice will of course need to be given most tactfully, no 'expert' likes to be given advice by a layman, but most teachers are working for the benefit of the child and co-operation is normally readily forthcoming.

The aims of physical education should include the following:

(*a*) The maintenance of bodily health and physique.
(*b*) The development of socially acceptable characteristics, e.g. co-operation, friendliness.
(*c*) Co-ordination of thought and action.
(*d*) Learning of new skills.
(*e*) Provide challenges which result in pride in achievement, self-control, self-examination.
(*f*) Pleasure from bodily activities.

How best to achieve these aims is at this time a matter for conjecture since like all educational media physical education is undergoing changes. The methods of physical education are in a state of flux with new ideas taking pride of place over older ones, which are being rapidly discarded. More and more importance is being laid upon the need for the child to express himself, and self-expression is the watchword in physical activities and dance. But there is in the secondary modern school with the dull and backward child a real need to learn self-control before self-expression. Self-control can only be fully learnt in a controlled environment and the more proved system of group and class work with the teacher in charge has much to commend it. Such a lesson gives the individual opportunities for self-expression but has the safeguard that the whole group is in the control of a responsible person.

The syllabus should include:

Exercises and activities – to encourage physical development.
Gymnastics – to develop bodily control, and to encourage the most economical use of energy.
Organized games – for their social training, because most children like them and because they may later play them in their own time.

Dancing – because of its unique and important contribution to education – especially good for girls but useful for boys.
Swimming – because of its completeness as a physical activity.

Before going on to the more practical aspects of P.E. lessons and the school's contribution, it may be as well to think a little of the material upon which it is intended to work. The secondary modern school life of a child spans one of the most critical phases of a lifetime – adolescence, and the onset of puberty. It is an age of irregular physical growth, adjustment to new codes of social behaviour, the passing of childhood characteristics and the awareness of adult qualities. It is an age of mental, physical, social, emotional change. The dull child best compares with his more normal companion in the physical sense. His intellectual activities may not be of the same standard as some of his chronological counterparts but his wrists will stick out of his jacket just as far and he can be just as gangling or covered with as many spots. Socially, too, he is on much the same plane and expects the same degree of social acceptance and wants to indulge in the same social activities as his superiors. It is in the mental and emotional spheres that he lags most behind. Adolescence in the normal child is a complicated enough problem, but add to it the retardations in the mental and emotional make-up of the dull child and the need for individual understanding and handling becomes imperative. It can be fairly said of secondary modern children that their greatest unity lies in their diversity.

The backward child will have to be studied, when lessons are planned for the following reasons also:

(a) His co-ordination is generally poorer.
(b) His span of concentration is less.
(c) He is more 'accident' prone.
(d) His reactions are slower.
(e) He will need more physical demonstration, and verbal commands must be clear.
(f) Activities will have to be carefully graded to bring success.
(g) He will be possessed of less of the skills normally expected of his age group.
(h) Progress will always be slower.

PHYSICAL EDUCATION AND HEALTH

(i) In many cases the degree of interest in the lesson and activities will be low.

(j) His mental age, and the characteristics of that age group, should be understood and catered for.

Many influences have an effect on a child at school but in P.E. rather more than any other subject the personality and attitude of the teacher has perhaps the greatest role. In the classroom the insincerity or lack of interest by a teacher can perhaps be camouflaged by the presentation of interesting textbooks or materials, but in the gym the teacher is the cornerstone and focus of attention. It will therefore be necessary for the teacher to present himself as someone worth emulating. His appearance should portray efficiency, smartness and readiness for work. Some suitably clean and smart clothing, worn by the teacher will put the children in a more alert frame of mind, and an attitude which suggests the importance of the lesson and of the gym is vital.

A tolerant discipline, with the judicious award of praise and the tactful restraint of the unruly should be aimed at. Good standards of personal achievement should be maintained. The P.E. teacher holds a very responsible position in a school. To him, perhaps more than any other teacher falls the task of setting standards of behaviour that the children will most readily accept, and acceptance comes unconsciously through the child's admiration of the teacher's physical capabilities, the desire to emulate them, and the wish to please through his own performance.

The content of any gym lesson will be governed by many considerations. The time of the year and even the time of the day must be considered. The age of the class, their standard of achievement, the teacher's long and short term aims will all have some bearing on the type of lesson to be presented. But all P.E. lessons should have one common factor and that is that they should all be as enjoyable as possible. Physical training should be enjoyable because (a) children and adults show themselves more efficient in those tasks in which they are interested and (b) the enjoyment derived from physical activity has a most beneficial psychological effect which is perhaps even more valuable than the physiological effect.

The enjoyment of P.E. as part of his school life will also have other beneficial advantages, perhaps the most important of which is the stimulation of the desire to learn. As has been already mentioned, the backward child is most akin to the normal in the physical and social spheres and in his desire to be like others will want to make the utmost use of his body. This inherent wish coupled with enjoyment and desire to learn lays a very firm foundation on which to build. Encouragement comes best from success and the teacher must see to it that all activities are so graded that, with effort, every step can be mastered and eventually the child can reach some definite stage of achievement. Naturally enough, the P.E. teacher likes to see progress being made as rapidly as possible, but with a backward class he may need to restrain himself from pushing ahead too fast and remember the need for the duller children to master and consolidate at a much slower rate than the A and B child. Then, again, some P.E. teachers prefer, for reasons of discipline or organization, to see classes in lines doing jumps and exercises in unison. This is often a sheer impossibility to achieve with the dull child and the P.E. teacher must be encouraged to accept a class scattered at random around the gym and a rhythmic exercise that is not as unified as that of other classes might be.

One often hears the complaint that C classes 'always need such a lot of watching' – or that 'you can't trust them to get on with anything without damaging themselves or the apparatus'. Such criticisms are not justified except perhaps as a criticism of the mode of training. Children are quick to assess their own capabilities and generally will not seek to emulate the few agile ones, unless of course, a common standard is demanded or some competitive element has been introduced. Common standards are not easily possible with dull children. They are more completely individual in their capabilities and diversities and the only standard which should be aimed at is the best standard of the child himself, and the only competitive element the competition of the child with himself to improve past performances.

The use of apparatus in a gym is another point upon which the dull child will need special guidance. In the handling of the apparatus he will need more supervision and help, and a certain routine to be followed every lesson is probably the best way to achieve the greatest safety. A certain group of boys should be responsible for the handling of the beams, another group the handling of the box and horse, and other boys should be given jobs with which they can easily cope, the carrying of mats, the putting away of balls, etc. There should be only one way to handle or carry any piece of apparatus and this routine should be established, practised and adhered to.

As to the use of apparatus by dull children, there is little to fear if 'standing by' is accepted as a necessity by the teacher in the first practices of a new activity and if boys are trained to 'stand by' for one another in familiar exercises. Children usually know their own abilities quite accurately and approach new apparatus or activities with great circumspection. But there must always be the reinforcement of the training in self-reliance and the careful gradation of tasks which brings confidence. The dull child can be trained to 'stand by' quite successfully and a poor performer who can 'stand by' in good fashion can receive quite a lot of confidence and self-gratification from so doing.

The amount of apparatus to be used in a programme of physical education for dull children is of prime consideration. Broadly speaking the criterion should be to give each child one item of apparatus each in almost every situation where the learning of an individual skill is the aim, e.g. catching a ball, kicking a ball, bowling a hoop, and as small a group as possible where combined practice is possible, e.g. pairs for bowling and batting, passing a football. If each child is equipped then more work can be done, and individual requirements are met. The class should be allowed to choose its own groupings – friends with friends always work better, but tact and firmness will be necessary with those who abuse this privilege.

It is generally accepted that a P.E. lesson should be divided into the following sections:

(*a*) Introductory activities.
(*b*) A table of exercises.
(*c*) Class practices.
(*d*) Group activities.
(*e*) A game.

and this scheme of work fits the requirements of most children, but the dull child has the following extra requirements to be catered for:

(a) He is not suited to a rigid programme of formal exercises and for him game-like exercises are preferable.
(b) He needs more variety – because his span of concentration is less.
(c) He will need more 'breaks', both of the kind which demands mental alertness and those included to ease stresses.
(d) His game will need to be simplified either in rules or in numbers taking part or both.
(e) In group activities he will probably need more supervision and these activities should always include some that are 'foolproof' so that the teacher can supervise those that are not.
(f) His slower speed of dressing and undressing.

An integral part of any gym lesson is the shower afterwards, and children should be expected to bring towels, and, if they wish, soap. Few children need to be permanently excused from showers and the teacher should be firm in his insistence that high standards of cleanliness are maintained. In addition to the consideration that the backward child is slower to dress and undress, care will need to be taken to see that he dries himself properly. These dressing-room activities will need to be supervised, and extra time for all of them will have to be allowed for in planning the lesson.

It is beyond the scope of this article to go into details of the various kinds of exercises that should be included, but for those who may be unaware of them a representative list of game-like exercises and 'breaks' has been included as an appendix. One point however is worth stressing and that concerns remedial exercises. Beyond the considerations of correcting bad posture at a class level or some other common fault it will not be expedient to attempt any remedial exercises. Remedial exercises are so individual that they cannot be attempted at all in a class and are best left to qualified therapists. If a child is so physically disabled as to need remedial treatment he should be passed on to the medical services. Few teachers have the qualification to tackle this branch of physical activity with any success and probably more harm than good would result from these efforts.

Organized games are a part of nearly every school's time-table but for the dull child and indeed for many children organized games as they are constituted are often of little purpose.

PHYSICAL EDUCATION AND HEALTH

Major team games are a very adult concept with their rules, organizations and leagues and their place in school is usually due to the enthusiasm of a master or some local tradition. To a dull child, an eleven-a-side game of football or cricket with its complexity of rules, tactics and its long duration must be a rather bewildering situation. He gets far more out of a six-a-side game, on a smaller pitch, for, say, ten minutes each way. He has fuller participation, the rules are less complicated, after a while he has a change of activity, and the achievements of those who are better at the game are not so obvious, conversely neither is the lack of ability in others so noticeable.

The insistence, too, that all boys should play football, because of football leagues, or because there is a nationally famous local team, is manifestly unfair. The teacher should be prepared to offer a variety of games both in summer and winter so that the child can at least choose the one in which he is most interested. Rounders, soft-ball, skittle-ball, single wicket cricket and volley ball are possible summer alternatives to a whole afternoon's cricket; six-a-side football, some elementary game with a rugby ball, a reasonable cross-country run, can be alternatives to full games of football.

To be a success at team games the child must be in possession of certain basic skills and if the child can be interested in the game he will be more prone to practise the skills and become more successful.

Organized games have a lot to offer and should be encouraged. They should lead to alertness, independent individual action, a quick answer to unexpected directions and a quick awareness of a situation. Detailed perfection cannot be expected – but every child should show effort. The social training and co-operation required in the playing of team games is immensely valuable; but perhaps most valuable of all is the thought that an interest created at school may carry on in after-school life and become a source of worth while leisure activity.

Despite the seasonal and administrative difficulties of organizing swimming periods, the efforts to encourage children to learn to swim are well worth while. From swimming a child obtains all round muscular improvement, indeed it is one of the few that produces symmetrical development, increases the efficiency of the nervous system, increases self-confidence, and, as the skill develops, self-reliance. It is no easy matter for a non-swimmer to overcome his natural fear of the water and then go on to be a proficient swimmer.

Most teachers will have evolved their own systems of teaching swimming and most of the conventional and popular approaches are equally useful for the dull child but it is as well to bear the following points in mind when the need for adaptation is realized:

(a) The class should either be smaller or there should be more supervision than usual.
(b) The lesson should be a little shorter on the instructional side and a little longer on the recreational side.
(c) The class may range between those with complete over-confidence who will willingly jump into any part of the bath and those with an exaggerated fear of entry into the water.
(d) It is a great help if the instructor can demonstrate frequently both in and out of the water.
(e) The lessons should be as frequent as possible and an all year round programme should be aimed at.
(f) Nothing should ever be permitted which would result in the fear of water or any lack of self-confidence.
(g) There should be a system of incentives – e.g. badges for stages of achievement.

There is every good reason why life-saving drill and instruction should be taken by the child and it may be possible for some children to take the examinations of the Royal Life Saving Society and be awarded the badges that the Society has for various stages of achievement. Such knowledge whether it results in the award of a badge or not can only be useful.

Modern dance and folk dancing are best taught at the junior school age or at the latest in the first year of the secondary modern, if it is a mixed school. Dancing has so much to commend it, social and physical rewards are so bountiful and it is to be regretted that many children spend their whole lives in single sex schools where they never receive any instruction or experience any of the delight that goes with dancing classes. If classes can be arranged, folk dances of a repetitive pattern are probably the best for the dull child of this age, but experiments and excursions into all types of dance should be made at the discretion of the teacher. The class will of course need a lot of space and gradual instruction, the teacher will need to have a full knowledge of the possibilities and limitations of dance and music and a very good approach to her class. 'Her class' is used advisedly for dancing is usually taught by a woman in a feminine way and with boys this may present difficulties which require real understanding to overcome. She will find, however, that her dull class is generally less lacking in inhibitions and that once she has them working with her the results are very satisfying.

There must be a very close, almost an infusion of dance, drama and music to enjoy the full scope of using the body as a means of expression. It is a means of expression that comes easily to most children and in their movements can be mirrored almost an undistorted image of their personality. There is no way that is better than another in developing a child's body, co-ordinations and movements to the full, all approaches, gymnastic, swimming, dancing, games have their own unique and subtle contribution to offer. In modern life the child is better fed and clothed and has more medical attention but there is no doubt that industrial development, the restriction of fields, the fast moving traffic in streets, the artificial amusements of cinemas and television, have all reduced the opportunities for sheer animal movements which most children enjoy. The 'gym' teacher has a very valuable and difficult role to play but played well it can be of outstanding value to the child, the school and the community.

Some Suggested Game-like Exercises
As tall as possible; as small as possible.
Bunny Hops.
Wheelbarrows that won't go.
Grinding Coffee (sometimes known as Grinding Salt).
Giant Strides.
Indians at Powwow.
Lift the Sack.
Hopping Charges.
Leg Wrestling.
Arm Wrestling.
Jumping the widening cavern.
Bear Walk.
Crab Walk.

'Breaks'

Jump to head an imaginary football.
Jump to save a goal (teacher indicates where ball is supposed to be).
Put your thumb on the floor and run round it.
Thunder 'stamp the feet'; Rain 'slap the knees'.
Lightning 'clap the hands' and combinations of these activities.
Crust and Crumbs } Running to touch a previously designated wall
Head or Tails } and back to your place.
'Reverse Files'.
'Skinning the Snake'.
Follow the leader.
Reverse running on whistle commands.
Indian War Dance.
Through your partner's legs and back again.

Bibliography

BRIDGES, C. E. and BRIDGE, D. E., *The Physical Training Teachers' Legal Rights and Responsibilities*, Foyle.
HALL, FERNAN, *The Anatomy of Ballet*, Melrose.
Health Education, H.M.S.O.
JARVIS, M. A., *Swimming for Teachers and Youth Leaders*, Faber.
KNUDSEN, *A Textbook of Gymnastics*, Churchill.
LABAN, R., *Modern Educational Dance*, MacDonald and Evans.
MARSHALL, F. J. C., *Physical Activities for Boys' Schools*, U.L.P.
Moving and Growing, H.M.S.O.
MUNROW, M. A. D., *Pure and Applied Gymnastics*, Edward Arnold.
Planning the Programme, H.M.S.O.
Reference Book of Gymnastic Training for Boys, H.M.S.O.
The 1933 Syllabus, H.M.S.O.

E. A. SAY

Chapter III

SPEECH AND ORAL WORK

I wonder how many times the command 'Stop talking!' is given in many of our schools. Have you ever been guilty? This section is devoted to suggesting that 'Start talking!' be substituted and some ways in which it may be done, in the secondary modern school.

It is the use of speech that distinguishes Man from the other animals and is a universal basic skill, essential to him in all his social groups. Since Caxton's day it has been somewhat overshadowed in the West by the printed word, a tyranny that lingers on in our schools today, but one which the gramophone record, the tape-recorder and the sound film threaten to overthrow.

Moreover, the oral communication of thought is the means of self-expression most easily learned by the normal child and valuable to the growth of his emotional self by providing an outlet for appetites and desires, denied to him by the taboos of society. You may reason that this skill is acquired during infancy and some degree of mastery should be achieved before coming to the secondary modern school. That is so, but it is equally true that many older children in our secondary schools and even adults seem to have lost the knack; some are morosely unwilling to talk, some unable to articulate their thoughts into words. What then has happened? Is adolescence responsible, or discouragement, or has an eagerness to teach other skills resulted in letting this fundamental one fall into disuse? What seems obvious is that there is a need for deliberate and consistent teaching of how to talk, even in our secondary schools.

So, convinced that 'Start talking!' should supplant 'Stop talking,' how can we make a start? The first absolute necessity is perhaps the most difficult requisite to furnish – atmosphere. There must be throughout the class a friendly and natural air, an absence of tensions, a mutual acceptance of one another. This is the challenge that confronts all teachers in the class situation: how by personal example, he or she can instil a spirit of understanding tolerance among children grouped together by an outside authority on a non-voluntary basis. There is no set formula for creating such an atmosphere. With devoted goodwill by the teacher and a preference for happiness by the child, it will grow and permit a certain degree of freedom or rather relaxation of restraint, without which there will be no talking-at-ease. Permit some fluidity of seating arrangements: the timid child may feel less diffident sitting next to a friend; the forward child some restraint from having to share the public ear on an equal basis with others. Perhaps some relaxation in the sitting posture may help children to feel at ease, especially with young fast growing adolescents who sometimes seem to find comfort only in ungainly attitudes.

Now, the stage being set to the best of our ability, when does the performance start and how long last? The answer is all day long. If we believe in active learning and acknowledge the difficulties that reading and writing have for the C and D streams, we are forced to a realization that most subjects must be taught by the active participation of our pupils together with the free speech essential to the situations you devise for each separate subject. 'On the bus', 'Shopping expedition', 'A visit to the tailor', 'Buying a bicycle' – such titles readily suggest real life situations in which the spoken word and arithmetical processes are exercised. Similarly geographical talks may be built up in a series round the subject we are teaching; 'Why we emigrated to Australia', 'How we got there', 'Finding a job', 'Learning sheep farming', 'Schooling in the wilds'. History eminently leads to similar treatment, and at the right moment the printed word and the written one can be introduced; but remember that the spoken one is always more important. Religious instruction, too, can be given in the dramatic form even with modern settings, so that the basic truths of Christianity are understandable by pupils in the lower streams. The titles 'Who's my neighbour', 'The Prodigal Son', 'The Great Supper', 'Talents' suggest by themselves the method.

You will note that the foregoing will serve to illustrate how the spoken word may be used to teach most subjects of the time-table and our efforts to encourage it, not narrowly confined to the English lesson. Facility in the use of the spoken word will come only through constant practice; and the English lesson of course is the chief opportunity to loose inhibited tongues, and to guide the direction of the talking from just aimless chatter to the target set by the teacher. But beware of insistence on purism of enunciation lest we block the very purpose we seek of natural easy oral communication, or create the disparity of one dialect for the classroom and another for outside. So 'Start talking' must precede 'Start talking properly'.

Hobbies always seem to offer a good way of inaugurating discussion. Most of us have some interest that consumes leisure time and this often is the subject we talk about to our friends, justifying our enthusiasm perhaps, or seeking to proselytize new devotees. Tell your class about yours and before you are finished you will have questions and some pupils literally bubbling over to tell you about theirs. Now slip into the wings and let each have full limelight. If one falters with his lines, your skilful question can get him going again. Let the speaker answer queries from the rest of the class. Discuss how this interest may be further pursued and brought into the classroom by pictures, catalogues and books if not directly. Encourage children to bring along their pets, stamp albums, model aircraft, model cars and railways. Recently Michael, an inarticulate 12-year-old boy brought along and expounded upon his collection of 1,000 match-box tops. You will be surprised at the richness and variety of your pupils' interests; Robert, a backward boy of 13, showed himself as a potential designer of women's dresses with an extensive collection of illustrations and a knowledge that certainly surpassed my own. In short let the hobby-horse have his head. He may lead into the pastures of reading books and writing letters, but remember his basic purpose is to start pupils talking freely, naturally and easily.

Just as these interests will tend to reflect themselves on the environment as collections and pictures, so will the reverse process happen. A rich variety of things and pictorial display will stimulate discussion. Hence the need to use wall space as astutely as the window-dresser and, even more important to keep it ever changing. Newspaper headlines will have to be selected with discrimination. A wall newspaper printed by pairs of boys in turn with single rubber letters mounted on blocks, has proved provocative of criticism and discussion, provided that the topic for the day be the boys' own and in their own words, even if the spelling is yours.

Television and wireless programmes will readily suggest 'games' in which the spoken word is practised. 'Twenty questions', 'Tell the truth', 'Dear Sir', with little modifications will be as popular in the classroom as over the air, and a little ingenuity will suggest others even more effective. 'Pot luck' has been a favourite with a succession of O Groups and D streams; all boys write a brief title of topic on a piece of paper; these are folded, put into a hat, shaken and singly drawn by lot; the drawer is required to talk about the topic he has chosen for one minute. Of course, the teacher himself has first pick to undergo the ordeal, but then maybe it is not difficult for some of us to talk about nothing for sixty seconds.

Be wary of correcting the speaker's grammar or pronunciation until the end of the minute and then let the class do it but make sure criticism does not dampen future contributions. Good habits of speech, like bad ones are acquired by example not by precept, and once there is freedom of flow, the pupil will pattern his on yours subconsciously. And here the results of teaching do not necessarily correlate closely with intelligence. So the more backward child can taste a degree of success, denied to him by more academic work. Furthermore he will be equipped to play his part in the world as a citizen.

The citizens of tomorrow certainly need to know how to talk; speech is the lubricant of democracy. Without an interested rank and file able to criticize, elect and voice a dissentient opinion, government will become an oligarchy of the more able, administering through an uncaring bureaucracy. There is no intelligence qualification for a vote. So the survival of our hard won way of life will depend largely on our success in teaching future citizens how to talk and think for themselves. The balance of rights and responsibilities, inherent in democracy, also can only be learned by practice, and the secondary modern school is an excellent rehearsal ground. Responsibilities are a wonderful steadying influence; by extending the school leaving age to 15 and by withholding responsibilities, many secondary modern schools have found themselves with pupils difficult to teach and apparently immature to fit vocationally or socially into the outside world. It may be salutary for us to consider how much of the blame for the Teddy Boy gangs may be attributed to the shortcomings of our secondary schools.

The solution will certainly not be found in automatically showering responsibilities on 'fourth year' shoulders unused to them; rather it will be in a carefully graded course of delegating them on pupils right from the first year gradually increasing the dose to the maximum the youth can bear. Youngsters of 11+ are quite capable of electing class captains and committees, using the democratic machinery of nomination, and voting by elimination. The class captain is of course not teacher's pet, nor chief policeman; he is the class leader, representative to other classes and welfare link with the class teacher.

Periodic meetings of the Class Council will provide plenty of practice in the use of spoken English, some training in the restraint of listening, much valuable information to the teacher on public opinion, and a steady growth of self-responsibility. Let the meetings be purposeful by including on the agenda anything directly affecting the school life of its members. It is as well to be chairman yourself at first with an elected secretary responsible for minutes. Do your best to implement any practical resolutions carried by a majority. Some years ago in a secondary modern school, it was decided to institute a school fund to purchase amenities not otherwise provided, on a voluntary basis of 1d. per week. It was a failure: seventy-five per cent. contributed to begin with; within three months less than twenty-five per cent. Yet in a third year D class the Class Council decided to contribute 3d. per week, per child. During the year over ninety per cent. kept up their voluntary contributions to the class fund, which was sufficient to buy baskets of fruit for sick members, toys for a local hospital Christmas tree, a coach trip to London Airport, with a surplus at the end of the year spent on a party. The difference between the two similar efforts is accounted for by the decision to contribute and the method of disbursement being taken by the children themselves.

Yes, there must be speaking with a purpose in the secondary schools; only thus can the irresponsible school child develop into the self-reliant adult, willing and able to shoulder the responsibilities of communal life. Responsibility is a wonderful steadier. The defect of the prefect system in most schools is that it relegates authority to the few, thereby denying it from the many. By his fourth year every child should be saddled with some responsibility to his school and, more importantly, for himself. He should have acquired such skill in the art of discussion as to be able to share the responsibility with his headmaster or housemaster of choosing the course of study best suited to his pattern of abilities and his vocational objective; moreover within that general framework there should be optional lessons, when he may be free to use, as it were, leisure school time as he may determine, perhaps even in a commonroom where he may just talk with his fellows.

The purpose of this section was to suggest that in the secondary modern school especially with the C and D streams, spoken English is an essential of top priority. To this end I have sketched a few suggested methods. Moreover I have tried to adduce adequate reasons for deliberate teaching towards this objective. But I shall have failed utterly if I have not made clear that the constant and ultimate aim is neither facility in spoken nor written English in itself, but rather to train skills in all children according to their abilities so that they mature into well-balanced people, able to face up to the challenge of a rather frightening new world.

L. H. LYON

Chapter IV

READING AND ENGLISH

The plight of a child who cannot read by the time he reaches the secondary school is a pitiable one and his subsequent achievements there are likely to be very meagre indeed, unless he can be helped to overcome this major difficulty. It is generally accepted that a pupil with a reading age below 7 is a non-reader but, in fact, those with a reading age between 7 and 9 are, for all practical purposes, non-readers, from the point of view of tackling reading or textbooks aimed at the average girl or boy aged from 11 to 15. Unless special provision is made either by the school or individually by their teachers for those who are so far behind in this basic skill, they will be condemned to spend the greater part of their final years at school at work which they cannot possibly do and which will, therefore, be of little or no use to them and may, in fact, be definitely harmful to their development. This wasted time, if usefully employed, could enable them to raise the standard of their reading to the point where it could be the start of further general all round progress. When this occurs and the retarded child begins to feel a sense of achievement at the very point where he has failed for years, he is far more likely to accept the school environment and avoid the extreme behaviour problems which can be so difficult to deal with at the adolescent stage.

It may be asked whether this problem does, in fact, exist to any large extent, or whether the child who cannot read by the age of 11 or more is so rare a phenomenon that it has no general significance for teachers in the secondary modern schools. The child who cannot read a single word cannot, of course, be missed, but the ones who can struggle through a certain amount can and do escape detection. For example, the case could be quoted of a second year girl whose reading age turned out to be well below 8. She was not a dull girl and, although she never achieved the results expected of her, it had never been realized that she could barely read. This particular girl was really doing marvels with the small amount of reading she could do, but she was always told she 'could do better'. Of course she could do better; she could learn to read well if she were given the help and training she required and then use her intelligence and this newly acquired skill to achieve the standard of work of which she was capable. But, unaided, she could not possibly 'do better'.

In my personal experience the incidence of non-readers varies considerably from district to district, school to school, and from year to year. Nevertheless, in practically every first year intake, two or three may be found, e.g.

School I	Year 1	14 girls with R.A.	between	5.9 and 8.0 yrs.
(approx. 420)	,, 2	10 ,,	,,	,,	,,	6.3 and 8.4 ,,
Girls' school	,, 3	4 ,,	,,	,,	,,	8.1 and 8.7 ,,
	,, 4	1 girl	,,	,,	of	8.3 yrs.
School II	Year 1	10 girls with R.A.	between	5.4 and 8 yrs.
(approx. 600)	,, 2	1 girl	,,	,,	of	7.3 yrs.
Girls' school						
School III	Year 1	8 with R.A. from 5.0 to 8.0 yrs.
(approx. 1,000)	,, 2	10 ,,	,,	,,	5.7 ,, 8.5 ,,
Mixed school	,, 3	3 ,,	,,	,,	7.9 ,, 8.9 ,,
	,, 4	3 ,,	,,	,,	6.3 ,, 7.1 ,,

On the whole backwardness in reading is a greater problem with boys than with girls, so it is probable that these figures rather underestimate the extent of the problem as the first two tables refer to girls' schools and in the last school only those put forward by class teachers were tested.

In some schools a great number of any given class may be non-readers, in others it may be very few, but, in either case, the child is entitled to help to overcome his difficulties and give him a chance to benefit from the education offered to him. It is liable to happen, in any secondary school, that two or three or more in any given group may be non-readers, so the problem is an actual one which deserves consideration. Added to this is the fact that there will be, in each case, a very much larger group which will fall into the 7–9 category, and it seems obvious that failure in reading is a very real problem in the lower groups of the secondary modern school.

The result of lack of reading ability, at this stage, is that the child may become a passenger for most of the lessons during the day. Practically every lesson entails some reading or some writing. The non-reader, is therefore, constantly being made aware of his failings, is probably being censured for not achieving results which are absolutely impossible of achievement and will, most likely, put up a defence behind which he retires, where the brain is inactive. The habit of not understanding becomes deeply ingrained until the simplest thing which in truth, could easily be grasped by the particular child, passes him by. He may make an effort to compensate by being 'good at oral work' or may become a thorough nuisance or may just sit. By the time he has reached the secondary school, still a non-reader, he has probably spent some part of each day for the past five or six years supposedly learning something, but, in fact, in all that time, he has learnt nothing of the reading processes. It is no wonder if he really believes it is impossible to learn, but the wonder of it is that so many keep on trying. In trying to help the non-reader or the extremely backward reader this must be remembered and some means must be found of replacing this deeply ingrained attitude with a belief in his own ability to read. However, there is one advantage, in a way. It is highly unusual to meet a non-reader who does not really desire to learn to read if only he can be given confidence to try, although it is not very unusual to find the senior child with a reading age of from 8–9 who is perfectly satisfied with that performance. 'I can read', he thinks or says, and that's all that is necessary is the idea, so he is inclined to lack purpose in his work for he sees no need for further improvement.

Some method, then, must be found, in the one case to replace the ingrained sense of failure by confidence, and, in the other, to stimulate the desire to do better, and to this end the child must be shown that there is pleasure both in reading and in learning to read.

Therefore it is important that, for all retarded readers, the reading lessons should be interesting from the child's point of view. So individual or group reading, in itself, does not usually meet the need.

It is possible to make provision in various ways. The most effective is to allow time for reading periods when small groups of children or even individuals can regularly be given remedial lessons which aim to bring their reading to the standard which they are capable of attaining. If there is some small room, other than a classroom, which can be used for this purpose, and it can be made attractive as well as suitable for work, it helps to create the right atmosphere initially. If this is not possible, then a classroom can be used.

The class teachers can then put forward, for testing, those children who, in their opinion, have the greatest need of help in reading. Those suggested are then given an individual intelligence test (e.g. Terman and Merrill) and one or two basic reading tests. This, naturally, takes some time, but it is time well spent, as it gives the child a chance to become at ease in the situation where he has the undivided attention of the teacher, and the response to the various tests in the intelligence test will often give clues to the cause of the backwardness in reading.

Having considered the chronological age, mental age and reading age of each child, they can then be put in groups for the remedial reading. Care must be taken that those in any group are of approximately the same mental level and reading level as, obviously, the same rate of progress cannot be expected from a dull child as from an average or superior one. As one of the main objects is to replace the attitude that they have always failed and will always fail at reading, with confidence in their ability to succeed, it is most important that no child should be placed in a position where he cannot possibly do as well as those learning with him. Therefore it is better, if necessary, to take one child alone, if he is much above or below in intelligence those in his appropriate reading group, than to jeopardize the success of all. If a child is very backward in reading but the individual tests show that he is not, in fact, retarded according to his mental age, then he is not a suitable case for remedial reading as he is already doing as well as can be expected of him. An added advantage of this system of giving help is that those of higher intelligence, but with some specific difficulty, can also be dealt with as well as the dull and backward. Having then decided who is most in need of help and how they can best be grouped together, the remedial programme can be begun and, in this, it is essential that the needs of each individual must be realized and catered for. To this end every effort should be made to get to know the child as a person, as a member of the family, of the class and of the school; to consider with whom he plays and how, his interests or lack of them, his likes and dislikes, his medical history and his educational history and any other factor which may give a clue to his disability. Everything cannot be learned at once, but if you can gain his confidence, by degrees you will find out what is necessary for him. The full discussion of the causes of backwardness in reading given in Schonell's *Backwardness in the Basic Subjects* gives the basic facts on the basis of which a reasonable diagnosis can be made. Sometimes one is lucky and the first impression is correct, but at others you must be willing to change or adapt the lessons if further knowledge suggests this would be an advantage.

In remedial reading, of course, impressions are not enough, and the work must be based on careful analysis of the child and of the reading. For this purpose the first step should be to list all the faults made in the test (which can be recorded quite easily during it) and analyse these and their frequency. For example reversals of letters or parts of words, omissions, substitutions, additions, confusion of vowels, wrong sounds, difficulty with the visual appearance of words, lack of confidence in attacking words, not consistent left to right attack on unknown words, all appeared in the analysis of one particular girl's reading faults.

If the child is in the lower stages of the secondary school I usually find it advisable, then, to give him a choice of books at about the same reading level, probably rather below what he could tackle, to give him confidence. The lessons must be carefully prepared and, at first, based on the knowledge gained in the testing period and later on the records kept of the work done. I always find it most helpful to keep the record in a large loose leaf file, with the plan of the lesson on one side and the exact record of it on the opposite. One example taken from an actual record reads:

(1) Matching sentences without pictures.
(2) Read page 4 from *The Fair*.

(1) (1 min. 5 sec.) Discussion of L's visit to circus and fair.
(2) Run-ran, stair-street, p-p-putting, over-others, does, watching-watched, ate-tea, last-lets.

(3) Cutting, pasting and colouring pictures in workbook.	(3) Postponed until Monday. Wanted to play Snap. Usually little enthusiasm or preference so I did it. Talked of family and desire to be hairdresser. (Mother owns shop. Sister already in it.)

Some find it best to give a whole battery of tests to find out the exact stage reached in every particular skill involved in reading, and some like to use a particular method in trying to improve each point. I, personally, find it suits me better to compromise and begin on a reasonably broad basis, becoming more precise as the remedial work continues and using whatever method or adaptation of method seems desirable.

Then, as particular points arise or the time comes to deal with a certain fault, suggestions can often be found in the well-known remedial teaching methods. For example Gates suggests that rhymes are very useful in teaching children to visualize words. Rhymes like silly sayings can be employed in various ways such as matching the rhyme to the correct picture, completing the rhymes where some words have been omitted, adding the last line to a rhyme, putting jumbled rhymes in correct order or playing rhyming dominoes. When dealing with weaknesses in using phonics, M. Monroe's programme can be invaluable in deciding in what order to tackle the faults and in giving some methods of doing so. Where the pupil needs practice in the visual discrimination of words, Schonell's suggestion of match-boxes containing pictures with somewhat similar names pasted on top can be used, or, where appropriate, small models can be placed inside. The cyclostyled sheets of letters described by Gertrude Keir will prove useful and, for each point, some device can be found, each one usually suggesting to the mind variations or adaptations which will be best in the individual case under consideration.

In my experience, with the older pupils in the secondary school, who have still not learnt to read, the kinesthetic method used by G. Fernald and Keller can be the best one. In these cases where practically no progress has been made in nine or ten years of learning to read, where there is no accurate knowledge of the techniques of reading on which to build and where the pupil knows himself to be in a hopeless muddle, a completely different method seems to give the best hope of achieving results in the time available. The tracing, the use of the alphabetical filing system, the constant revision of the words learnt, the direction of attention to the initial letters of words and the possibility of directly using the pupils' strongest interests, all help to overcome the ingrained faulty habits of these older girls and boys. Difficulties can arise in it, too, where the pupil is of very low I.Q. and has very few interests but, in that case, the method can be adapted in the later stages. I have found, however, that in my case, I have only been able to achieve success with this method with very small remedial groups. I have not been able to adapt it successfully for class use. It has been very easy to create a great enthusiasm at the first instance in class, but I have not yet been able to sustain this, except in isolated instances where someone with an extreme disability in spelling has continued to use the tracing for this purpose only. (Working with adults, Mr Phillips also found this method useful, and his comments complement mine. See Chapter XV.)

In the secondary school it is extremely difficult to ensure that all non-readers shall be taught to read before leaving school unless some special provision is made, at least for the elder ones. Starting in the first year, I believe they can be taught in class, but, if they are in the third or fourth year then the time available is so short, and the difficulties of such long standing that special remedial lessons are really a necessity.

This may not be possible if staffing or accommodation are limited, so other means have to be found. An expedient often used is to create one or more special classes in which the backward or retarded children can be placed. The numbers here can generally be smaller and those with reading difficulties will probably be placed in these classes as this has the greatest effect on their general work. I have never had any personal experience of dealing with one special class with the full four-year age range, as I am convinced that with the secondary school pupils at least, the advantages are strongly outweighed by the disadvantages. In my experience many of the pupils resent very much being placed in a special class with even a two-year age range and, although this can to a certain extent be overcome, it makes the establishment of a stable class atmosphere very difficult and, even when apparently achieved, it is more easily upset than in other types of organization. This may vary according to the school, the tradition and the type of child, but I speak as I have found it, not only in classes I have taken, but where I have later taught children who have been in other special classes. A typical example of this is where one of them said: 'I'd much rather be in this school than the other one. You know there they used to put me in a special class.' I am convinced that this particular girl had been very much helped by her period in that class, but nevertheless, the fact of being in it had had a strong emotional effect. If there is no other way of giving the help needed then it must be used, but, personally, I would avoid it with older pupils if I could. In Dr M. F. Cleugh's book *The Slow Learner*, the advantages and disadvantages of various types of special provision are discussed. The other method of dealing with non-readers is to attack the problem in the ordinary classes which, in the usual 'streamed' school, means the C or D class. It is possible to do so, providing the class is not too large and specialization not too widely applied to the lowest streams. There should be a basic organization of the regular reading lessons which does not change and which the child knows and understands. Within this framework each child should get variety of work which may include, for example, reading, writing, pasting, matching, crayoning, painting, games, drawing or puzzles. If the child is gradually trained to prepare the room for the lesson and to go to the place assigned for the material and to do the particular activity he has reached, then he not only uses his time adequately, but is receiving training in good organization and methods of work. Provision is also being made for controlled movement around the classroom which is so necessary for the dull and backward child to prevent restlessness and disappointment. Remembering that whatever the original cause of the reading failure it is certain to be complicated now by emotional factors, it is extremely important to help the child from this point of view. He must be convinced that he can and will read.

The teacher's own honest conviction will achieve a great deal in this direction but if the general opinion among the staff is either, that if the pupil cannot read by the secondary school stage the Special School is the only possible place for him or her, or that if he has not already learnt he never will, or that it isn't our business to give practice in basic reading for we have other more important work to accomplish, then there is little hope for the non-reader. Sometimes an attempt is made to deal with the problem by allocating a simple reading book and giving reading practice when the class is otherwise occupied. For the non-reader this is highly unlikely to solve the problem, though it may be useful with those of rather higher reading attainment.

No, any child with sufficient intelligence to be kept in the ordinary school system at all, can learn to read if time, thought and patience are given to his problem. The main difficulty is to find the method to which he will respond. If the teacher is really convinced of this, the afflicted child catches this conviction and, once basic confidence is established, something can be done for and with him.

As previously stated for individual cases in remedial reading, a few tests must be given, so that you have a basis from which to work. Generally one has to be satisfied with a group intelligence test as there is never time for individual testing of a whole class in the normal school routine. It also requires careful planning to ensure that the other information needed about each child is collected and studied; but unless this is done as carefully as is humanly possible, the chances of finding the causes of retardation are minimized considerably. When, on giving the reading test, you realize that the child can barely recognize a word, or may not even know a single letter or sound, great care must be taken. This is a very difficult moment for the child, who is probably very tense, and ashamed that a new person in a new environment is going to know of his absolute failure. As always, as much encouragement as possible must be given, but no surprise should be felt and most certainly none shown. An attempt can be made, at this stage, to put him more at his ease. It is not much use telling him he has done very well in the test if he knows perfectly well he has not been able to do it, but he can be approached something on these lines: – 'Do you find it rather hard to read? I expect some little thing has held you back. Perhaps you were away from school when you were little and missed a bit. I've known lots of people like that, but we'll just have to find out what it is and help you with it and then you'll be able to get on very quickly. Would you like to be able to read well? Oh, well, that's all right then! If you want to do it and I know how to help you, in the end you will find it's quite easy for you.'

If there can be found out in advance some obvious factor which may have retarded him, e.g. absences, changes of school, hospital treatment or something of that sort, which will be comprehensible to the pupil, then the explanation is less of a shot in the dark. The child is usually delighted to find a sympathetic ear and to have it suggested that there is a reason for his failure which is no fault of his own. Naturally the approach would vary according to the child and his age, but I have always found a ready response and a great relief when he is approached on these lines. Sometimes it seems to act as a release, and the pupil may talk quite freely about his previous history which may help in diagnosing the cause or, at least give an insight into his thoughts and feelings.

The practical difficulty is, of course, dealing with the few non-readers in a class where others can read. How are they to be kept occupied in a useful way, when there are so many things which the others can do and they cannot? In any lowest stream there is likely to be a very wide range of reading ability. From complete inability to a reading age of 11 or 12 is quite common and every gradation and complication may be found within that range. But, when this fact is recognized, part of the problem of providing adequate reading lessons for the non-readers is solved, because it is obvious that the class cannot be taught as a homogeneous unit, so it has to be organized for group and individual work for a large proportion of the English lessons.

We will take it, then, that you have a new class of first years to be taught English. It will, of course, be very much better if you are also taking them for a number of other subjects so that you may get to know them really well and can co-ordinate one subject with another more easily. After testing all on a graded word reading test and all except non-readers on a silent reading comprehension test, they should be listed and grouped according to reading age.

There should be available, in the school, a number of series of reading books with graded vocabulary which can be roughly classified according to reading age. These books should also have either a workbook or questions which ensure that each child must not only read the text, but also refer to it constantly in order to answer the questions and carry out the activities suggested.

A Survey of Books for Backward Readers gives considerable help here though individual circumstances and tastes will affect the choice made.

The non-reader, by the time he or she has reached secondary school age, will not learn to read simply by practising reading to himself, in a group, or to the teacher. Constant practice should be given, but, of itself, will prove insufficient. He must read, write, and use each word in a dozen different ways. The principles which have to be borne in mind in all teaching must be applied to a greater degree and the child cannot be expected to remember words unless they have been used frequently in different ways.

Many good and interesting series are now on the market for the non-reader, but considering results and the fact that they are very inexpensive, I have found 'The Adventures in Reading' series by Gertrude Keir the most useful for me personally. There are three sets of these books with six titles in each set, and each book is accompanied by a workbook which need not be expendable. These books are intended for use with retarded juniors, but, as they deal with subjects interesting to every child, e.g. *The Circus, The Farmer* and so on they do not antagonize the senior by their topic nor by an infantile appearance. The books are short and so avoid the spending of endless ages before having the satisfaction of having finished the book.

In the Teachers' Companion to this series the author gives numerous helpful suggestions on the correct use of the books and the approach to the backward reader. As she points out, if the child cannot read at all he must be placed on the first book *Red Indians*, and, at this stage actually be told every word probably. No attempt should be made yet to persuade him to sound any. If the child has some slight knowledge and makes an attempt himself, then that is different, but the teaching of sounds, phonograms, etc., should be left until later when a larger reading vocabulary has been acquired and when he has more confidence in his ability.

At this stage the pupil should read to the teacher at least once a day. If it is not possible to do this each time in the lessons he will usually be willing to come at the end of a session for a few minutes reading practice on certain days. At first this may mean reading each sentence to the child first, but, with the pictures to help, the first few sentences will be memorized quite rapidly. Then he can return to his place to answer the questions in the workbook. At first, until he gets used to the system, he may find it difficult to read some of the questions although they consist mainly of the reading text with perhaps a word left out. He can, though, always be asked to come out and read the questions to the teacher before he answers, or he can be asked to check with another child of higher reading age. If one of his friends in the class is at a higher stage, they may enjoy sitting together, and the poor reader, reading the question to his companion before he answers. This does not mean constant interruption and holding back the more advanced reader as there will be many times when the non-reader is doing something else which does not need help, and the actual writing of the answer takes some time at this stage.

Now, unless the rest of the class is to be neglected, all the reading lessons cannot be spent on these few very difficult cases. Probably all the pupils in the class need extra help with some section of reading, so what is to be done when the non-reader has been heard and has practised the new sentences for a short time? At this early stage there are many things which he needs to do, some of which can be done by himself in the course of the lesson. Apparatus is needed at this point and, in my opinion, may be the thing which will tip the balance from failure to success with the non-reader.

As a general rule two lines of approach should be borne in mind. The first is to isolate and deal with particular difficulties, which entails keeping an exact record of all mistakes, and the second is to expand and increase ideas, facts and vocabulary.

For the non-reader the following kinds of apparatus have proved useful: *Matching cards*. The first set should have on it a sentence with a picture underneath it in clear, large print. The same sentence is printed on a separate strip of cardboard. Put half a dozen of these picture cards in an envelope and mix up the sentences. Half a dozen of these matching cards in an envelope will give the child necessary practice in recognizing and matching sentences, to which the pictures will give a clue.

The pictures are more attractive to the child if they are drawn and painted but, if this is not possible, one extra copy of the book cut up for this purpose, is sufficient and every picture can be used for a very long period if mounted on a card with a fairly wide margin for handling. Then it can be kept clean and remounted if necessary.

The first progression on this is to use the same thing again but to add to it a third sentence cut up into groups of words. Then the sentence is matched to the sentence and then the phrases to the correct part of it.

The next progression is to cut the sentence into words to be matched to the sentence under the picture.

One or two sets of matching cards should be made for each book in the series. I find it better to expect no further progressions in the earliest stages, but the instructions for using the cards can be printed on the front of each envelope if the vocabulary is carefully chosen and repeated, in each case, with only minor alterations.

When some progress has been made sets of cards can be introduced as follows:

(1) A set of pictures only with one sentence to match each.
(2) A set of pictures for which a correct sentence has to be found in the book.
(3) A set of pictures, with the sentences cut up into phrases to be fitted together and matched to the picture.
(4) Pictures with separate words which can be made into sentences to match the pictures.

Now all this is necessary work, very useful to the child and takes him some time to do. The teacher need only check, in a few seconds, when he reports he has finished.

The extremely retarded reader will not learn to read unless his attention is constantly being directed to the words, not in one way only, but in as many ways as can be devised. Obviously if he is given a word or a group of words or a sentence to learn he will become bored and listless or restless if expected to go over them again and again. He will probably eventually know the sentence by heart and repeat it without, in reality, looking at the words at all. The basic necessity in reading is to recognize the printed symbols on the page, so this repetition will probably defeat its object by gradually persuading the child to look at them in the most cursory fashion.

Nevertheless he must look at the words dozens of times before he is going to build up a vocabulary of words which he will recognize instantly and which will form a nucleus which can be expanded in various directions to change him from a non-reader to a reader.

Devices for directing attention to words must be used and, if the apparatus appears different, interest can be maintained even when the exercise is basically of the same type.

Again matching cards are helpful. A picture of a simple object is pasted at the top with the word underneath. A number of words with a similar sound are placed in a column underneath. Each word is then cut out of cardboard and has to be matched to the original. This is easily checked and can be copied into the child's book. The simplest way to keep the single cards is to paste a match-box on to the bottom and cover it with a piece of coloured sticky paper. As a change some cards may have the original picture word repeated in the list and the card can be copied into the child's book and the right word underlined again. Instructions can be written on these cards, with slight variations. For example: 'Copy this card. Draw a line in red pencil under the word which is the same as the word at the top'. Another one may ask for underlining in a different colour. Asking the child to carry out a simple instruction, which you know is in his power, is good training, as the backward children very often lack confidence to translate words, particularly written words, into action. He may need a little help at first, but, by degrees, he will do what is required without finding it necessary to ask first.

Some can be asked to make their own similar cards for words they find difficult. A picture can be found from a magazine or from sets of pictures. If necessary they can be coloured or painted and then pasted on the card. He writes the word underneath and then finds a few matching words in his own reading book. If well done these cards can then be used by more advanced pupils for phonic work. This cuts down work for the teacher and also gives a sense of achievement to the very retarded reader when he sees his work used by those at a higher level than he is.

Sets of pictures such as those for a room in a house or for a shop also prove useful for matching or for games.

Where there are numerous reversals or it is necessary to direct attention to the initial letters of words, jumbled sets of words beginning with say four different letters, can be placed in an envelope or tin. These have to be arranged in columns according to the initial letter. This can also be used for middles or ends of words, or for vowels. It does not matter if all the words cannot be recognized as that is not the purpose of the exercise.

Games can also be useful in directing attention to the form of the words and give practice in recognition in a pleasing way. Snap cards are easily made by cutting up sheets of cardboard into cards about 4 in. by 3½ in. It can be a useful exercise in arithmetic to get the older pupils to measure out and cut up these cards explaining the purpose of them and letting them use them on completion. Whereas simply measuring, or drawing lines may have little or no interest for a backward pupil, the same task, with a definite purpose in mind gives the necessary practice, with an incentive to doing the work well.

With the secondary school pupil it is wiser to make the cards as near the ordinary pack as possible, so thirteen words, each repeated four times will give a good game. The smaller number of pairs suggested for younger children are not sufficient. The extremely retarded reader will need sets of words very dissimilar in appearance but a set can be prepared for any book, so they will have the satisfaction of doing the same kind of work as the better readers, apparently as well.

The same cards can also be used for playing 'Pairs' or 'Pelmanism', where all the cards are put face downwards on the table or a couple of desks and each player, in turn, turns over two cards. Where a pair is turned up he keeps them and has another turn. When all the cards have been won, the player with the most pairs is the winner.

Narrower but longer cards can be made into word dominoes. In every case the words used should be carefully chosen either from the reading book or from words recorded in the reading record as unknown or confused.

As has often been pointed out, it is particularly important to see that each child has a chance of winning fairly frequently so, if possible, he should be playing in a group roughly of his own ability. There will usually be two, three or more in a class of about the same reading level, so these can play together. Sometimes a child of low attainment can hold his own with others because of his interest in a game or his concentration on it or because he is of higher intelligence than the others. However, if there is, in the class, one non-reader or a child so slow mentally that he cannot ever achieve success against the others in the group, then the groups must be rearranged or the teacher must play with him and ensure that he sometimes wins. It must be remembered that the majority of backward children are likely to be even more backward in emotional development than in other ways and that it is highly unlikely that they will be sufficiently mature to be able to lose constantly and still have any incentive to keep on playing. The objective of the games is to arouse interest so it is a complete failure if further discouragement is the result.

Similar types of games can easily be devised to deal with a particular fault. For example, let us say a pupil has great difficulty in rapidly recognizing the vowels and often confuses them. Now this, in my opinion, is a very common fault among backward readers and one which it is essential to remove, as it can give rise to a tremendous number of reading errors and sometimes persists even when the reading level is quite high. The pupil can be asked to find a picture for each vowel sound in the pictures or magazines and to paste it in his notebook with the letter and the word. But, obviously, this can only be done once, though it is available for reference when mistakes are made again. He could also be asked to cross off the vowels in a prepared sheet of letters, but this, though helping him in the future to recognize them, will give no practice in using them nor in picking them out by the sound. Doing one or two things is, however, generally useless in eliminating a fault in a pupil old enough to be at a secondary school. If a card game can be devised the children need no persuasion to play it several times, but are very eager to do so. Something on the lines of Housey-housey would serve the purpose. A number of pictures of articles with the basic vowel sounds in them, e.g. apple, dog, hut, chips should be mounted on cardboard, perhaps eighteen at first, adding more as they become familiar. For non-readers the word should be printed under the picture, for others it is not necessary. For each picture a separate word card is also printed and there should be five extra pictures, one for each vowel. A 'banker' then places the five vowel cards in a row on the desk:

a e i o u

READING AND ENGLISH

He shuffles the pictures and deals out the words. Then he takes one picture at a time from his pack, and places it in the appropriate line according to the vowel in it. He asks the player with the right word to put it in the correct column. The first one to put out all his cards is the winner.

All these games can be adapted to remedy other faults or to give practice on other points, e.g. initial letters, ends of words, common phonograms. The use of the right words or combinations can make the same game serve different purposes. To give variety a card game can be made from many of the individual books. Take *Tracking Adventures* in the 'Adventures in Reading' series in which certain tracking signs are given. These sentences can be used instead of pictures and one sentence card given to each player. The separate words in a pack can be left in the centre after three or four cards have been dealt to each player. In turn, each player can pick up a card from the pack and discard an unwanted word until he has all the words of his sentence. Similarly, sentences can be taken from any book the pupils are reading and used in the same way.

At this stage different types of games can be devised and introduced. These also give variety in the practice and repetition of words and phrases. A cardboard base for the game can be divided up into numbered squares. Each player has some sort of coloured counter or figure to move along, the objective being to reach the end first. The games can either be played with dice, in which case various traps and rewards are written in several squares, or the instructions can be printed on cards which can be picked up, in turn, by each player. For example, a game could be based on *White Hawk* in the 'Active Readers' series. Indians normally arouse interest and small models can be bought very cheaply in Woolworth's or collected from cereal packets. Or cowboys might also be introduced and words from La Bonté put on the cards.

In connexion with these figures it is usually the case that models are attractive to children and this fact can be used to help the reading programme. Instead of confining oneself to apparatus made from cards and pictures, a pleasant change can be introduced by using models of a farm or town or any similar set which fits into the scheme. Instructions can then be written on cards for setting out the models in a particular way. For example, a model of a village proved particularly popular. Some of the cards read:

(1) Put the houses in two rows;
(2) Put the green house next to the red house;
(3) The red car is in front of the black car in the road.

Again the practice in following instructions will be good for the backward child and it will take only a second or two for the teacher to check the finished version.

The motifs for sticking on walls or furniture can also be used in a similar way by attaching them to pieces of wood or hardboard when, for example, a farm can be assembled or a set of birds. As these can be cleaned with a damp cloth they last a very long time.

This type of activity serves not only to interest the child but also to increase vocabulary and to give useful reading practice.

A different method of achieving an increase in reading vocabulary on certain topics in the reading books is to use prepared sheets of strong paper with pictures, word matching and choice exercises. In these a large attractively coloured picture can be stuck on in the centre panel, with the names of the main objects around. Exercises which require the use of these words, questions on them, missing words, jumbled words or sentences can be devised around this topic. For example work sheets such as 'The Lion Tamer' or 'The Big Top' can be used with 'The Fair', 'The Postman' or 'The Policeman' with Pathfinder Book I; 'Bob the Sailor' with Pathfinder Book II; 'The Birds' or 'The Birthday Party' with stories from The Wide Range Readers. Suitable coloured pictures are frequently published in magazines and these can form the basis of the work sheet.

This type of apparatus, without pictures, is particularly useful for those few senior pupils who feel that the pictures make their work too infantile. This point seldom arises with the non-reader, probably because the mental effort needed for them to do the work, even with the pictures is enough and because they generally recognize their need. With more advanced, but still backward readers matching practice may be necessary, but it has to be disguised in some way. So, with books such as the Pathfinder Books III to V, or later, the Active Readers, the pictures can be discarded and the work can be more in line with the pupils' actual age. Sentences can be chosen from the text and typed and mounted. These are put in envelopes with instructions, which vary slightly, on the outside. Some of the sentences can be cut up to give some elements of a puzzle to the task.

When the pieces are correctly sorted, the sentence has to be found in the book. Sometimes this sentence has to be written out, sometimes the one above or below it; or a number of sentences may be mounted on a card and cut out to form a jigsaw puzzle. Sentences with a missing word, separate words to make sentences, sentences to be put into the correct order, all serve the purpose of letting the older pupil look at and match words, with that need of a little extra thought to do the job properly. He must also refer to the printed text to complete the job.

Other kinds of expression may also serve to help the reading and so use the childs' interests to give them an incentive to recognize the words. They usually enjoy using 'instruction cards' on which are printed instructions to do certain things. These can be used with any age of child, varying the actions to the age. The first years are quite pleased to 'Walk to the board, write the date and then go back and sit down at your desk', while the fourth years have no objection to following instructions which will take them, for example, to a certain place in the school. While this is being done the cards can be read out to the class and they can say where, in fact, the absent member should arrive. They can later prepare their own cards and put their ability to give clear directions to the test, by sending someone to follow them.

This can be developed by putting short simple dramatic situations on the card. A volunteer reads this silently and mimes or acts it. Then the rest of the class say or write down exactly what was written and the results are compared with the original card. This is usually enjoyed, but care must, of course, be taken that no one is given a card to read which is quite beyond his or her power.

It is also necessary to give visual and aural discrimination exercises to those who particularly need them and it is possible and I think useful, to give them occasionally to a group or the whole class. Similar words to use for the exercises should be taken from the records of reading and, for the individual child, written or printed. When the teacher has read out the word in each group to be underlined, the paper can be pasted in the notebook. For the class the groups of three or more similar words can be written on the board to be copied in the exercise book. Then one word from each group is said clearly and each child underlines it in his copy. It may be objected that the pupils will be at various stages and should not do them together, but my experience is that, with a little tact, they can all join in. The worst readers can be given a choice of joining in or not but they always want to and can be highly praised for getting some right. In fact their difficulty may not be mainly aural and they may be able to do quite well, as it is not necessary to recognize the word, but only to discriminate the sound of either the beginning, middle or end of the word. These exercises can also be used with any year in the secondary school by varying the difficulty of the words and the speed of saying them.

Flash cards can also be adapted for class use and nearly all children love to do them. Single words help recognition and phrase cards help to increase eye-span. They are fascinated by the explanation that three, four or more words can be seen at the same time, and with practice more and more. Depending on the known ability of the class, the flash cards can be read out or written down, but the older pupils generally prefer to write them. Providing the ones who are bound to fail are given their flash cards another time, by the teacher, the rest of the class can usefully do them altogether, provided the words or phrases are carefully chosen and the progressions are well controlled.

Other points which must be dealt with in a reading programme designed to help those who have failed, in a greater or less degree, are giving help and practice in blending the sounds together to form words and teaching them to guess words, intelligently, from the context clues. Giving phrases or sentences with one word missing, except for the first and the last letter, will help in this. It must be remembered that those things which are done naturally and automatically by the average or more intelligent child, have to be taught to and practised by the dull or specifically retarded ones.

Although the apparatus and individual work cards may take some time to make, it can be collected together by degrees and if, as mentioned before, the class is trained by careful introduction to it and supervised closely in the early stages, it will last for a long time and only require replacement as any piece becomes dirty or battered. It is worth doing, because I am sure that the consideration of the individual difficulties and needs, which forms the basis of the apparatus (and without which it will not be very effective) is often the final point which brings the child to success after so many years of failure or partial failure. They are often very impressed and flattered that you are willing to put yourself to this trouble for them and respond to your interest with their own.

One other point to be considered is that, although there is an extremely good chance of success when non-readers are started on this type of programme in their first or even second year at the secondary school, the problem becomes much more complicated in the third or fourth year. All the added difficulties of adolescence may complicate matters; the pupil may be very mature in some ways and will probably have already set his or her ambitions to the time when school will be left behind and a new start made where, he hopes, his failures will no longer dog his footsteps. At this stage they will probably be less responsive to the adult than before and it may be much more difficult to get a personal response and create a belief in your ability to help them, or they may even have reached the stage where they no longer think it worth while to make the effort necessary to overcome the long-standing difficulty. This needs very careful handling as their needs, in reading, may still be very similar to those of an infant, but an attempt to give them these things will be resented and only serve to antagonize. Many ways must be thought out to get round this, but, in connexion with the point of apparatus making, one solution is to appeal to the older boy or girl for help to make apparatus for younger ones, or to check it to see if it is in good order with no parts missing. This gets the practice done without any injury to pride.

Other difficulties which arise with the older ones are that they may not have adjusted themselves to their limitations and may, either from themselves or their home, have set themselves a target (e.g. a job) which cannot be attained. They may also have set ideas on how certain lessons should be conducted and can be made to feel insecure or resentful at changes introduced. As an example of this, at one school in a fairly good district a reading programme as outlined above was put into practice with a third year class. Reading ages were from below 7 to over 10 and, as it was an extremely difficult class to handle, as many of the girls were very tense and emotionally immature, individual work cards were prepared for each girl and filled in each week. Reading, writing and related activities were set and the response seemed very good, as all worked well, with only two exceptions who needed a lot of pressure. After one term great progress in mechanical reading could be recorded and better work habits were being developed. It was something of a surprise when one parent arrived at school to complain that the girl was playing games instead of learning English. The girl in question was being given every personal consideration and had made far more progress in that one term than ever before, but the family had firmly decided that an office job had to be attained somehow and that as the English lessons were being enjoyed, they could not be achieving their purpose. This illustrates the point that explanations of the purpose of the work, especially when different methods are used, should, whenever possible, be made to the older pupil.

It might appear that, with so much attention given to reading, the English for the backward secondary school child would be limited, but this should not be allowed to happen and where these classes have a block time-table and spend a good part of their time with one teacher, this can easily be avoided. Integration of one subject with another needs no consultation and the child can be introduced to practically all aspects of the school activities. As wide a basis of experience as possible should be given, as only in this way will it be possible to give each dull or backward child a chance to find something in which a good standard can be reached.

This concentration on reading and work connected with it is not an end in itself, but a means by which it is hoped that each individual child, however handicapped, will reach the standard of fluency of which he is capable, and so be enabled to tackle work of a more advanced kind. It is just as bad to demand too little as too much. So it is necessary to realize that most children in the D stream will become ready, at one time or another, to progress, if the reading programme is successful. Although all in the first two years will benefit from, say, two lessons given to work similar to the most retarded ones, and some will need to continue to the end of their school career, yet there are many who can advance further. They must be taught how to read for a particular purpose, how to find out the main idea, how to skim, and, in fact, be trained in the many different ways in which comprehension and fluency can be increased. Useful material and suggestions which can be adapted for the older pupils, can be found in *How to become a Better Reader* by Paul Witty, published by the Science Research Associates Inc. of Chicago.

When the pupil has reached a mechanical reading age of about 9 and the mental level is not very low, it is also necessary to give some time regularly to comprehension exercises such as are done by the more average classes. The material must be easier and the questions fairly straightforward, but if the passage is well chosen this kind of work is enjoyed. For example the series called 'New Reading' in the two series one red, one blue, provide very useful work for backward seniors. The fact that it is connected with *Readers Digest* also adds to its attraction for older ones and the questions can be supplemented with more difficult ones where necessary.

This type of short article, containing interesting facts or a short extract from a longer story or book, can be carefully studied and the comprehension tested either by oral or written questions.

These, or other extracts read for the purpose, should be used also to try to stimulate the pupils to take books themselves from the class, school or public library, or, if their ability is insufficient, to ask the teacher to read it to them.

Where there are any difficulties at all it is wise to use some of the English lessons for reading aloud to the class, books or stories of a higher level than they can tackle themselves. Pupils with ability to read aloud well should be asked to prepare such stories for the pleasure of the class. Some of the more self-reliant or self-confident pupils can also prepare a few simple questions on the text or teach some simple point to another group or even the class.

How much formal English or composition should be done with the better children in the D stream is a very debatable point, but it depends a great deal on the standard of ability and attainment in the class, which may vary very widely. As a general rule free written composition for most of them is not very productive and often serves only to give practice in errors and disappointment in the result. However, the final end of the teaching of all written English is to give the child ability to express himself in writing and if he can learn to do so, it will be to his advantage. So all those who can reach this standard should be encouraged to write something of their own, perhaps when more handicapped pupils are doing their basic reading and written work.

The English training from the beginning of the secondary school should include the writing of sentences. I believe it is wise to insist on a full sentence always, when answering any questions. In this way a habit is formed and a sentence is written automatically whereas these children might never understand what you were talking about if you tried to explain to them what constituted a sentence.

Imaginative written compositions or essays cannot be expected of a really dull child and they see little purpose in them, but they can be taught to write simple, straightforward paragraphs on things they have learnt or seen or heard. A certain amount of the time for English should be given to the preparation of notes or paragraphs for their other lessons. Again this is much easier and more productive if one teacher is taking a number of subjects with the same class.

For example listening to the B.B.C. programme 'The Jacksons' is often an enjoyable experience which may lead to written expression of the incidents or of opinions on the points raised.

They should all be taught to write a simple, straightforward letter, both a business letter and a friendly letter, but the same principles apply as in teaching a dull child to read. They will need frequent repetition, but if the exercises are varied, they will be more successful. Any excuse can be seized upon which necessitates the writing of letters, absent pupils, girls on holiday, invitations to staff or children to visit some small exhibition or show prepared by the class, or thanks for educational visits. Anything of this sort can be used, and, in doing project work or arranging school visits, business letters can be sent to firms or offices. The typed reply usually received pleases them and does more to convince the child that there is a recognized form of setting down a business letter than any exposition by the teacher.

Nearly everybody agrees that formal grammar lessons should not be given to dull children, but, in my experience, the child is handicapped in making further progress if he cannot master a few very simple grammatical points. He is likely to be poor at spelling and to have a meagre vocabulary and less general knowledge than the average child. If he can be taught to use a dictionary and an encyclopedia then he has the means of at least partially overcoming these handicaps. But he cannot use the dictionary at all accurately unless he knows what a noun and a verb are, singular and plural, tenses of verbs and a few facts of this nature. Therefore the teacher should be on the alert to find pupils who are ready to understand these things and teach them to all those who can benefit by it. This would not, of course, be the whole class. If in the first and second year personal dictionaries are kept (even the poorest reader can make his own picture dictionary) then, by the third year, the great majority of pupils are ready to do some useful work involving the use of the dictionary. Although the work may be 'formal', the method of teaching need not be.

It is, of course, even more important that the pupils should leave school able to talk, so they must be given opportunities to speak. This aspect of English has been discussed by Mr Lyon – so it need only be mentioned here.

The less able senior pupils should also be given training in using the school library (*The Library in Education* by R. G. Ralph gives many valuable suggestions for the lower classes in this). In fact, if any sort of topic or project work is to be attempted, it is necessary for them to be able to understand where to find the kind of book they need, or how to use an index, or the difference between the fiction and non-fiction section. Even before they have reached the stage when they will want to use the ordinary library books, when they must still rely on supplementary reading material provided in easy form in their own classroom, they can be given short practices in finding a given book and on putting it back in the right place, with the rest of the class.

Unless basic training of this kind and in getting information from books and presenting it in their own form is given, then there can be little or no progression in the type of work produced. This training is invaluable in giving the pupils a chance to use their own interests as the basis of their work. It is, however, no use expecting to take any backward class, to stimulate their interest in some particular topic, however well this may be done, and then hope for the work to flow smoothly on to completion. The children will not achieve the standard which will satisfy them, unless they have previously learnt to work from books by themselves, for it is impossible for the teacher to deal adequately with individual work in a class when each member of it constantly needs help.

The basic reading lessons which formed part of the earlier work are a good basis to start from, because there they do learn to use a book for themselves and to use the classroom, the necessary tools and the apparatus.

Once this is established routine, it is possible to get all the class started on a piece of English work in which all can share. It is best not to be too ambitious at first. The thing which seems to work best with me is to take some interesting short story, perhaps set in another land, and to read it to or with the class. Discussion of this follows and as each point arises someone may volunteer to find out more about it, until eventually everyone has contracted to do something either in a group or alone.

A few English lessons at strategic intervals are then given to going to the library and finding the information needed. The better reader can use the normal books, the poorer ones must find something there which they can use.

A supply of simple reference books should be gradually built up by the teacher of a backward class and the County Library is usually very helpful in lending particular books on a topic, both for normal readers and, within limits, for those with difficulties.

Eventually the information can be copied out with illustrations, maps, etc., and mounted for display on the walls.

From this beginning advances can gradually be made and more difficult topics tackled, based on visits, exhibitions or almost any subject in the curriculum.

This type of work is generally enjoyed and even a senior girl in her last year, who might well lose all interest in school, can respond extremely well to a 'Health and Beauty' or a 'Home' topic. At this point, I will refer those who would like detailed suggestions for working on topic lines to Mr Beagley's chapter.

Teachers in the secondary school who have to deal with pupils who are retarded must be prepared to spend time and thought on the problems the individuals present, must have confidence in the probability of succeeding but not be depressed by some apparent failures; and while isolating and dealing exactly with each fault which may be the cause of the difficulties, must try to widen and expand the outlook of the backward child so that he may develop into a person who has tasted success and knows that many things can be interesting.

References

Bristol Institute of Education, *A Survey of Books for Backward Readers*, University of London Press Ltd.

CLEUGH, M. F., *The Slow Learner*, Methuen.

DUNCAN, JOHN, *The Education of the Ordinary Child*, Thomas Nelson and Sons Ltd.

FERNALD, G. and KELLER, H., 'The Effect of Kinaesthetic Factor in the Development of Word Recognition in Non-Readers', *Journal of Educational Research*, pp. 355–77, No. IV, 1921, University of Bristol.

GATES, A. I., *The Improvement of Reading*, The Macmillan Company.

— *Interest and Ability in Reading*, The Macmillan Company.

KEIR, GERTRUDE, *Adventures in Reading Teachers' Companion*, Oxford University Press.

MONROE, M., *Children Who Cannot Read*, University of Chicago Press.

RALPH, R. G., *The Library in Education*, Turnstile Press Ltd.

SCHONELL, F. J., *Backwardness in the Basic Subjects*, Oliver and Boyd.

— *The Psychology and Teaching of Reading*, Oliver and Boyd.

WITTY, PAUL, *How to become a Better Reader*, Science Research Association, Chicago.

JOSEPHINE STOPA

Chapter V

ARITHMETIC

The Problem

The problem of teaching arithmetic to a backward class in a secondary modern school is necessarily a complex one. The children will probably have been drawn from a number of junior schools and will have been taught by different methods. Their levels of attainment in arithmetic will vary very much and will very often not correspond with their intelligence levels. The children are often dispirited and feel that they are failures, having no inclination to try the work at which they have so often failed. From this rather unpromising material the teacher has to try to give each child as much understanding as possible of the uses of number which he or she will meet in after-school life.

The traditional academic approach to arithmetic when used with backward children is impracticable for one simple reason: the backward child has insufficient imagination to visualize the concrete form of the written number. The child may have limitless imagination in the fantasy sense, in that it can, and will, daydream and live in a world of its own, but the deliberate conjuring up of pictures relative even to as simple a thing as adding 3 and 3 is beyond its ability.

It is bearing all these things in mind that we should begin to assess our class.

Assessing the Class

As teaching should begin from where the children are, and not from where they are assumed to be, there is an absolute necessity for diagnostic and attainment testing before we can begin to teach arithmetic to the backward child in the secondary modern school.

Ability will be mainly low in a backward class but there may be a retarded child with higher ability. Record cards usually give results of intelligence tests; when averaged over several years these give a

ARITHMETIC

good enough idea to work on. If there is no record card then a child must be tested. The range of ability may vary from those with Intelligence Quotients or Standard Intelligence Scores of about 70 to those with 90 or more. My present class varies from 59 to 110, the latter being a very maladjusted girl whose attainments are difficult to assess accurately, varying as they do with her attitude.

Terman and Merrill's tests of intelligence give accurate results, but need a trained tester to administer them and take quite a long time with each child individually. If this is not possible there are several tests which can be more easily administered and give as accurate an assessment as the usual group intelligence tests. Of these Sleight's *Non-Verbal Test of Intelligence* and the *Simplex Intelligence Scale*, both published by Harrap, are perhaps the most widely used.

The child's attainment level in mechanical arithmetic may be on the record card. If not it can quite easily be found by one of the recognized tests, but this will only reveal a child's aptitude. A child with a Standard Score in arithmetic of 96 will be good at number, for a backward class; but this score does not show whether she has ever learned long multiplication or whether she really knows how many feet are in a yard.

In any case, a teacher will wish to find the child's general level herself and a test of the four rules in number and money will reveal this.

The following is an example of the sort of observations that might be made from the results of this test:

Janet Sainsbury

This girl has mastered the four rules in simple number. She is not absolutely certain of her × combinations, having said $4 \times 7 = 26$.

In Number 14 she has forgotten to multiply the tens figure.

Her addition of money is accurate but in subtracting she has used 10*d*. for 1*s*. She has made two small mistakes in multiplication of money but obviously knows how to multiply and divide.

With a little practice in the four rules of money Janet should be quite ready for more advanced work.

A more accurate assessment can be made by using carefully graded tests such as *Beacon Survey Tests* or Schonell's *Diagnostic Tests*. This will reveal at exactly which step the child is failing.

Here are some examples of the sort of comments that I would make after studying different children's performances in *Beacon Survey Tests* in the four rules of number.

Beryl Aldridge. Beryl knows these additions although she has made one slip.

Cynthia Bell. Cynthia obviously has no idea of addition at all when more than units are involved.

Valerie Britton. Valerie fully understands all the subtraction sums.

Jane Christie. Jane has no idea how to subtract when any 'borrowing' is necessary.

Pat Clements. Pat knows the process of multiplication but is unsure of 7, 8, 9 times tables.

Jennifer Tait. Jennifer knows how to divide although she has omitted the tens figure when it is 0.

Gay Martin. Gay seems to know how to divide but has made such silly mistakes in Numbers 7 and 8 that she obviously needs much more practice or was not giving her full attention to the test.

The level of attainment found by testing will only reveal the child's level of mechanical arithmetic when written down. It does not give any indication of how much number really means to her. Whether the number 7 really conjures up a picture of 7 marbles or 7 cakes, or whether 5 + 3 really conveys 8 automatically, can only be found by a careful individual study of each child and her work.

Objectives

Ideally the teacher should aim at giving these children as clear a conception of basic number as they are capable of, and if possible, a working knowledge of the aspects of number which will be necessary to them in adult life. Unfortunately it may be necessary to add to these requirements other work which is necessary for them as part of a school pattern. If they are near the top of the backward class they may have to be taken into a higher group to make room for a new child of much lower ability. In this case the top children in

ARITHMETIC

the backward class may perhaps be expected to work on a syllabus similar to that of the higher stream. In some schools the teacher is required to use a 'watered down' version of the general school arithmetic syllabus, but fortunately these are rare.

The limited arithmetic requirements of these children in adult life can be more or less tabulated, though there will naturally be a little deviation, since occupations vary in their demands. In home life, shopping lists, the working out of the family budget, the everyday dealing with bus fares, the following of cooking recipes and the measuring of such things as curtains, wood for shelves, quantities for home decorating, etc., are for the main part nearly all the arithmetical problems that will be met. In the factory there will be little demand for great powers in this direction and few backward children find jobs where much calculation is needed. They should have some idea roughly what deductions are likely to be made from their wages, even if they cannot work it all out to the last penny. They should also have some idea of buying things by instalments and realize that paying for articles on hire purchase increases the price of the goods. The ability to use a ready reckoner may also prove useful.

Although the children should be able to work neatly if the occasion demands it, the aim should be to work out necessary problems speedily and accurately and more emphasis should be placed on this than on the very careful setting down of every sum, and perfectly formed figures.

Methods

The ability to use numbers must be acquired through a steady mental growth in mathematical awareness, and the child must thoroughly grasp each stage and live through it before proceeding to the next one. It is not a ladder with a fact on each rung so that a child may miss a rung out completely, or barely touch it and yet still reach the top. Each step must be learned thoroughly.

So often the backward child is one who is frequently absent from school. We must be prepared to realize that many children will have missed vital preliminary stages and with some of these children it may be necessary to go back to the very beginnings of number experience.

This may mean going back to the beginnings of number language, to counting shells, cotton reels, etc., sorting large and small, heavy and light, to playing with scales and weights, shop articles and money, and using blocks and templates of different shapes and sizes.

A very useful general piece of apparatus is the board with holes cut out. The loose shapes can be fitted in holes or used to draw round. Many children will never have met triangles, semicircles, etc. They will enjoy fitting in the shapes and using them to make patterns with. The names triangle, square, oblong, circle, etc., can be introduced verbally.

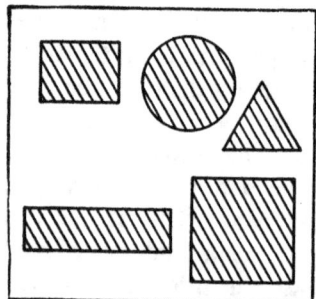  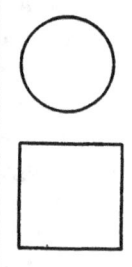

No opportunity of number language should be missed with these children, e.g. How many girls are here today? Mary does not have milk, so how many bottles shall we need? This will be followed by practical number combinations, such as: 2 shells and 3 more shells make 5 shells, etc. These should be practised with simple numbers until the response to some of them will be automatic, and until the children can state clearly on paper what they have found.

When they have learnt to state their findings clearly and correctly, then they can proceed to simple sums based on reality and given verbally, e.g. How many marbles altogether in these two boxes?

Box 1	.	.	.	.	.	.	5 marbles
Box 2	.	.	.	.	.	.	4 marbles
Altogether		.	.	.	.	.	9 marbles

Leading to 5
           +4
            —
            9

ARITHMETIC

When they have grasped the four rules by actual experience of meaningful things, then I think there is a place for mechanical practice.

Many children will say that they have 'done' much more advanced work than tests prove that they know. Very often this means that they have been used to class teaching as opposed to individual teaching; the class must necessarily work at the speed of at least the average in the class, and much work is then done which the more backward children will not have understood. The use of different text-books from those used in the contributory junior schools may help to obviate the feeling many children have in this case, that they are going back to junior work.

Mechanical practice will help the children to learn the simpler number combinations by heart and when this is completed, the basis is there for all arithmetical processes.

Practical experience is very necessary to these children at all stages. They must learn the concrete before they attempt the abstract. Measuring, weighing, capacity, time, etc., should all be introduced at the right points, followed by appropriate exercises, not as isolated units. The weighing of sugar, fat, etc., which the children can actually use to cook with, or the measurement of material, wood, etc., which they are really going to use will help them to learn to weigh and measure accurately. If it is possible to correlate arithmetic and domestic science as discussed later by Miss Devereux and Miss Cooper, it makes weighing, etc., much more realistic. Reference should also be made here to the linkages suggested by Mr Beagley between arithmetic and social studies and projects.

Work other than arithmetic, but with a definite number bias should be allowed whenever possible. If a school shop is practicable perhaps some girls could do it each week, checking their sales, banking their money, etc. The whole class could make notebooks one week, make toffee-apples another week, and so on. This work which holds the interest of the children from the beginning is of much more value than many lessons of straightforward 'teaching'.

Mental work is very important to backward children. When they eventually leave school and use whatever knowledge of number they have retained, very little of their working will be on paper.

Mental exercises help the children to listen, especially if, after the first few, each sum is given only once. Wisdom's *Arithmetical Dictation Books 1 and 2*, and similar sums are very useful for this. These sums also give practice in terms plus, minus, double, etc. Quick addition, subtraction, etc., round the class will help the children with their number combinations and encourage quick thinking. A continuous sum given fairly slowly to give the children time to work, such as . . . Start with 6, add 4, take away 2, divide by 4. How many have we left? . . . will encourage mental working and help to revise number combinations.

Many backward children find a pen and ink difficult to control. Children should be encouraged to set down their work clearly, always putting the date, page, or exercise, for their own convenience and that of the teacher who corrects. However, in view of the little written work they will ultimately have to do, and of their limitations, do not be too insistent about neatness and ink until they have thoroughly mastered each process. When they have learnt it then they can practise it using ink and taking care with their figures. It is important to remember that to many of these children neat work is as difficult to achieve as the actual working out of a sum.

Number games can serve a very useful purpose. Most children enjoy them and they can be yet another way of practising the basic number combinations as well as specific games for different processes. Competitive games are usually enjoyed by children, but care must be taken that the less able ones do not feel frightened because they cannot do very well, and that the teams do not bully or scare their less able members.

With four teams and four sets of numbers and signs +, −, ×, ÷, =, a great variety of team games can be made. This gives the children practice in quick thinking and the competition encourages them to do their best.

Children always like to use the blackboard and many games can be devised with working or answers on the board.

Games with Simple Number Combinations

For team games divide the class into four teams and number each team up to the number of the largest team. For example, if there are twenty-seven children there can be three teams of seven and one of

ARITHMETIC

six, but if each team is numbered to seven one of the small team will be 'running' twice.

1. (a) Teacher calls out 4×2 ... number three, and each number three runs and writes answer on the board. First one with the correct answer scores a point. This can be done with +, −, ×, ÷.

(b) Loose numbers can be put in front of each team and the player must find the right number for her answer.

(c) Numbers can be taken to front by players but not shown until all are ready. Each one with correct answer scores a point.

2. (a) Teams in groups with numbers and signs in centre. One team calls. Number one calls out: e.g. 9+3. The other teams look among their numbers and lay out 9+3=12. Each team with a correct sum scores. Number two then calls.

3. Teacher puts part of sum on board and calls a number: e.g. 12 4 = 3 ... number six. Number six then runs out and finds the correct signs: e.g. ÷.

Many variations on these games can be made.

The purpose of arithmetical skill is to solve personal problems. Dull children are not good at the transference of ideas, and so problems should be kept constantly on personal things ... stations, pictures, post office, etc. Many games can be based on a set of prices for railway journeys, pictures, etc.

Example.

Railway Fares
Maidstone to London

3 monthly return	Adult	12s. 10d.
	Child (3-15 yrs.)	6s. 5d.
Single fare	Half return fare.	
Day return	Adult	9s. 0d.
	Child	4s. 6d.

Children can make a list of their proposed family.

e.g. Grandmother
Mother
Father
Mary, 13 yrs.
John, 7 yrs.
Betty, 2 yrs.

If tickets can be made then they can go and collect the appropriate tickets for their journey from the ticket office ... (no money as this proves too much working out for the cashier, and causes a lot of waiting).

They then return and add up their fares. Cashier should note number of tickets 'sold' and work out total cost. This can be varied by taking dogs, bicycles, etc. Intermediate stations may be introduced later.

Nearly all children like shopping. Shops can be made from empty cartons, from pictures pasted on card, or from any articles in the room. It is a good idea to have several shops and avoid queues. Each 'shopper' should list her purchases and their prices, which can be checked by the teacher.

Organization

Backward children need an arithmetic lesson of not more than thirty minutes each day. A short period of really hard work is of far more value than a long drawn out lesson when the children get bored and tired.

Each lesson should have a short period of mental work all together: this can be table practice, answers to questions, games, etc.

Following this each girl should continue with her individual work unless she has a job such as checking sweets, etc. When work on an exercise has been marked, corrections should be done before continuing to the next exercise.

There is always a very varied ability in the backward classroom and although no school today is able to have classes small enough for the teacher to give the child as much individual attention as she needs, yet the teacher must not despair and resort to class teaching in a frantic attempt to 'do her duty' to the children. The solution to the apparently insurmountable problem lies, for the main part, in the teacher's ability to organize individual work so that, recognizing certain stages in a child's mental growth, she allows and encourages her to progress from stage to stage at her own rate.

The ideal method would be to allow each child to pursue her own interests and learn through the arithmetical problems involved. Mary and Joan would work hard and would learn a great deal of arithmetic if they could always run the tuck shop unaided. Susan and Jane

ARITHMETIC

would probably learn a lot from their pets in weighing food, measuring wood for cages and so forth. Joyce would learn accurate measuring very quickly if she were allowed to make all the notebooks she wants to. Unfortunately since most of these children are unable to follow written instructions and therefore need continual guidance, it is not always possible to let them do these individual things. Also, there may be some very necessary stages in arithmetic which are not included in the practical projects that the children suggest.

It is very rarely that two children in a class are at exactly the same point and work at exactly the same speed. A child must be allowed and encouraged to work at the greatest speed which is possible for her, so individual work is necessary.

This need not be as complicated as it so often appears, if it is competently organized, and the class well trained in what they should be doing. It is, however, much more effort for the teacher because instead of explaining a process to the whole class, she may have to explain new processes to any number of children during the course of a lesson.

These are some important points to remember in organizing individual work in arithmetic.

(1) There must be a progressive scheme based on carefully graded books or cards.

(2) Children who finish an exercise must be able to find out if the answers are correct. It is usually quite practicable to let them mark their own sums. It will soon be found if there are the odd one or two children who will copy the answers.

(3) It is not always possible for the teacher to teach a child the next process at the exact moment she finishes the exercise before. There should be some exercises that the children can get on with while they are waiting.

(4) If cards are used each process should have a special coloured card so that the children can see at a glance which are theirs: e.g. +pink, − blue, × green, ÷ yellow.

Cards on money could be slightly larger, or have a special picture and the processes coloured as before.

Each set of cards should have problem cards to go with them. These could be number 1, 1P, 2, 2P, etc.

Cards with pictures or printed in colour are always more attractive to children. The cards should be printed or written clearly, and as nearly as possible in the style of writing which the children are expected to use if there is a fixed style. A coat of clear lacquer such as that obtainable from E.S.A. will help to preserve the cards.

(5) It is necessary to introduce some practical work for individual children when they reach certain stages. Practical work done as an isolated section is no use; it must be connected with the appropriate work and introduced when each child is ready. When a child is ready to work in feet and inches, she must do plenty of measuring first. Practical work is essential to the backward child because she cannot grasp abstract ideas, and to a child who has never measured a foot 12 inches = 1 foot is a completely abstract idea.

A set of cards of practical work on length, time capacity and weight are very useful, and each child can work through the appropriate cards when she reaches that stage, e.g.

CARD 4
1. Measure the depth of each bookshelf.
2. I have five books. The first is $11\frac{1}{2}$ in., the second 8 in., the third 5 in., the fourth 10 in., and the fifth $7\frac{1}{2}$ in. Which books would go on the top shelf? Which books would go on the second shelf? Would they all go on the bottom shelf?
3. Measure your height. (With help.)
4. If I am 5 ft. 10 in., how much taller am I than you?

If each set of cards . . . weight, capacity, time, etc., is done on different coloured cards, the children will find them easier to sort out. Always try to use figures written as the children will write them

Any practical work that can be used to real purpose is the best possible help to the children. If a real shop is possible then the working out of prices, giving of change, checking of stock, and banking of money provide experience which will prove invaluable to the children because they will see the purpose of it.

The following examples are taken from an actual school shop.

ARITHMETIC

	Stock	Sold	Left	Takings
Caramel	69	14	55	4s. 7d.
Crisps	14	8	6	2s. 0d.
Lollies	33	18	15	1s. 10½d.
Flakes	16	9	7	1s. 9d.
Liquorice	72	31	29	7d.

17s. 2½d.

(16s. 11d.)

This page from the shopkeepers' daily record shows the number of each item when the shop was opened, the number left at closing time, the number sold and the cost of these. The money in brackets is what they actually took, showing a deficit of 3½d., due to incorrect change, incorrect counting or other causes.

Here are a shopkeepers' weekly entries of money taken:

Date		£	s.	d.
9th June	Monday	1	2	4
10th ,,	Tuesday		17	1½
11th ,,	Wednesday		9	8
13th ,,	Friday	1	1	3½

3 10 5

In this chapter I have written with the needs of girls in mind, but as in fact backwardness in arithmetic is usually more of a problem with girls than with boys, this is not a disadvantage.

The same principles apply, although the type of examples will naturally differ, in a boys' school.

Grading of Work
The following is a suggested outline of work for backward children in a secondary modern school.

It is divided roughly into eight sections. Testing at the end of each section, or alternatively at the end of a set period of time, e.g. six weeks, is essential.

It may well be found that girls have not really grasped one piece of work, although they did the given examples accurately after they had been taught. This will mean repeating the work with examples taken from other sources. Some girls may never progress further than perhaps Section V.

Girls of very low intelligence may never be able to understand such things as percentages, although they may learn how to work out examples mechanically. The use of figures thus involved will be good practice, but if they cannot understand them, further work on them should be omitted. In testing it may be found that a girl does not know one process in Section II. Once she has grasped this it is not necessary for her to continue through Section III if she obviously knew this work when she was tested.

In some large schools it may be necessary to introduce the brighter girls to work which they would not otherwise do, in order to keep them level with the stream above and facilitate movement to a higher group.

Suggested Grading of Mechanical Work

I. (1) (a) Number language ... how many, less, more, etc.
   (b) Conception of numbers up to 20.
   (c) Addition and subtraction up to 20, no carrying.

   e.g.   4   7   5   6
         +3   +1   −2   −4

   (d) With coins $\frac{1}{2}d.$, $1d.$, up to $10d.$
       Use of pennies in + −.

   e.g.   d.   d.   d.   d.
          3   6   5   7
         +2   +1   −3   −4

(2) (a) Make-up of tens and units,
       e.g. 36 = 3 tens 6 units.
   (b) Conception of numbers up to 100.
   (c) Addition with 10's, no carrying.

   e.g.   42   31
         +21   +14

ARITHMETIC

(d) Addition with carrying.

 e.g.   27   45
     + 6   +17

(3) (a) Addition with $\tfrac{1}{2}d$.

 e.g.   d.   d.
    $4\tfrac{1}{2}$ 7
    +2 $+1\tfrac{1}{2}$

(b) Addition with two $\tfrac{1}{2}d$.'s.

 e.g.   d.   d.
    $4\tfrac{1}{2}$ $7\tfrac{1}{2}$
    $+2\tfrac{1}{2}$ $+2\tfrac{1}{2}$

(c) 1d., 3d., 6d., 1s.

 e.g. How many 3d. bits make 1s.?

(d) Counting in tens.

Simple problems should accompany each step,

 e.g. Jim saw 9 rabbits and his dog chased 4 more.
 How many did they see altogether?

Practical work with money, such as simple buying and selling may be introduced at the end of this section.

Telling the time on the hours.

II. (1) (a) Inches.

 Measuring small articles such as a pencil, a book, etc.

(b) Feet.

 Measuring door, table, etc.

(c) Straight lines.

 Which articles have straight sides? Blackboard, door, etc.

(d) $\tfrac{1}{2}$ inches.

 Measuring given cards, etc., which have $\tfrac{1}{2}$ inch.

(2) (a) Subtraction sums, adding 10 to each line.

 e.g.   9   19   29
    −4   −14   −24
    ——   ——   ——
    5   5   5 etc.

This leads to subtraction with "borrowing",

 e.g. 24
   −15

As you cannot take 5 from 4, add 10 to each line

  2 ¹⁰4
  −2 5

(b) Multiply with one number below 6.

 e.g. 4 7 3
   ×5 ×2 ×6

(c) Divide with one number below 6.

 e.g. 2)18 8)16 5)5
    ― ― ―

(3) (a) Money to 24d., with coins if necessary.

  e.g. How many pennies make 1s. 4d.?
    How many shillings and pence in 15d.?

(b) Feet to 24 inches (as above).

(c) +, −, of shillings, pence.
 ×, ÷, of shillings, pence.

 e.g. s. d. s. d. s. d. s. d.
   3 3¼ 8 5¼ 1 2 4)4 8
  +1 2 −1 3   ×3   ―――

(4) (a) Writing hundreds.

  e.g. Write two hundred and sixty-one.

(b) Addition with carrying to hundreds.

 e.g. 57 136 154
   +26 +225 +272

(5) (a) Right angles: trying corners with a right angle paper.

(b) ¼ inches.

  e.g. How many inches in 8 ¼ inches?
    How many ¼ inches in 3 inches?

(c) +, −, feet and inches with ½, ¼, no carrying.
 ×, ÷, feet and inches.

ARITHMETIC

e.g.
```
ft.  in.      ft.  in.     ft.  in.     ft.  in.
 4   2¾        5   4¼       2    1      3)9   6
+1   3        -2   1        ×4
```

Simple problems as before, and practical work in measuring. Telling the time on half-hours.

III. (1) (a) × by 0, and with both numbers greater than 5.

    (b) ÷ with 0, and with both numbers greater than 5.

```
e.g.    9      7     0     7    0)9   9)54   6)0
       ×0     ×6    ×5    ×8
```

    (c) + with three sets of figures.

```
e.g.   25      36
      +14     +11
      +12     +45
```

    (d) × hundreds, tens, units by numbers up to 5.

```
e.g.  341    212    301
       ×2     ×4     ×3
```

(2) (a) + of s. d. with shillings to carry.

    (b) + of ft. in. with carrying.

```
e.g.   s.  d.     s.  d.      ft.  in.     ft.  in.
       3   9      2   7½       2    9       1    8½
      +1   3½    +4   8       +1    7¼     +1    6
```

    (c) − of s. d. with borrowing.

    (d) − of ft. in. with borrowing.

```
e.g.   s.  d.     ft.  in.     ft.  in.
       3   5       5    4       3    6
      -2   7      -1    9      -1    8
```

(3) (a) Oblongs, rectangles and squares.
Definitions and finding which articles are this shape.

    (b) Names of thousands.
        e.g. Write in figures one thousand, five thousand, etc.
What is the name of this number: 2,000?

(c) $\frac{1}{2}, \frac{1}{3}, \frac{1}{4}, \frac{1}{5}$, by drawing and practical work.

e.g. Copy the oblong and colour $\frac{1}{2}$ of it.

Copy this square and fill $\frac{1}{4}$ of it with dots.

(d) How many in 1 dozen, 2 dozen, etc.

(4) (a) 10 × table.

× and ÷ by 10 where dividend ends in 0, by short method.

e.g. 7   6   15   10)130   10)90
     ×10 ×10 ×10

(b) 11 × table.

× by 11 up to 5 × 11.

e.g. 4   3   11
     ×11 ×11   ×4

(5) Addition of pennies and halfpennies, with coins if necessary.

e.g.   d.   d.   d.
      $4\frac{1}{2}$ $2\frac{1}{2}$ $3\frac{1}{2}$
     $+1\frac{1}{2}$ $+1\frac{1}{2}$ $+1\frac{1}{2}$

(6) (a) × with carrying up to 9 ×.

e.g. 35 ×   26 ×   38
       4   5   ×7

(b) ÷ of hundreds with no remainders.

e.g. 6)246   5)525   4)832

Practical work with measuring $\frac{1}{4}$ inches, $\frac{1}{2}$ inches and $\frac{3}{4}$ inches.
Practical work dividing up articles into fractions.
Telling the time on quarter hours.

ARITHMETIC

IV. (1) (a) Longer addition.

e.g. 431   343
       24   156
      179   48

(b) × by 11 and 12.

e.g. 23   31   24   35×
     ×11   ×12   ×11   12

(c) Longer subtraction.

e.g. 592   436
     −347   −251

(d) ÷ with carrying.

e.g. 5)325   8)264   4)764
      ─────   ─────   ─────

(2) (a) Addition of *s. d.*, ft. in., with carrying.

e.g. *s. d.*   ft. in.   ft. in.
       2   4½   1   7½   1   8¾
      +1   9½   +1   8¼   +1   6½

(b) £ *s. d.* Four rules with no carrying.

e.g. £   *s.   d.*   £   *s.   d.*   £   *s.   d.*
      1   13   2½   7   14   8½   2   4   3¼
     +3   2   4   −1   3   1½   ×3
     ─────────────
     5)£15 10*s.* 5*d.*

(c) +, −, £ *s. d.* with carrying in *d.*

e.g. £   *s.   d.*   £   *s.   d.*
      3   4   9½   4   14   4½
     +2   6   8½   −1   3   9½

(3) (a) Feet and yards.

e.g. How many feet in 4 yards?
     How many yards in 21 feet?

(b) Four rules: yds. ft. in. with no carrying.

e.g. yds. ft. in.   yds. ft. in.
       4   1   7   7   2   8
      +3   1   2   −4   1   6
      yds. ft. in.   yds. ft. in.
       3   0   2 ×4   8   2   6 ÷2

77

TEACHING THE SLOW LEARNER IN THE SECONDARY SCHOOL

Telling the time on every five-minute mark.

V. (1) (a) +, −, of £ s. d. with carrying.
e.g.
£ s. d.   £ s. d.
3 13 9½   5 11 4½
+4 17 8½   −3 14 1½

(b) ÷ by 10 with remainder.
e.g. 10)472   10)398

(c) +, −, yds. ft. in. with carrying.
e.g.
yds. ft. in.   yds. ft. in.
 4   2   9½   5   1   7¼
+1   2   4¼   −2   2   3½

(2) (a) Time: up to 1.55, 2.35, etc.
    (b) Writing numbers up to hundreds of thousands.
        e.g. Write in words 837,514.
            Write in figures two hundred and fifteen thousand, eight hundred and ninety-two.
    (c) Circles and diameters.
    (d) Roman numerals up to 10.
    (e) Further fractions.
        e.g. Measure this line and draw ¾ of it.

(3) (a) ×10, 20, etc., cwt., tons; seconds, minutes.
e.g. 43×   621   437
       20   ×60   ×30
How many cwt. in 72 tons?
Change 84 hrs. to minutes.

(b) Long multiplication.
e.g. 37   432   321
   ×24   ×56   ×17

(c) Long division.
e.g. 42÷21   352÷32   531÷21

(d) Longer subtraction.
e.g. 9,413   4,132
   −1,586   −2,371

ARITHMETIC

(4) (a) Fractions of shillings, pounds, etc.
  e.g. What is $\frac{1}{2}$ shilling, $\frac{1}{4}$ score, $\frac{1}{8}$ £?
 (b) Area.
  e.g. Draw a rectangle 4 in. × 2 in.
  What is the area?

(5) (a) Multiply pence and halfpence.
  e.g. d.   d.
      $5\frac{1}{2}$ $8\frac{1}{2}$
      ×4   ×6
 (b) Reduction.
  e.g. How many pennies in 8 shillings?
  How many feet in 18 yards.?
  How many shillings in £4. 16s. 0d.?

Practical work with clocks and time.

VI. (1) (a) ×100, 200, etc.
  e.g. 37×   421
      200   ×300
 (b) ×, ÷, £ s. d.
  e.g. £ s. d.   £ s. d.
     4 11 $5\frac{1}{2}$ ×   6)8 7 $7\frac{1}{2}$
       4
 (c) ×, ÷, yds. ft. in.
  e.g. yds. ft. in.
      4   1 $5\frac{1}{4}$ 5)7yds. 1ft. $2\frac{1}{4}$in.
          ×4

(2) (a) Roman numerals up to 50.
 (b) Fractions $\frac{2}{3}$, $\frac{1}{2}$, $\frac{3}{4}$.
  e.g. Draw a circle and colour $\frac{3}{4}$ of it.
 (c) Writing millions.
  e.g. Write in figures seven million.
  Write in words 1,342,000.
 (d) Time before and after twelve o'clock.
  e.g. How long is it from 8.30 a.m. until 2.30 p.m.?
 (e) Reduction and expansion.

e.g. How many pence in £2. 14s. 9d.?
Bring 384 halfpennies to s. d.

(3) (a) Four rules of weight.
   (b) Four rules of liquid measure.
   (c) Four rules of length.

e.g.

tons	cwt.	qrs.	gal.	qt.	pt.
3	17	2	5	1	0
+1	5	1	−1	2	1
+3	16	3			

miles	furlongs	yds.
5	6	89 ×
		5

VII. (1) (a) Reduction of liquid measure.
      e.g. How many pints in 9 gal. 3 qt. 1 pt.?
  (b) Long multiplication £ s. d.
      e.g. £ s. d.
          4 13 8½
            ×23
  (c) Long division £ s. d.
      e.g. 21)£39. 18s. 8½d.

(2) (a) Roman numerals up to 90.

(3) (a) +, −, of fractions with same denominator.
      e.g. $\frac{3}{8}+\frac{1}{8}$, $\frac{6}{7}-\frac{3}{7}$
  (b) ×, ÷, of fraction by whole number.
      e.g. $\frac{1}{3}\times 4$ $\frac{2}{5}\times 3$
            $\frac{2}{3}\div 2$ $\frac{3}{4}\div 5$
  (c) Division of whole number by fraction.
      e.g. $4\div\frac{1}{4}$ $7\div\frac{1}{2}$

(4) (a) $\frac{1}{10}$, $\frac{1}{100}$ as decimals.
  (b) +, −, decimals.
      e.g.   4·92   5·17
           +1·37   −2·31

ARITHMETIC

VIII. (1) (*a*) Percentages.

e.g. What is 5% of 340?

(*b*) Costs of dozens, short method.

e.g. How much will 2 dozen oranges cost at $3\tfrac{1}{2}d.$ each?

(2) (*a*) +, −, mixed numbers, different denominators.

e.g. $4\tfrac{1}{2}+3\tfrac{1}{4}$ $7\tfrac{1}{3}+3\tfrac{1}{2}$ $4\tfrac{7}{8}+3\tfrac{1}{4}$

(*b*) Cancelling fractions.

e.g. $\tfrac{36}{60}=\tfrac{6}{10}=\tfrac{3}{5}$

(*c*) × mixed numbers.

e.g. $3\tfrac{1}{2}\times 4\tfrac{3}{4}$

(*d*) ÷ fractions.

e.g. $4\tfrac{2}{3}\div 1\tfrac{1}{4}$

(3) (*a*) Long multiplication, division, all measures.

e.g. 3 days 16 hours 25 minutes × 14

319 tons 18 cwt. 2 qrs. ÷ 30

(4) (*a*) ×, ÷ decimals.

e.g. 3·41 × 7 59·82 ÷ 6

Books for use with Children

(1) *Beacon Arithmetic*, Books I to IV each in two parts, Ginn and Co. A well-graded book in easy stages that I find very useful as a general basis.

(2) *Oxford Graded Arithmetic Practice*, Holland, O.U.P. Each book contains graded sums on one or two rules, e.g. addition of number, addition and subtraction of money, etc.

(3) *New Way Arithmetic I*, Boyce, Macmillan. A clearly and pleasantly set out book giving very first stages in number and money.

(4) *New Primary Arithmetic I and II*, Whitwell and Goddard, Schofield and Sims. Some exercises give very useful practice in such things as beginnings of fractions.

(5) *B and A Arithmetic*, Books I and II, Gatehouse, Cassell and Co. Books giving practice in much more advanced work, e.g. long multiplication, with problems.

(6) *Primary Mathematics*, Basic Books I to III, J. S. Flavell and B. B. Wakelam, Methuen and Co., 1960-1. A new course, making for understanding rather than rule-of-thumb computation. With separate teacher's books.

(7) *Number Work*, Books I, II and III, E. Kraft, Methuen and Co. Applications of arithmetic in household and life situations.

Suggestions for Reading

Arithmetic in Primary Schools, Longmans.

BALLARD, P. B., *Teaching the Essentials of Arithmetic*, University of London Press.

BRIDEOAKE, E. and GROVES, I. D., *Arithmetic in Action*, University of London Press.

Cheshire Education Committee, *The Education of Dull Children at the Primary Stage*, University of London Press.

DRUMMOND, M., *Psychology and Teaching of Number*, Harrap.

LLOYD, F., *Educating the Sub-normal Child*, Methuen.

MONTEITH, A., *Teaching of Arithmetic*, Harrap.

SCHONELL, F. J., *Diagnosis of Individual Difficulties in Arithmetic*, Oliver and Boyd.

SMELTZER, D., *Man and Number*, Black.

SUMNER, W. I., *The Teaching of Arithmetic*, Blackwell.

M. E. RICHARDS

Chapter VI

ART

First of all, I wish to apologize to two groups of teachers; to all those who teach backward children – and teach them well. For their experience has taught them so much more than I could hope, or would presume to do. Also to all competent art specialists – whose knowledge of the technique of their subject is so much greater than that of a mere 'jack-of-all-trades'. It may well be that nothing in this chapter will be found that is new or of any practical value to the more experienced teachers in secondary modern schools. On the other hand there may be a few, perhaps less experienced either in teaching art or in teaching backward children, who may find here something of interest, some odd scrap of information or a fresh idea – something to start a discussion or to provoke an argument. This chapter tells only what I have learned whilst 'on the job' – what I have found to be practicable, acceptable, and, occasionally, successful. Nothing here is revolutionary; much must already be known by some; most of it is common sense plus enthusiasm. Some of what I have to say is probably controversial and part may meet with downright disagreement. But nothing is intended as a hard-and-fast rule, for the approaches to art teaching are as many and varied as the teachers themselves – and many are the different roads which lead to success.

The Children
Those who make up our D streams will be backward for many reasons; some will have poor intelligence, some suffer from bad environment, a few may be E.S.N. children who for some reason have not been sent to a Special School, and one or two may be intelligent but maladjusted and may have graduated into these forms on nuisance value. In the lower forms they will not yet be welded into

a group – in the higher ones they may have welded themselves – into 'gangs'! They come from different junior schools and many different homes. They have been subjected to many different kinds of teaching and have many different preconceived ideas of 'art'. Temperamentally, they may be restless, apathetic, stolid, aggressive, inarticulate, suspicious. They may be suffering from a feeling of failure – may be allergic to all forms of artistic expression – may greet you with the ominous words, 'I HATE art'!

It is important, therefore, to give somehow to these children a feeling of success, of achievement and enjoyment early in their secondary school life – before that deadly apathy which all too often pervades the upper part of the school sets in and gets a hold. Bernard Shaw once observed, 'Art is the only teacher, except torture'. We must take care that art is not also torture! It must be remembered that as many of these children are backward for environmental reasons, and come from homes where they have no artistic experience except that provided by television programmes, and where they have certainly not had the incentive to 'make pictures' for themselves, it is up to the art teacher to provide both the experience and the incentive. If a good beginning is not made, art will later on be regarded as 'kid's stuff' and the art lesson as merely an opportunity to 'lark about'; whereas, approached in the right way it can appeal to the highest emotions and can sharpen the perception of beauty in the everyday world. Moreover success in this field will spread, and enthusiasm will overflow into other school subjects.

The Teachers

The art teacher in the C and D streams of a secondary modern school may be one of many kinds. He may be the form teacher (with or without a particular interest in art); he may be an untrained graduate or an art student; he may be an enthusiastic artist, caring more for his subject than anything else in the world; may belong to the conventional 'realistic' school (still-life model, perhaps a bottle and an orange, carefully outlined in pencil and 'filled in' with paint or pastel); may be even (dare it be said?) plain lazy. "Copy a picture out of your reading book; trace something—no paint, mind! you'll only make a mess; draw what you like." (So long as you don't bother me!)

ART

Well, who *should* be in charge of the art teaching in the C and D streams? There is always controversy about specialization in these forms – in all subjects – and this is fully discussed in chapter XVI; but art teaching is rather a special case and I feel it needs to be considered here.

Let us first assess the advantages of the form teacher as an art teacher. He knows his children and there is some affection between them (it is to be hoped); at any rate there will be a certain amount of understanding. A friendly, relaxed atmosphere is most important during the art period. No artistic feeling, and certainly no inspiration can survive if the air is charged with animosity, strain, or even the nervousness engendered in diffident or nervous children by being confronted by the unfamiliar. It might with profit be asked at this point 'Why is this particular teacher in charge of a backward class?' If it is because he wishes it – has a vocation for the work and is genuinely interested in the children – then he may be the best person to teach them art (or indeed anything). But if, as is unfortunately so often the case, it is someone whose 'turn' it happens to be, or the newest and least experienced member of the staff – someone who welcomes the chance to 'Get away from them' for a time – then the children will be better off with an art specialist, who may at least pass on to them some of his own interest. The form teacher can often use 'odd times' to finish off paintings, and if the time-table is flexible enough, can take extra time if he feels it is needed. Even when the official art lesson is taken by a specialist teacher it may be an advantage for the form teacher to do some as well. This, of course, presupposes a sympathetic Head teacher, since extra stock will be needed!

Working negatively in favour of the form teacher is the fact that an art specialist may care more for his subject than for the children. He may be impatient with the efforts of the duller ones; and in a large school where there is more than one art specialist a certain amount of 'jockeying' for the A and B forms may take place. One often hears staff room complaints (sometimes good humoured – sometimes not so good humoured) such as, "I won't have anything to show this year; I'm landed with all the duds!" Of course one may hear the same from a form teacher – and not only about art – but I am presupposing him in this case to be the *right* kind of form teacher.

But caring for the children, vital as it is, is not enough. The teacher should also care for the subject enough to want to draw or paint for his own amusement. If the form teacher is not an enthusiast, not hitherto even interested, yet finds himself having to teach art, then it is much better if he will 'have a go'. He can even try *with* the children. If he is interested enough in *them* no one will suffer, and it will certainly make for a pleasant pupil-teacher relationship if he is frank and friendly enough to say, 'Let us all paint a picture of a fair (or of the seaside – or whatever it may be). I don't know much about painting, so we'll all try together.'

Lest the foregoing remarks may have given the impression that I consider the skill of the genuine artist is of no value and that artistic talent in an art teacher is to be deplored I hasten to correct this, and to add that the advantages of a talented art specialist are very considerable. First, he knows his subject, and by having been trained in the 'beginnings' is able to give a good groundwork and is ready for the snags and difficulties that are likely to crop up. Secondly, he is likely to be a practising artist – and therefore an enthusiast. Enthusiasm is infectious! Again, by dealing with the same children year after year as they progress through the school he is able to give them continuity. He comes to know their capabilities and their possibilities; he knows when to encourage, when to instruct – and when to give them their head. But he needs also to be patient and tolerant – two qualities that are not usually associated with the artistic temperament!

To sum up; perhaps the ideal art teacher for these children would be someone who would be willing to specialize in the lower streams throughout the school. An artist himself (though not necessarily a very skilful one) yet able patiently to encourage the clumsiest attempts of the most unpromising. Someone with the vision to inspire the most unimaginative of dullards, yet able to deal with the practical problems set by poor co-ordination, defective eyesight, inattention – or just common-or-garden naughtiness. Someone, in fact, who is very rare!

Not so rare, and a good second best, is the right kind of form teacher; interested in his children – and interested enough in art to try to learn something about it.

ART

Aims

It is important, I think, to decide why we teach art at all, since our reasons will influence our attitude and our methods. The following list is not comprehensive, but includes some of the 'aims' which occur among teachers of art.

(1) Talent spotting. (With vocational training in view.)
(2) Teaching accuracy. (Training hand and eye.)
(3) To achieve a good 'show' on Open Day. (Results all-important.)
(4) To keep the children quiet.
(5) To kill time.
(6) 'Art' is on the time-table, so it must be 'taken'. (Rather like a dose of medicine!)

How will these aims work with your backward children?

(1) is unlikely to work at all. There may be the occasional child with a little more ability than the others, but the reasons for his general backwardness will render him unfit for any training his teacher may have in mind for such jobs as tracing, draughtsmanship, designing, etc.

Observation and feeling can be directed; colour sense can be encouraged. But vocational training is a very different kettle of fish, and presumes enough talent for the child in question to go on to a technical college. If a C or D stream child is considered able to do this, then he is in the wrong stream.

(2) Again, very little likelihood of working. Presumably continual practice must make for some improvement – in some children; but at what cost in the teacher's temper! And with how little enjoyment for the children! Insistence on rigid accuracy will become just a dreadful bore.

(3) Is doomed to disappointment. Contrary to opinions still held, duller children are *not* 'compensated' by extraordinary gifts in art and craft.

(4) and (5) may work for a short time, but it is very hard work to *make* them work. After about fifteen minutes the unfortunate teacher who hoped for peace and quiet will get 'I've done it' from half the class – and 'I've done it wrong' from the other half.

(6) will meet with the disaster it deserves!

If the foregoing aims appear to be wrong when dealing with C and D stream children, what are the right ones? You may have noticed that I have used the word 'enjoyment' two or three times when speaking of art teaching – and in my opinion this heads the list.

(1) To give enjoyment.
(2) To stimulate imagination – the use of the 'inner eye'.
(3) To encourage observation – remember the story of 'eyes' and 'no-eyes'?
(4) To help appreciation – in its best sense. Appreciation of the efforts of others, of good design in everyday life, and of beauty wherever it may be found.
(5) To promote a feeling of 'belonging'; of serving the community; of being appreciated and recognized as someone who matters.

To me No. (1) is the most important. If the children really enjoy their art and gain from it a feeling of satisfaction there is no need to strive for anything else. In fact, the other aims help enjoyment – and through enjoyment the other aims are achieved.

But it is not easily come by. Enjoyment does not automatically follow on sitting down in front of a blank piece of paper and some paints. At the beginning it often depends on children's previous experiences of the subject and some prejudice may have to be overcome before the word 'art' always arouses happy anticipation. Nothing worth while is ever easy; so the teacher must be prepared for plenty of 'spade work'.

First, practical measures can be taken. Good preparation, not only of the subject matter but of the room is essential, and time spent before the lesson is well spent. It is a good idea to train and use reliable 'monitors' so that everything is ready before the children come in. To have to sit and wait while water, brushes, etc., are given out is frustrating; but the sight of a well-prepared room (newspapers spread on tables or easels in position, clean water, tins of bright paint), give a feeling of eager expectancy. Plenty of space is a great help, though I realize it is often impossible. But some moving of formroom furniture may make the most of what space is available; and do try for really suitable equipment. If each child has *two* brushes, one thick and one thin, he will feel well armed to tackle anything, and paper that is just the right size, colour and texture

ART

seems to demand to be covered with lovely shapes and colours. Jam jars, which are fairly stable and reasonably heavy, *half* filled, are better than paste pots filled to the brim. (This may seem superfluous advice to many, but it is surprising that many teachers do use small water pots.) There should be a good supply of clean water for changing, for nothing is more discouraging than to try for a clear bright picture when there is only half an inch of muddy sludge left in the bottom of one's jar – and teacher won't let it be changed. Children, even the most backward of them, can be taught to move round the room with water pots without inconveniencing others, and can cope with water changing with a minimum of mess – even when the available supply is only in a couple of buckets. This is part of their training. (Would that every room could have a sink!)

Next, it is essential that what I call the 'atmosphere' of the art room is good, for without a happy relationship between teacher and children any art lesson is foredoomed. Everyone should feel relaxed and at peace with the world and there should be no 'hangover' of nagging for past misdeeds. From this point of view it would be desirable for art time always to come in the afternoon – after the midday recess has given time for the irritations and frustrations of the morning to be forgotten – although, again, this cannot always be arranged. Once the right atmosphere has been achieved it can be a wonderful experience to see a group of children 'in action'. All petty quarrels and accumulated fatigues are forgotten; a boy can be seen sharing a water pot quite amicably with an erstwhile sworn enemy; or co-operating in a group picture with a gang that cuts across his own 'gang'. The almost fierce concentration is so tangible that it can be felt! And the span of attention and interest shown even by the most volatile and restless is quite amazing – and cannot fail to be beneficial. Whilst on the subject of atmosphere it cannot be over-emphasized how important is the teacher's influence, and his attitude towards minor mishaps. However carefully one may prepare, the occasional water pot *will* go over, since many of these children have poor motor control, and then the teacher needs not only to control his own annoyance but placate the possible victim whose painting has been flooded. It has been my experience, on (fortunately) rare occasions, to see a room full of children, arms folded, glowering at half-finished paintings, forbidden to move, as a punishment for the carelessness of a couple of victims who have spilled their water or overturned their paint – whilst the (also glowering) teacher kept them subdued by sheer will power. The atmosphere could be 'felt' all right in this room! But it is debatable how much enjoyment was derived from the art lesson.

Of course, one needs to learn discrimination. I hold no brief for the pest who deliberately sets out to spoil the enjoyment of others. Unfortunately, the informality of the art lesson lends itself to indiscipline if the teacher is unsure of himself or the children especially difficult; but it is a fact that once their interest is caught even the most intractable cannot resist the fascination of making pictures. One offender can be judiciously removed to a more isolated position, or the lesson can be tactfully shortened if interest is flagging and restlessness beginning; but in the interest of future art lessons recriminations should be avoided and the relationship kept friendly.

'Clearing up' should be part of the lesson. (Contrast with the beginning when everything was ready.) It is something these children can be trained to do well and methodically, each taking part – and should be praised. Incidentally, it would be a very good plan if each child could have an apron, but as I have found this not always practical, a generous supply of 'paint rag', collected and kept in a labelled box has proved of great use. Absorbent cotton, such as old handkerchiefs or old sheets, is the best kind and an occasional 'washing day' keeps them usable for some time (especially if one has that coveted sink!).

Teaching

Now we come to a controversial question. How are we to teach – what are we to teach – are we to teach at all? In my own lifetime I have seen a complete swing of the pendulum and I am wondering if it is due to swing back – and how far it will swing? As a small child I had 'drawing' lessons, when I had to copy from a card on which was a copperplate 'design', complicated, symmetrical and deadly dull, but which had to be reproduced with accurate precision. Later, I was subjected to 'models', consisting of once white cones and cubes piled on top of each other in extraordinary combinations – to be copied in pencil and 'shaded' – with geometric precision. Later still came the excitement of colour – three tiny blobs of water colour squeezed on to little porcelain dishes as I sat still in breathless expectancy whilst the teacher paced the rows, dispensing this magic. With this I was expected to copy one daffodil or one tulip on a narrow strip of paper – with photographic precision. Even my first post as an 'art' specialist was with a head teacher who insisted that all lessons should be devoted to copying 'Old Masters' – again with precision!

Then came the swing to absolute freedom. But does this always work with older children? Infants draw and paint as naturally as they breathe, and nearly always, symbolically, but is it not possible that self-conscious secondary modern children will flounder in this sea of freedom if given no direction? ("Must we *always* draw what we like?") In my opinion (though I admit that many will disagree with me) a certain amount of instruction is necessary. Children of this age tend to be self-critical. Those in the D stream know something is wrong with their drawing but don't know what, and if help is not forthcoming they become dissatisfied with results and will eventually lose interest. They cannot enjoy what they cannot do – they often need telling *what* to do. Not that I think originality should be discouraged. If a boy or girl has a burning desire to paint a particular picture the opportunity should be provided. But be wary; you will often find this individualist (if a boy) going in for an orgy of violence – guns, rockets and bullets tracing their path all over the paper and dead bodies in generous heaps. This is one child I would definitely give other subjects to occupy his art lesson! It may be said that this is wrong psychologically – if given his head he will work the aggression out of his system; my own feeling is that he may become better at it with continual practice – will merely learn to draw bigger and better wars. These pictures are not good artistically and will certainly not help your young artist to appreciate beauty. In any case I very much prefer leaving any psychiatric treatment of this kind to the experts at the child guidance clinic.

There should, I feel, be definite instruction, in the right way and at the right time (often unobtrusively) on the following:

(1) The technique of paint mixing and the difference between the thickness of powder or poster paint and the transparency of water colour.

(2) The care of tools and materials. It is a good idea sometimes to let the children look at a catalogue. The high price of brushes, etc., might command respect.

(3) The 'drill' for preparing a lesson and for clearing up. Monitors can be replaced easily if all know what the job is, and the clearing up routine must be taken step by step for a long time until all are familiar with it.

(4) Paints. The difference between the various kinds of paint and for what they should each be used. Oil colours, of course, may possibly never be used; but they should be shown and explained just the same. How else will children ever appreciate a visit to a gallery? Some teachers deplore the use of water colours, but it must be remembered that any children who have a 'box of paints' at home will almost invariably have water colours, and were probably using them before they ever reached the secondary modern school. Moreover, water colour has its use for charts, maps and illustrations, so it is a good thing to practise washes occasionally.

(5) Colours. Primary and secondary colours should be known by name, and, in the upper part of the school, complementary colours. Colour charts can be made by each child and the colours named. (A help to reading.)

(6) Other media which may be used; charcoal and white crayon, pastels, tinted paper, different textures of paper. You will probably find many children wanting to cling to a pencil-rubber-ruler combination as if it were a life-line. I usually try to woo them away from this as early as possible in their secondary school life. By demonstration it can be shown how much bolder and more 'important-looking' is a black brush stroke or a thick charcoal line than any feeble pencil mark – and as for the ruler, a straight line is a lifeless line – sometimes necessary for machine drawing but not in art. Look at the human body; it is alive – and where is there a ruler-straight line? Look at animals and plants. Even the pine tree trunk is made up of thousands of tiny lines – none of them dead straight. (It is significant that the word 'dead' is used!) If you want something to *look* straight, the hazard of a series of brave free-hand strokes with crayon or brush results in a far more lively and interesting picture than that achieved by an anaemic pencil-ruler line – often drawn over a messy, much-rubbed patch of paper.

(7) Covering the paper. This is something children find difficult. Left on their own they will often draw a tiny object bang in the middle or right on the edge of a large piece of paper. Help can be given by always seeing that the paper is the right size; not so small that the child feels cramped and not so large that he is terrified of the huge space to be covered. 12 in. by 10 in. up to 16 in. by 12 in. is about right for the lower forms and up to about 24 in. by 20 in. for older children. These are approximate suggested sizes, as the measurements of paper delivered to schools varies with different types of paper and in different districts; and it is often convenient to divide each sheet into halves or quarters. It should be noted that larger paper can be managed better on the easel than on a flat table. If the latter has to be used drawing-boards are ideal because with them one can work at a comfortable angle, and from time to time they can be propped up so that the children can walk away and view their work from a distance. Except in the case of small repeated designs this 'standing back' is essential. Similarly, the holding of the brush well up on the handle and the use of the whole arm in large sweeping strokes; once the children have mastered this technique they will find it easier and less tiring than crouching short-sightedly over their work, with the brush gripped tightly close to the hairs. Yet this is the method children will use if they are not taught a better one. I usually have a 'brush drill' lesson early in the first year, using several different colours to add interest, and the 'doodles' often result in some lively and original line patterns.

(8) Overlapping, two-dimensional pictures, space relationships, use and abuse of heavy outlines – all these need to be *taught*. Children cannot be expected to find out about all this by instinct – any more than reading will 'come naturally' if they are left alone.

At the secondary modern stage symbols can be discarded in realistic pictures – although some might argue that since the C and D stream children have usually a lower mental age than the others they are not yet ready to proceed beyond the infant stage. But their 'Painting Age' (if there is such a thing) may well be much in advance of their mental age. An interesting book by Helga Eng, *The Psychology of Children's Drawings* shows the gradual progress in the free drawing of a bright child from 1 year old to 8. It is a pity it did not go still further! But it should be possible to find the stage at which children are, and then lead them on. In any case, one must not forget that many of these children are backward for environmental and emotional reasons and are quite able to cope with the same kind of painting as those in the A and B classes. Even in the case of the duller ones, it is a matter of degree rather than kind, so the art they do need not be very different from that of the others. I feel they need guidance to lead them forward to observe the world around them and to draw what they see. Evelyn Gibbs, in her book, *Teaching of Art in Schools*, says that if children can see, they can draw – but our job is often to teach them to see! In expressionist pictures, when imagination is given full rein and children draw what they feel, they may be free to mix realism and symbolism; what they see, what they know and what they feel.

Does the foregoing smack of reaction and rigidity? Much depends on how the teaching is given, for the teacher must be sensitive enough to pick the right moment for instruction – when it is actually needed – *not* stopping the children when they are absorbed in what they are doing and impatient of interruption. On the other hand it is no use always waiting until the C and D stream children *ask* for instruction; some of them never will ask – but the need is there just the same. Much can be done individually, during the lesson; but if it is something you want them all to learn, much can be done by 'walking them around' at the beginning of a lesson, to gain their information practically, e.g. take them out to *show* how the sky appears to meet the ground (or the roof tops), to *see* where a boy's shadow lies on the playground, to *watch* the trees all bending the same way in the wind. Much also can be taught by demonstration – though this, again, is controversial, many teachers feeling it 'unethical' to 'show' how to do things. But with slower children at any rate (and quite often with brighter ones) I have found five minutes' demonstration to be worth more than half an hour's talk – and much more interesting to the children, who will give you the most flattering attention directly you 'draw' for them. And where is the so-called 'cheating'? The demonstration sheet is not left up for the children to copy slavishly, but it is hoped that just enough will linger in their minds for the lesson to have gone home. Nor need it be argued that demonstration is fraught with peril for any except a skilful artist, for your drawing need not be 'clever', but only just ahead of the children's.

ART

Let us take an example: you want your class to paint a picture in which one person is partly in front of another. This is a difficult thing for children to visualize – left to themselves they always draw things where there is a space, and always draw the *whole*, never part, of an object. Very well. First you demonstrate practically by standing two children out in front; then you show two *things* (to show that the rule always applies). There will be no need for talk – the children will tell you what they see. Next you demonstrate by a large painting. Any easy objects will do – a ball and a book, or a box and a jar. It can be shown that there are two ways of making the picture look right; the front object (or person) can be painted first, then the piece *you can see* of the back one – or you can paint the whole of the back object, as you know it looks, and then paint the front one on top and partly overlapping it. You can often get the children themselves to tell you how to tackle the job. Perhaps the first lesson will 'click' with only a few – but next week can be used for consolidation; and things learned this way will stick and the children will apply their knowledge in other pictures, enjoying the feeling of achievement. As a boy once remarked to me after he had learned to apply the first simple rule of 'perspective' (that things look smaller when farther away), 'It looks better when it's *right*, don't it, Miss?'

The teacher who does not give any instruction, but leaves his pupils condemned to eternal 'free expression' is not helping them at all. Time for free expression there should be – but even this will be more enjoyable, and the young artists will be able to express themselves much more 'freely' if they can apply unconsciously the simple techniques that have been given them – instead of sitting hopelessly looking at the empty paper – 'I don't know what to paint' – 'I can't DO it' – 'I don't know how' – and eventually and inevitably – 'I HATE art!'

At some point the children will need to be shown the things already mentioned (perspective, the horizon, overlapping). At some point they need to be shown light and shade, the simple proportions of the human figure, 'tricks' that help to gain a pleasing effect – e.g. light tones against dark, dull colours against bright, large shapes balanced by small. Observation needs to be trained and imagination stirred. Children can be asked: which shapes are angry shapes and which are happy shapes? Which colours make us feel lively?

Which are sad colours? Which lines seem to be hurrying and which are at rest?

Pattern in Nature and in our own lives should be pointed out. The complicated and lovely arrangement of feathers on a bird's wing; the intricate leaf-mosaic of trees; the brilliance of a butterfly; the ripples on water; these can be first-hand experiences. Children may well ask (and if they don't the question should be raised) – is all this of any use? Many of them are completely lacking in artistic experience, and come from homes where no value is recognized that is not strictly utilitarian or commercial. Here is an opportunity to introduce applied art. A visit to the Design Centre may well be enjoyed by the older ones, where they can see good design in useful things, and critically discuss, for instance, whether a certain chair is beautiful as well as comfortable. Design in glass and china, carpets and curtains – all can come under their critical gaze; and even if the teacher feels that some of the tastes expressed are crude and coarse, the very fact that they are expressed, and that 'design' in living is recognized, will be of inestimable value. Other visits found to be of pleasure as well as profit; – visits to art galleries – in small doses. The Tate for Turner and Blake I feel is essential if you teach in London. Visits to churches – for the stained glass and for the murals; visits to exhibitions of contemporary art (again in small doses). Even the most advanced and controversial of contemporary paintings can be 'taken' by the older children. One can say to them, 'This man painted what he *felt* about something, rather than what he saw.' (Could you paint in the same way?)

In the classroom posters, advertisements, cartoons, illustrations – all can come under discussion. Children are usually amazed to find out that the lovely pictures in a well-known story book were all drawn or painted first by an artist, and that practically everything we use had its first existence on a drawing-board. Some of the best London Transport posters may be shown with benefit, and the fact pointed out that it is thought worth while to commission first-rate artists for this work.

Art and Craft
I feel that it is a great advantage for the art teacher (or form teacher, as the case may be) to teach simple crafts to backward children.

ART

Art and craft are very closely allied and in a big secondary modern school, with its emphasis (even in the lower streams) on academic subjects, often the only 'crafts' taught are woodwork and/or metalwork for the boys and domestic subjects, such as housecraft and needlework for the girls. Whereas pattern work could be applied to simple pottery; baskets could be 'designed' and then made; papier-mâché, puppetry, paper sculpture, simple bookbinding – all could follow so naturally from the art lesson that it might be worth while sacrificing some painting time to them. Or even begging a sympathetic head teacher for extra time in which to do things with one's hands! I realize of course that there are some schools where these crafts and many others are available and excellently taught; I merely suggest the above for those where this is not the case.

Service to the community is important to these children. When there is a school play the performers are rarely (if ever!) chosen from their ranks; but they can play their part in making props and helping to paint scenery under direction. Inspired by having seen good murals they may even 'take over' a piece of corridor wall and decorate it, either with their own stencilled designs or a series of wall pictures. In the same way, having practised '*appliqué* work pictures' they can make some on a piece of cheap material (dyed hessian is suitable) and use it as a curtain in front of some classroom shelves. Or they can print their own designs on a piece of fabric to make 'teacher's cushion'. Tremendous pride will be felt in knowing that their work is really of use.

Because, as has been stressed, there is no sharp dividing line between B children and C; or between C children and D, the actual subjects taken in the art lesson need not be very different from those of the higher streams. But the teacher must be prepared to go more slowly, not to expect such a high standard of achievement or such length of concentration, not to tire by too much repetition (two lessons on the same subject in succession are the most for which interest can be expected to hold), to give more help, both by suggestion and by demonstration, both collectively and individually, to make all instructions simple and to use more 'word pictures'. For example; to A stream children one could say, 'Paint a picture called "Joy" '. But to D stream children one would say, 'Have you ever been very happy and full of joy? Think of something that made you happy. Shut your eyes and try to see joyful colours – or shapes – Could you paint a picture of something that made you happy – or of someone who feels very happy?'

Some Suggestions

The following notes are not intended to be used as an 'Art Scheme', although they could supplement one that is already in use. What they are intended to do is to offer some ideas that have been well and truly 'tried out' and have been found workable with the children in the lower streams of secondary modern schools. They are by no means comprehensive and the experienced art teacher will probably find nothing new. But I include them because they are fairly practicable, and may, perhaps, help one or two who are newer to this kind of work and may be sometimes 'stuck' for an idea. The subjects are divided for convenience into Lower, Middle and Upper School – but naturally some overlapping will be found.

Lower School (11 to 12 or 12½)

Design. Abstract patterns. (It seems strange that these children who so often find abstract thinking difficult can produce some striking and original abstract patterns!) Free use of brush to outline shapes boldly in black paint. The teacher can demonstrate how to cover all the paper and how to make the lines cross each other. Fill in shapes with different colours and textures. Teaches colour mixing and overlapping. This is a fairly 'foolproof' exercise in that some good results are almost certain and the children are pleased with the result. Self-criticism should always be encouraged – 'How could I have made this look even better?' 'Let us try again next week' – with different shaped paper – perhaps a circle? (prepared by the teacher.)

Repeating patterns and alternating patterns. I should like to emphasize here that the first art lesson is not the time to teach accurate measurement – the paper can be folded (*with* the teacher) into the desired squares or rectangles. The unit of design should be kept very simple (homely objects such as a jug or a dish can be used). Tile patterns, all-over patterns, using simple flower, leaf, fish, bird and beetle shapes, templets, stippling, stencils, potato prints, paste papers and marbled papers may all be attempted – the last few being put to practical use when the opportunity arises, for decorating book covers, art packets and wall notices. Writing patterns (the finished pattern disguises the original letter) 'stained glass window' pictures – which bridge the gap between abstract design and pictorial work.

Many will divide pictorial work into realistic and imaginative; but I maintain that imagination and feeling must be part of every picture – otherwise it is not alive. The children should realize that if thirty of them paint a picture of Mother doing the washing there will be thirty *different* pictures! Before such a picture is painted it needs preparation for a few days (the form teacher as an art teacher is at an advantage here, because the children need constant reminding). Example: Look at a bus on your way to school. Look at the back of the bus, look at a bus queue, look at people getting off a bus, look at the driver, look – look – *look*. Then paint your picture; a man running after a bus; a conductor helping a woman with her shopping; a child falling in front of a bus. Or look at a fruit stall; see how the fruit is arranged; notice the people buying fruit; see the bright colours – the sunshine – the shadows. To show how figures look so dark as to be painted black against a very bright background, stand a child up against the window, and challenge the others to name the colours she is wearing. There are countless 'pictures' to be found in the home or in the street; the children soon learn the habit of observation and then paint their own feelings into the pictures.

Imaginary pictures can use observation as well as imagination if the titles are well chosen; and subjects suggested by literature or poetry can be included. Some ideas for titles – 'Shipwreck', 'The Highwayman', 'Harvest', etc.

Figure work. Charcoal or black crayon for quick sketches of each other; or 'action' pictures using matchstick figures. White crayon for highlights. (Tinted sugar paper best here.) Another 'foolproof' idea (in that a result pleasing to the child is almost certain to be achieved) – 'silhouette pictures' – factory chimneys against a sunset sky; camels and palm trees on the horizon; bare branches against a grey wintry sky; painted in black against a contrasting background. This also drives home the lesson that the sky always appears to meet the earth.

Applied art. Decorating end pages and covers of books; painting papier-mâché masks and ash-trays in oil or enamel paint; making design to go on tiles or other simple pottery; fabric printing (at this stage potato prints can be used), beginning with one unit of pattern in the corner of a handkerchief (a present for Mother!); painting patterns on plastic beakers (a present for baby brother or sister!); decorating glass jars for use as classroom vases.

Middle School (12 to 13½)
Design. The abstract pattern can be extended. It may now be the time to look at abstract paintings by famous artists – see how ordinary objects, or even portraits, are sometimes incorporated in the design. More selective use of colour; (earlier attempts used all the primaries, with a few secondaries when there were no more primaries left); a pattern may now be tried using two or more tones of one colour, with black and white. Most of the pattern work suggested for younger children can be taken a stage further. For instance, when preparing the paper for alternating and repeating patterns the spaces may be set out by the use of marked distances on a strip of paper – which allows for more variety than merely folding, and is a little more advanced – yet not fraught with the difficulties of measuring with a ruler. When using templets two different shapes can be cut, and used in the same pattern; and a large potato print can be interspersed by a smaller one in a different colour.

It is useful to collect pieces of patterned material and old wallpaper books, to see how the designers have used the available space. Then large 'all-over' designs for dress or curtain material can be tried (without attempting the difficulty of showing a repeat of the pattern); different colour combinations should be tried – the children looking for the reason why some are more pleasant to look at than others.

Pictorial work. Silhouette pictures can be continued; portraits (of real or imaginary people). 'Try making a frame for your picture.' In illustration the process of black-and-white reproduction and that of colour printing may be explained simply. Good colour prints of artists' work (Medici prints excellent, but expensive) can be shown. Some of Van Gogh's pictures and the rather over-simplified landscapes of John Nash can be well appreciated by children of this age. Poems and short stories can be illustrated.

At this stage there is often a striving for perfection. The question is often asked, '*How* do you draw – a man, a dog, a horse?' etc. Usually the child can be encouraged to 'go and look', but sometimes this is not possible – especially in the case of a horse! Most children want to draw a horse at some time, but town children rarely see one – except pictured in 'Westerns'. So why not encourage them to collect pictures of horses – and other animals? After all, no commercial artist would be without his 'library'! When needed, this 'reference library' can be consulted – the animal drawn several times 'for practice' and then adapted to the picture in hand. Another tendency is for children to ask others who are 'good' at it to help them – 'Draw a dog in my picture for me—'. My own attitude towards this is that help given should be acknowledged – 'Both John *and* Pat's names shall go on the finished picture'. Treated thus casually, with no emphasis on 'morals' the affair assumes no importance, and the child in question will soon wish to stand on his own feet and want his pictures to be 'All my own work'. *Appliqué* needlework pictures can be introduced at this age (can lead to a useful boy-girl partnership); group pictures, with half a dozen working on one project, and more complicated scenes to be observed, such as 'The Crossroads', 'The Dancing Class', 'Christmas Day'. Then there are 'descriptive' pictures – the teacher describing a scene (imaginary or otherwise), the children listening with closed eyes. Help can be given with composition, proportion and perspective – 'The tree in the picture is not quite in the middle, but a little to one side. It is so tall that the branches go right off the top of the picture . . . children are playing on the other side of the field . . . they are so far away that they look like tiny toy figures . . .'

Applied art. Simple lino cuts, Christmas cards, book-plates (which may be either individual or designed to be used in, say, the school hymn-books), fabric printing, progressing to using simple blocks and dyes, School Journey books or books of 'Visits' and simple rhyme sheets combining good script printing with illustration.

Imaginative work. The expression of emotions – 'Joy' 'Sadness' 'Surprise'; dreams – peaceful dreams, strange dreams; imaginary places – 'The Moon', 'Other Planets', 'Fairyland', 'Under the Sea'; fabulous animals, witches, gnomes (word pictures in books such as Macdonald's *Princess and the Goblins* can be read to the children).

Upper School (13½ to 15)
There is a case here for specialization. If the children have been in the

hands of a good teacher they will by now have confidence and can be bolder and more adventurous in their art work. Classes are likely to be smaller, and often divided into boys' and girls' classes. Individual work is possible and special interests can be followed.

All the subjects dealt with in the lower and middle parts of the school can be taken to a more advanced stage; from two-dimensional to three-dimensional pictures; from flat surfaces to solid forms showing light and shade. Poster work can be attempted at this stage, using simple lettering – but as little as possible; accent being on the illustration. (Point out that just as in 'good' cinema, the maximum of 'action' and the minimum of 'talk' should be the rule.) The knowledge of facts gained in other lessons can be used – pictures of lumber-jacks, Eskimos, cave men, etc., being attempted. A picture a child particularly wishes to finish may be continued for two or three weeks – if the interest lasts; while at the same time quick 'memory' paintings or an 'impression' of a vase of flowers can be included. Outdoor sketching can be tried, perhaps included in a visit to the country, and expeditions to galleries and museums organized. At this age the practical use of the art work can be pointed out – interiors, 'Plan a room *you* would like to live in'; exteriors, 'What would you like your own house to look like?' and in the case of older girls, 'Design a party frock you would like to wear' – usefulness in the school, decorating a spare piece of wall; helping with scenery painting; making a model for a younger group of children. There are many opportunities for these boys and girls who will soon be leaving school, to do something to help the community and perhaps to realize that they will later on be able to help the larger community outside school.

Finished Work, Storage and Display
If children's work is to be shown at all, it should be shown to the best advantage. White paper makes the best background, except in the case of 'snow scenes' which can be shown on black. Each child's picture should be clearly named, paintings should be well spaced as near to the eye level as possible and the title of each group clearly printed by the teacher. (Unless it so happens that one of the children is particularly good at printing. Poor lettering should never be shown.) The 'show' should be changed frequently and the utmost effort

made to give every child a turn. Since all the paintings cannot be up on the wall each week the rest should be somewhere in the room – perhaps clipped together in book form and labelled – where they can be looked at occasionally by the children; or in the case of older ones, kept in individual portfolios made by themselves. I feel very strongly that a painting should never be destroyed or thrown away in view of the children. It is true that pleasure is in the *making* of a picture, but how soul-destroying it must be for a child to see the work into which so much effort and feeling have gone just thrown callously into the wastepaper-basket! This is even more true of D stream children than of any others; and at the end of the term, if they do not wish to take their own work home the greatest care should be taken that any necessary destruction takes place in secret.

Two ideas – which have both worked. (1) A voluntary Sketch Club with weekly meetings – sometimes for outdoor sketching or (in winter) weekly subjects set and brought in for criticism. (2) A termly 'Academy' when each child selects for himself his favourite painting of the term to put on show.

Book List

BARRETT, H., *Suggestions for the Study of Colour*, P. Carpenter, School of Art, Rochdale. An old book, but simple and useful.

Dryad Leaflets, 153, *Paper Sculpture*, 102, *Fabric Printing*.

ENG, HELGA, *The Psychology of Children's Drawings*, Kegan Paul, Trench, Trubner and Co. Ltd.

GIBBS, EVELYN, *Teaching of Art in Schools*, Ernest Benn, Ltd.

HOLMES, K. and COLLINS, H., *Child Art Grows Up*, Studio Publications.

HUNT, ANTHONY, *Textile Design*, Studio 'How to do it' series, No. 15. Interesting for children to look at when doing fabric prints.

LEVY, M., *Painter's Progress*, Phoenix House, Ltd. More modern.

SHARP, DOROTHEA, *Student's Book of Oil Painting*, Pitman.

TOMLINSON, R., *Children as Artists*, Studio Publications.

— *Picture and Pattern Making by Children*, Studio Publications.

WITT, R. C., *How to look at Pictures*, Bell.

JOYCE MYERS

Chapter VII

MUSIC

General Characteristics of Dull Children as they affect Musical Learning

Some of the characteristics of dull children are low mental ability, limited powers of learning, inability to form highly organized concepts and lack of the power of insight. These disabilities, though

they may not always be present, occur so frequently that consideration of them is an essential part of our planning. Their low mental ability – usually general – is often accompanied by poor perceptual power: they may thus be innately and organically incapable of hearing in music what a more intelligent child hears. For example,

---

[1] These items of the Wing Tests are quoted with permission of Dr. H. D. Wing, who has also kindly consented to the quotation of his findings on the development of musical ability in normal young children.

out of twenty-two dull boys who took Test V of the *Wing Standardised Tests of Musical Intelligence* only five selected 'A' opposite as better than 'B'. In a similar group of normal children over 70 per cent. expressed a preference for the better version.

Their limited powers of learning necessitate realistic goals, slow progress and finely graded steps. Their inability to form highly organized concepts reduces the effectiveness of long-term motives and intensifies the appeal of the immediate distraction. Their lack of insight inhibits their powers of sympathy, makes for a less sensitive response and strikes at the very roots of musicality. The effects of these disabilities are sometimes aggravated by a deep sense of long-continued personal failure which often lessens still further their powers of learning, lowers their self-regard and adds to the difficulties which they already experience in their personal relationships. In a group activity like music these difficulties are likely to be more disruptive than in a subject where the work is on individual lines. We can therefore expect that teaching them music will be hard work, that apparent results – if judged objectively – will not be particularly stimulating or rewarding, and that effective teaching will require much energy and firm purpose on our part. Because of this our own feelings and convictions are of great importance. Their low ability is not their fault, nor anyone else's – that's how they are – and if they are inattentive, easily distracted and generally difficult, as they often can be, some of these things may be a reflection of an unrealistic programme or unsuitable methods. Dealing with such difficulties is part of the job, a fact recognized by Mursell and Glenn (1938, p. 32), who say 'Music education has a mission and a responsibility to children who at the outset may seem rather hopeless cases'.

Musical Ability and Needs of Slow Learners
Before we can *really* teach slower children we must value them so that our attitudes will be right, we must know their capabilities so that the standards we set will be suitable and we must have a wide knowledge of current practice and belief so that our aims, methods and techniques will be soundly based.

About music teaching in general the reader will already be well informed and the subject is well covered in the books listed at the end of the chapter. But little has been written about the musical characteristics of dull children and about the type of response to be expected. What seems plain sailing when written in a book often turns out to be very different in the classroom with a backward group. Why is this, and what can we do about it? These are the questions which are important to us as teachers and it is these which will now be considered.

To set up a minimum range it is useful to know what the severely handicapped may rise to. Nameny (1949, pp. 134–8), speaking of Special School children aged 6–17, says that the more able could sing rounds and two-part songs, though much patience and drill were required for this. It is interesting to know that the very dull can hold parts but it is doubtful if the effort is economic. I have heard excellent unison singing by classes of girls in three Special Schools and feel sure that this example could be repeated many times over. Pichot (1949, pp. 6–10) has shown that mentally defective children have the same rhythmic aptitudes as children of their own mental age, and Coffman (1949) has shown that the sense of rhythm is subject to training. This is useful. But what is more important for the purpose of planning our programme and setting our standards is a study of normal musical development, so that we may consider how far and how quickly our pupils, with their slower all-round rate of maturation, may be expected to progress.

Valentine (1914) has shown that young children make no distinction between dissonance and consonance and that their powers of discrimination are developed by about 12 years of age. It would be unusual for slow learners to reach this stage at 12 and some will not reach it until 15 or later. Wing (1941) states that a feeling for melody develops before the rhythmic sense in young children. This is contrary to what seems to be usually assumed but it is certainly true of slower secondary children: tune is comparatively simple to master; *accurate* rhythm is difficult. Even amongst adults only the more musical can produce the precision that results in perfect rhythm, though ability to accurately reproduce melodic shape is widely spread. In teaching a song to a slow class, then, it is profitable to direct specific attention to the rhythm. This is especially so of songs we wish to sing well. Wing considers that the appreciation of good rhythm begins at about the age of 10. Many of our slow learners will not reach this stage before the age of 12 or 13. For normal children

MUSIC

Wing recommends early training based on sense training, on the singing of various songs, including ones that modulate, and on creative work such as the answering of phrases and the insertion of passing notes. He says that the average child of 8 knows whether there are two or three notes in a chord, can tell whether a melodic line moves up or down and has memory for the immediate recall of a tune a few notes in length. We may therefore expect our older slow learner to have reached this stage. His powers of perception are poor, therefore it is no use trying to teach the finer points which he cannot grasp. By the age of 11, Wing says, the normal child is beginning to appreciate harmony, intensity and phrasing. Slower children may never in their school life reach this stage. Wing's findings are confirmed by Jersild and Bienstock (1934). They found that the child's ability to sing tones of a given pitch matures early. They investigated the effect of training on children's ability to sing and concluded (1934, p. 494), 'The children who received practice made large gains'. These gains persisted over several months of no practice. Speaking of the relative influence of learning and growth they stated '. . . singing was the one outstanding performance in which the trained children gained a significant advantage over control subjects'. This emphasis on the importance of singing in music education has also been stressed by the Scottish Education Department (1952), who say that singing should always be the principal part of the music course and that more of the time available for music with dull children should be devoted to the singing of songs. Winn (1954, p. 87) is another advocate of singing as part of the music course for less able children. 'Moreover, in singing, more than in most other activities, they can work quite happily, with no sense of inferiority with their fellows.' Mursell and Glenn (1938, p. 278) state, 'Singing is the core of school music work', and speak highly of its power to deepen appreciation. All this is borne out in practice. My own observation of slow learners leads me to believe that musically they lag behind their more able contemporaries, but that there is still a wide range of musical ability amongst them, and that occasionally one or two with special talent – contrasted with their low mental ability – occur. In a recent application of *Wing's Standardised Test of Musical Intelligence* to twenty-two dull boys, three had average musical ability, seven were classified 'D' on a normal five-point scale and twelve fell within the most unmusical 10 per cent. of the population. This is quoted to show the wide range that existed in a group who from the intellectual standpoint were much more closely knit. Dearborn and Rothney have shown that growth in its different aspects is not only irregular but also disharmonious, so that we should be prepared for wide variations in special aptitude and should watch closely to discern the boy or girl for whom music may be a specially important factor in producing wider means of expression and deeper powers of feeling. Burt (1927, p. 42) and Wing (1941, p. 320) both bear witness to the existence of special musical ability independent of general intelligence. Unless cross-setting for music is possible – and if it is at all practicable I believe it is desirable – the music programme for a group of slow learners must cater for a wide variety of children who vary from the bottom of the scale to the normal. It must drive along, as it were, on two fronts, the one extending the more able and the other nursing along the less responsive – and both these things have to be done to some extent in each lesson.

Our programme should be suited to the child's capabilities and musical characteristics, should accord with our ideals for his education and be capable of practical application within school. The general principles which apply to teaching other subjects apply also to music. We must work from what he has; give him a mass of sense impressions – visual as well as aural – and train his perception; work through the concrete by providing him with opportunity for active music experiences; base these experiences on his interest pattern; arrange for his efforts to produce an appropriate reward, and finally do this in a progressive and ordered way throughout the school.

Creation of a Musical Environment

One of the first essentials is the creation of a musical environment so that the child hears much good music, sees pictures of musicians and instruments and comes to regard musical sights and sounds as part of his daily life. This can be done by the regular reproduction of good music and the maintenance of attractive displays connected with it. It is particularly profitable if the same piece of music is repeated frequently within a short period. For example, the same

MUSIC

piece of music can be played every day for a week at morning assembly. By this means the best items of the classical repertoire can be put in front of the child with an impact comparable with that of much of the trivial music he continually hears outside school. His interest can be aroused by an up-to-date display devoted to the weekly music, in which the title of the music and the name of the

composer are clearly shown, pictures of composer, artists, instruments and orchestra are attractively mounted, and in which background information such as anecdotes about the composers, performers or music is provided in a simple and striking way. The interest aroused by the display, and the enjoyment felt if the music is suitable, interact to reinforce the one and deepen the other and are of great value. The developmental possibilities of the experience can be exploited by giving the children opportunity to respond to what they have heard by talking or writing about it. One method of doing this is to include a notice-board as part of the music corner (see diagram). The children will be encouraged to pin up their comments if suitable small sheets of paper and a ball-point pen are conveniently provided, and if they know that their efforts will be properly valued. Their misspelt, short phrases are the equivalent of the sixth-former's magazine article and deserve no less appreciation. One record a week done like this amounts, in a year, to thirty or more pieces of music heard effectively, and the result is that the child gains great familiarity with a worth while selection of good music by the time he leaves school. Slow learners acquire musical taste in the same way as their brighter brothers, but take longer in the process and require more repetition. The above system gives them this repetition, and at the same time has been found valuable for the whole range of children within the school. Finally, some form of record keeping is necessary so that the planned ground is covered and adequate revision done. The teacher will keep his own record but the boy or girl can with advantage do likewise and keep a music diary, making a written record of his music experiences. I believe this is most fruitful when on a voluntary basis – better half a dozen good records kept in a creative way by interested children than thirty mechanical ones that mean nothing. This is where some of the individual attention, encouragement and work comes into music teaching, and a lot of it has of necessity to be done at odd times outside the lesson. A few words with one or a couple of minutes with another, perhaps between classes or in the playground or wherever the occasion offers, are of great value to the children concerned and help not only all the music work but the school in general. Any child with a real live interest of his own acts as a leaven. As the researches of Diserens, Lombard, Binet and Courtier showed, and as our own experience convinces us, music is an influence of great power. Surely, in addition to being far more widely used in school as a stimulating and enriching part of the environment it could, if properly developed, provide an absorbing personal interest for many of the slow learners.

Training of Powers of Perception and Provision of Active Experiences
The training of their powers of perception and the provision of active music experiences must be purposefully done in the set lessons. Some music should be heard in every music lesson and the child's perceptive powers and critical ear should be developed by setting him suitable listening objectives: listen carefully for one or two

MUSIC

minutes, pick out certain sounds or distinguish certain instruments. Dull children need careful instruction if they are to recognize the instruments of the orchestra but it is worth while as a means of widening their interests and sharpening their senses. Active experiences include not only listening but performing, and it is this which can so often prove difficult.

The slow learner, unless he is a monotone, expresses himself musically most easily and most fluently with his singing voice. For this reason singing is the best avenue of attack. If he is a monotone he is deprived of a great natural gift and his powers of personal expression are severely curtailed, perhaps for life. Most monotones can be taught to sing so for them singing is as worth while as for normal children, in fact more so since their need is greater. For all our pupils then – singing. Singing, starting at their level and going as far as possible in the time available. The physical joy that singing can be, the deep emotional outlet that it can provide and the expressive power which it brings out are advantages of such great worth in the personal development of children that its inclusion in the programme is a matter of prime importance: no matter what other activities may be done singing should never be omitted and there is much support for its claim to the main share of the available time.

The Development of the Singing Personality

The critical factor in the development of the slow learner's 'singing personality' – remember we sing with our whole selves, not just our voices – is his will to sing. Given this, the work is possible and worth while: without it, it's back-breaking and the final result is limited to the production of singing, which though it be in time and in tune, is unfelt, expressionless and with little value in the personal development of the child. But it is precisely this will to sing that is most often lacking. And that it is which we must essentially seek to implant and nourish. Intimately bound up with its growth are three things over which we teachers have direct control – the songs he is given to sing, the standards he is expected to reach and the methods we use to help him to reach those standards.

The Choice of Songs

In choosing songs we should give him something worth while to express – worth while in content and worth while in terms of the sensations which the act of expression arouses in him. Slow learners are poor at phrasing and slow at snatching a quick breath where no rest is provided at the end of the phrase, so from the technical point of view it helps if the songs chosen have simple phrases with the words and music well matched and plenty of breathing spaces. In addition to a suitable voice range there should be no exceptional intervals, not too florid a melody and a helpful accompaniment. Common sense and the response of the child are good guides to the selection of songs. Good musical content is more important than the words. Experience shows that it is the appeal of the whole song that matters – and for dull children the appeal goes to their emotions rather than their intellects. Once a song has been selected the real test of its suitability is the reaction of the children, and it is better to scrap a song that has become really 'bogged down' than to waste time and kill interest in learning it just for the sake of being 'dogged'. There is such a wealth of good music they really enjoy that it's worth trying out a few songs with them to find the ones they like best. Not only is their interest in learning the song of their choice greater, but their powers of attentive hearing and critical appreciation are exercised. Every time they make a considered judgement – on no matter what subject – they are developing a faculty which is a highly necessary part of their personal equipment in the complex world of today. The fact that they may not be able to verbalize their reasoning does not necessarily detract from its value. The provision of real judging situations like this is one of the ways in which suitable music education can help to improve the quality of their learning – something we must particularly bear in mind when teaching slow learners. Having given our pupils some measure of choice, however, we must still be prepared to slog on through the normal tough going that comes along occasionally. Music is a discipline demanding hard work and perseverance, and willingness to abandon the unprofitable does not mean abdicating the responsibility of making the final decision as to whether or not our pupils are working to capacity.

Slow learners like songs by the Masters equally as much as Negro spirituals, shanties and traditional tunes. The Scottish Education Department (1952) recommends teaching a large number of easy songs quickly and aiming at a high standard in one or two each term. This works out well in practice. Like good folk songs many classical songs almost sing themselves once they've been learnt, and a good selection from the finest composers greatly enriches the children's repertoire. As well as being added to, the repertoire needs continual and systematic revision: with less able children the process of consolidation, like the initial learning, is a slow one and more attention than with normal classes needs to be given to it. In this connexion, Mursell and Glenn (1938, p. 275), referring to the 'creative reviewing of music already learned', describe all musical learning as 'a constantly deeper insight into the expressive possibilities and demands of music'. In this sense, some of the songs comprising the repertoire should afford opportunity for subsequent musical development during the routine work of consolidation. Songs of this nature, too, will be sung by the child time and time again in his free time when he's in a singing mood. A 'top-ten' tune gets plugged on radio, TV and record player for about two months, and a boy will sing it for just a few weeks longer than this. A song like 'How Beautiful Are the Feet' or 'Lend Me Your Aid' will, if well learned, be repeatedly sung by some of the dullest of slow learners and will last them through life. The songs which have given them the deepest experiences are remembered long after they have left school. My own observations in a residential school have been that during their free time they spontaneously sing songs of this kind when they are happy and relaxed, and I have no doubt of the joy children get from singing the best songs or of the value of such songs to them.

Appropriate Standards

The standards we expect our pupils to reach are reflected continually in the methods we use to teach them, and, to some extent, become clear to them through those methods a little at a time. But *we* should always have a clear vision of what we are ultimately seeking to produce for it is only a sure knowledge of our final aim which will give directness to our efforts and endurance to our purpose. With suitable training, our pupils should be able to sing a well-chosen song in tune, in fairly good time and with controlled voices. Shouting and roughness should not be accepted. The singing should be accurate, the intonation perfect and the feeling of the music expressed. Fineness of interpretation and sensitive dynamic shading cannot be expected. Lively attack, good rhythm and good ensemble should be striven for, but will only come late if at all. The standard of diction is often poor and an indication of what to expect can be gained from observations of their everyday speech. 'I left it on the dest'; 'chron*i*um-plated handlebars'; 'walking on s*k*ilts'; 'the pottery kil*m*' and so on. The effects of the lack of perception which underlies these common mispronunciations are usually intensified by their inability to read. For many of them, their only guide to the sound is what they hear. The brighter child not only hears the sound but sees it as well and it is the visual impression which in the end is the master one. It is commonplace for people to say words like 'terrestial' and 'unwieldly' for years until with a shock they see the correct forms in print. 'I couldn't believe my eyes' is a more emphatic denial than 'I couldn't believe my ears'. Many slow learners have only their ears to guide them in correct pronunciation. The unaccustomed physical co-ordination and the sustained mental effort involved in articulation which is appreciably more precise than that which they habitually use in ordinary speech interferes with the more musical aspects of expression and is seldom an economic expenditure of energy. But we sometimes have to carefully teach the words of a song in order that a sensible idea is presented to the child: we should be prepared to point out the obvious and should refuse to take anything for granted. Good phrasing is essential but will only be attained with training. A good working guide – especially useful with slow children – to the soundness of our teaching is not only to listen but to watch. When the right standard is being reached in a song which they have made secure the children become a responsive group, subordinate themselves to the music and, in some indefinable way, live in it. At these times what is achieved is not only worth while as music but is intensely satisfying to them. It is precisely the experience of this satisfaction which is the greatest aid in the development of the will to sing. Therefore it is profitable to aim at producing it right from the beginning. Each song learnt should give an immediate reward when it is sung. Unless a real response in the children is aroused and a satisfying experience shared the song has failed in its purpose and its effect in the musical development of the child has been negligible if not negative. As we have seen, slow learners are easily distracted and lack mental vigour. Expression of any sort requires concentration and musical expression in particular needs alertness, if only because of its intimate connexion with time. This concentration and alertness must exist in all the group together – it is not as in art, language or number, where a boy can work at his own rate and take a spell when he chooses without disturbing his companions. The expression is corporate, the teacher is dealing directly with a group and all must give of their best at the same time. The enthusiasm of the teacher – which he must not be afraid to show – and his ability to make the music live will be a powerful influence in securing the necessary discipline and hard work. We must demand this from slow learners in no less degree than from bright children but can only do so for much shorter periods. Five minutes' well-timed, carefully prepared, intense effort will accomplish more than a quarter of an hour's work where the effect of continual if slight inattention is reinforced by a general lack of purpose on the part of pupils or teacher. This does not mean to say that consideration for individual differences and the maintenance of a permissive, happy atmosphere have no place in the music lesson. As in all work with all children, they have, and they are especially necessary to enable slow learners to do their best. We must always bear in mind the necessity for experience of music to be joyful and must help the children to enjoy their singing. But they'll never *really* enjoy it unless it's their best, and it won't be their best if there's any slackness while they're at it. The right attitudes must be carefully cultivated, and right conduct encouraged and if necessary enforced. In the majority of cases the response can be expected to be good, but there may be a sizable minority who, but for imposed standards of attention and application, would be a disruptive influence on the work in hand. Contrary to what one often reads, or what is sometimes implied, everything isn't always easy: it means hard work by pupil and teacher. It's not sufficient to put the music before them, so to speak, and let them lap it up. One or two may, but the majority won't. If a good standard of musical expression is aimed at some element of compulsion is unavoidable. At the same time one must always watch for the odd difficult child who genuinely needs special consideration. Mursell and Glenn (1938, p. 55) sum up the question of standards very well when they say '. . . it is always desirable to push every learning undertaking to a definite achievement level as high as the pupils' age and capacity will permit'. Good singing by dull children demands vigorous teaching directed to a clearly visualized goal. It involves making quite heavy demands on the children in terms of patient application and steady attention. Success in this kind of work has to be underwritten by the establishment of a good relationship in as many ways as possible and through all aspects of school life. The deepest joy and the greatest satisfaction in music come from doing something really well, and are of such great value in the personal and social development of our pupils that we should demand their best and be satisfied with nothing less. Our own belief in this is the bedrock on which our teaching must be based.

Teaching Method
Most lessons should provide listening experiences and at least half the time should be devoted to singing. Good class organization helps – fixed places for the children so that they know where to go, and all sized so that they can see and be seen easily. A clear plan of how the lesson should go is a great aid to maintaining a spirit of work in the class. The easiest method of learning a song is by imitation of the teacher's pattern, a phrase at a time, singing the tune to the correct words. The class should have heard the tune sung, with accompaniment, right through first. When this has been done it is useful to build up a framework of reference which will help the children, with their limited mental powers, to assimilate the song easily. It is not technical information which is wanted, but descriptions which will bring the ideas of the song more vividly before them – a word-picture of the song as a whole, or perhaps an explanation of certain lines. Anything which helps to present the phrases of the song as meaningful units and any relevant pictures which stimulate the imagination will help the slow learner to grasp whatever it is he has to express. It is better to write the words on the blackboard or large wall-sheet than to have papers which are an added source of distraction. Music copies should, however, be provided for three or four songs a year so that the children gain some experience of following a copy. Most slow learners are poor readers, and some are non-readers, so they should be taken through the words on the black-

board slowly and carefully. The boy who sang 'I Fought on the Land of God' for 'I Thought on the Lamb of God' did not merely misapprehend the words, he misunderstood the sense and feeling of what he was singing. So careful teaching is necessary. On the other hand, the words should not be laboured and it is sufficient if the general idea of each phrase is grasped. Understanding comes slowly to slow learners, and they will often be able to feel the meaning of things sufficiently well to express them musically before they are able to put them into words. The song can now be played through a second time while those who are able to read try to fit the words mentally. When they come to sing the phrases of the song it is better to reverse the blackboard so that they give full attention to the teacher who, having sung the phrase first, plays it with them and, looking directly at them, at the same time mouths the words silently while they sing. This contact of teacher and class is most important. We should aim at trying to express the feeling of the song from the beginning and try to get results quickly. These may initially be personal to the child but will be most worth while to him – perhaps the physical thrill of singing a few good notes which suit his register, perhaps the gripping experience of being dead on the beat in some exciting rhythmic passage or a brief realization of the beauty of part of the melody as he sings it. We must look for these things and be prepared to point them out. The fact that he doesn't experience them without being shown doesn't mean that he can't do so once he has been helped. What the bright child may perceive for himself the slow one will often be unaware of, but once he's seen it – and *we* have to show him – his joy will be equally great at his own particular level of feeling. It pays to teach him more slowly and to be prepared to point out what to us may seem obvious. When the first two phrases have been learnt they can be sung through together, and so on till the first verse has been done. Care should be taken all the time not to exhaust the class or to strain attention. Long phrases should be subdivided where this is musically possible. Just as we work in short spells because their attention span is short so should we present learning material in small quantities which are within their conceptual grasp. Tonic Sol-fa is a useful aid for difficult parts of the melody. Where the rhythmic pattern causes trouble the French time names give added help. It is helpful to practise the rhythm on its own; it is useful to sing difficult parts of the melody several times. Repetition is not necessarily boring. The mind grows through real effort, and if the repetition is presented as real work which is helping them to progress they will tackle it cheerfully. A frequent reminder of purpose encourages them and us. When a song or phrase is repeated the specific object of the repetition should be made clear – insufficient time-value at the end of a line, sloppy attack on a large interval, a break in the wrong place, etc. – and the correction required must be exactly demonstrated to an attentive class. Not singing to the end of the line, for example, is a common fault with slow learners and they have to be held to the full value. Two or three inattentive children may finish singing the final note of a phrase before the remainder, and the effect of this destroys clarity of outline. They must be spotted and corrected individually. If there is a sloppy attack on a large interval it is often necessary with dull children to practise the interval on its own apart from the phrase, and only to sing the phrase when the specific skill of singing that particular interval correctly has been mastered. In cricket, for example, we coach children in specific strokes. Dull children will practise with enjoyment and keeness, say, a forward defensive stroke, till they master it. And master it they do, eventually, but after much more practice than a bright child. It's the same with music – to sing a fifth cleanly, if they're shown how to do it and helped in their efforts, is something they can see as a target and a skill they will work hard to acquire. Another common fault is that several will sing a small fraction of a beat behind the group. This is to be expected and the answer is to arouse their interest and get a better grip on them so that by crisp conducting their attention is alerted and a sharper response secured. Restrained conducting is all very well for trained musicians but it can lull a backward class into lifelessness. We should not be afraid to let ourselves go in order to get the response we want. Banging out the beat with the hand or the foot, bad as it may be in theory, works well in practice as an occasional aid to a vigorous response. Whatever the fault and whatever the remedy, we must give detailed guidance and wherever possible show by personal demonstration exactly what needs to be done. We can best cure one fault at a time. The slow learner should see his immediate objective as a real target which he can reach, and his training should not be laboured. Hard work in short spells, well-timed intense effort and the production in our pupils of insight, interest and will are the psychological fundamentals of sound method in music teaching. In singing with dull children it is useful to try out the songs in different keys. Their voices usually spread over a wide range and a pitch that is just right for one may be too high for another. The feeling of comfort that comes with a song which is rightly placed, is a great help in the production of an expressive and enjoyable performance: repetition of a song at a higher or a lower pitch increases the number of children who are able to sing it easily.

Changing Voices
It is frequently recommended that a simple bass part be written for older boys, and for one or two songs a year this will be profitable. But the usual result of part singing by slow learners – no matter how simple the parts – is that the tone suffers and expression is lost. It is useful and interesting to give them experience of singing a simple part, but the best way to cope with the lowering voice of the adolescent is to gradually drop the pitch at which he is asked to sing. In this way strain is avoided and he continues to use his singing voice on musical material. As his voice deepens it is important to check undue forcing when the music calls for vigorous singing – this is where the dull child needs extra help for he is less inclined to sing sensitively than the brighter child. The successive lowering of the pitch of the song to accommodate the maturing voices does not, however, mean that the children should willy-nilly be allowed to sing an 'octave below'. Slow children are very prone to do this, and many who produce a gruff undertone are well able to sing without strain in a lovely head voice but consider it unmanly to do so. It pays to point out that singing demands physical fitness and vitality, and that a wide range is something worth cultivating. We can be much surer of what to work for in this respect if we have tested the children's voices individually. If they can be brought to realize that through their personal effort the brilliance of the treble content of the singing is sustained, and that the teacher values this effort, they will be much more ready to sing up. Good advice on the treatment of changing voices is given by Mellalieu (1957), who recommends the use of the medium register – a practice also commended by

MacMahon and Chamberlain (1951). Much useful material, too, has been set down by Jacques (1934).

Growlers

One of the problems which looms large in backward classes is that of the 'growler' who is unable to place his or her voice or to sing a note in tune. In fact, very few children turn out to be absolutely tone deaf, and with help most monotones can be taught to sing. This is not just another pious platitude – it's true. But patience and persistence are necessary. We should try to give unobtrusive individual help during a lesson and special attention at some time when the child can be taken on his or her own in a small sympathetic group. Once a start has been made it doesn't take long – the real problem is to find time to take them on their own. It is easiest to start on the notes they can sing, and play or sing with them a note or two either side. Their first efforts may seem very unrewarding. They need liberal encouragement and praise for their efforts, and any slight success should be recognized for the really great step forward that it is. Once started they soon improve beyond recognition. Their voices may still lie within a low register and will probably be coarse, but the important thing is that they'll be able to sing a melody in tune. Once they discover this they cease to think of themselves as musical outcasts and make positive efforts to contribute to the music-making experiences of the class. This is of great value to them and helps the music work of the school: from all points of view it is worth taking time and trouble over. Any teacher who has seen one such child improve will have no doubt of the value of help of this kind.

Aural Training

Slow learners benefit greatly from aural training and from an attempt at sight reading. One French time pattern a term can reasonably be taught. Tonic Sol-fa intervals should be taught on a planned basis – say one interval a term. The time and Sol-fa names should be used incidentally during song teaching, especially for teaching difficult parts of the melody or for correcting faults. In this way slow learners gradually acquire an easy familiarity with the basic materials of ear training. Easy songs, rather than exercises, will give good practice in reading and some should be included, say for five minutes or so, in most lessons. Pitch is most easily read from Tonic Sol-fa and rhythm from staff notation. Two or three copies of good songs should be provided each year for experience in following a printed copy. Pupils should have a copy between each two at least, and the music should be in staff notation with the Tonic Sol-fa printed below. A good aid – very popular with slow learners – is a weekly sight-reading competition. This is all that is necessary.

A phrase from a song or hymn they are currently singing is taken and written down clearly in Tonic Sol-fa, the time values of the notes being shown in staff notation. The chart should be large and attractive to stimulate and hold the children's interest. The response from the slowest is really amazing. They look on it as a puzzle, and will discuss it with each other, guess at the tune and try to sing it. Time has to be found to hear their efforts individually – which usually means during breaks – but it is well worth while and doesn't take long. They enter into the spirit of the thing well and if they don't succeed at the first attempt will continue to try. A competition like this has no effect on the least musical of our slow learners, but about half are found to be interested in it and this amply justifies its use. In an easy and pleasant way they are developing their musical interest and adding to their ability. The fact that they come up to try the tune out increases the teacher's opportunity for individual contact and develops the child's freedom of response in that he will, without self-consciousness, sing a few notes for someone else to hear. All this has a good effect on the singing programme and makes the work easier. All the incidental ways in which direct teaching can be reinforced should be exploited as fully as possible.

Creative Music-making

Creative music-making is so often recommended (Wing, 1941; Scottish Education Department, 1952; Mursell, 1951; Mainwaring, 1951; Hooper, 1946, and others), that consideration of it for slow learners cannot be omitted. To find time for it during class periods cuts down that available for activities where the reward is more readily apparent, But there are some who can benefit greatly and all should have the opportunity so that some help in this direction becomes necessary. What can be done is to show them how some phrases in the songs they sing answer others, to ask them to supply a final note to musical phrases or to complete the last two or three notes of a song. Activities like these can be used as 'breaks'. The children who are interested can be picked out and given extra help outside the lesson, encouraged to make up simple tunes with a given start and so on. Their tunes should be played over and harmonized for them. Very often one can get gifts of unwanted instruments to keep in the classrooms – a discarded harmonium, a mandolin or an old violin – and if these are made available at playtimes the keen children will make good use of them, picking out tunes, making up tunes or just producing sounds from them. Circumstances may make it impossible for this to be done, but where it can without disturbing others there is no lack of interest and it is advisable to make a rota so that one child at a time gets uninterrupted use of one instrument. Chime bars can be purchased or water-tuned bottles arranged to fulfil the same purpose. If it seems that the child is aimlessly wasting time or making an unpleasant noise in activities like this, it is well to think of the number of times we, as children, have sat at the piano playing notes at random and of how we thus gradually acquired a basis of sense impressions and experience which have helped to form an organized musical background.

MUSIC

Instrumental Music

So far as instrumental music-making proper is concerned I am not inclined to advocate it for slow learners. The development of the will to sing must come first since it is such an important factor in personal expressive ability. Instrument playing introduces difficulties which are generally beyond the ability of slow learners and any skills learnt are not likely to be made use of in after-school life. To learn to play the harmonica in his spare time is a useful accomplishment for a boy, but I would be reluctant to devote part of the set music time to it. Having said all this, however, I freely admit that only the teacher himself can decide what is best in particular circumstances. Where there is a strong instrumental tradition, or where a pupil shows special talent or inclination or the teacher is particularly attracted to this form of music-making it may well be absolutely the right thing to do. Teachers will no doubt concede the same with regard to singing where these conditions do not exist.

Corporate Activities

The corporate activities of the school also afford good opportunity for participation by slow learners: they should have opportunity for membership of the school music club, choir, gramophone club and so on. Visits to concerts are valuable avenues of experience for slow learners no less than for intelligent children. They will need encouragement to join in these activities, and giving that is a necessary part of the music work. It is unnecessary to indicate ways in which music can be correlated with other subjects in the curriculum, but perhaps it will bear stating again that the more pegs one can provide on which to hang the framework of musical experiences available to the child the more deeply, extensively and lastingly will those experiences affect him.

Conclusion

Putting these ideas into practice, however, depends on many things – the ability of the child, the general teaching situation, the amount of time available, the attitude of the school to music and so on. Some of these factors are outside our own control and it is as well to be aware of this. What we *ought* to do is very often governed by what we *can*. What is desirable may not always be practicable, and what is possible may sometimes not be worth while. It is better to do one or two things really well than to unsuccessfully attempt too much. Backward children require patient, continued teaching. Very often the critical factor in their achievement is persistence: and achievement to them is so eminently worthwhile that persistence to success along one or two lines – provided they are educationally sound – is better than half-developed effort over a wider field. Failure to achieve success with some of these activities should not cause us to condemn them as educationally unsound or as unsuitable for slow learners. Sometimes teaching them is like stirring a newly-opened tin of lead paint: as with the one the remedy is to keep stirring so with the other the answer is to keep trying. If we keep trying we can be sure of eventual success, though at the same time we can expect the objective results to fall far short in quantity, and slightly short in quality, of those produced by more intellectually favoured children. This success will lie in the boys and girls themselves, in their attitudes to music, in their increased powers of feeling and expression and in the deeper capacity for future joy which their music education is developing. Though the work is sometimes arduous the real results are of fundamental value to the children, and whatever efforts we share with them to this end are richly repaid both to them and us.

Bibliography

BURT, C., *The Measurement of Mental Capacities*, Oliver and Boyd, Edinburgh, 1927.

COFFMAN, A. R., 'Is Rhythm Subject to Training?', *School Musician*, 1949, XXI, 1, 14, 45.

HOOPER, C., *Teaching Music to Classes*, Arnold, Leeds, 1946, pp. x + 11–312.

ACQUES, *Voice Training in Schools*, Oxford University Press, London, 1934.

JERSILD and BIENSTOCK, 'A Study of the Development of Children's Ability to Sing', *American Journal of Educational Psychology*, 1934.

MACMAHON and CHAMBERLAIN, *A School Music Course*, Novello, London, 1951, pp. iv + 72.

MAINWARING, J., *Teaching Music in Schools*, Paxton, London, 1951, pp. viii + 64.

MUSIC

MELLALIEU, *The Boy's Changing Voice*, Oxford University Press, London, 1957, p. 34.

MURSELL, J. L., *Music and the Classroom Teacher*, Silver Burdett, New York, 1951, pp. vii + 304.

MURSELL and GLENN, *Psychology of School Music Teaching*, Silver Burdett, New York, 1938.

NAMENY, G., 'Inaugurating a Music Programme for the Mentally Retarded', *Journal of Exceptional Children*, 1949, XV, 5, 134–8.

NIBLETT, E., *School Music*, Blandford Press, London, 1955, p. 119.

PICHOT, P., 'Effect of Rhythm and Functional Music on Mental Defectives', *Mental Health*, London, 1949, IX, 6–10.

Scottish Education Department, *Music in Secondary Schools*, H.M.S.O., Edinburgh, 1952, p. 23.

VALENTINE, C. W., 'Aesthetic Appreciation of Musical Intervals Among Schoolchildren and Adults', *British Journal of Psychology*, 1914, VII, 108.

WING, H. D., *Musical Ability and Appreciation*, Ph.D. Thesis, Psychology, London, 1941.

— 1941, *Tests of Musical Ability and Appreciation*, C.U.P., 'British Psychological Society Monograph Series', 1948.

WINN, C., *Teaching Music*, Oxford University Press, London, 1954, p. 93.

Note: The Standardised Tests of Musical Intelligence referred to on p. 105 are now available in Great Britain and the U.S.A. from the National Foundation for Educational Research, 79, Wimpole Street, London, W.1.

WILLIAM BRIEN

Chapter VIII

DRAMA

It teacheth audacity to the bashful. It not only emboldens a scholler to speke, but instructs him to speke well and with judgement; to observe his commas, colons and full points.
           Heywood's Apology for Actors

If we agree with Maria Denisch, writing in *World Theatre* that 'drama is no longer a performance which children attend, but an artistic activity which they practise themselves', then our minds are already half made up as to whether to adopt a formal approach with a written text or whether to encourage improvised activity wherein the child creates his own forms. If we agree with Herbert Read that '*all* children are born with a natural aptitude for artistic expression and that our educational methods effectively destroy this as far as most children are concerned', then let us practise our drama with the slow learners, for therein lies a training in social sympathy and an unforgettable lesson in co-operation. How can we encourage this vital activity and develop it within the limitations of our pupils and ourselves?

The class is the lowest stream of a secondary modern school. It has a room of its own, furnished with movable chairs and tables. It has an open time-table in which will be inserted "Drama" for two half-hours a week.

It maybe that, for these occasions we envisage something reminiscent of the picture-frame stage; a period which begins with a kind of reading lesson, with those children who are able to read, taking parts, while we hope that the 'uncast' will be quiet and listen. Perhaps we give vague hints and promises about performance on a school stage with costumes, make-up, lighting and, almost certainly, prompters (if they can keep the place). In my opinion this is unsuitable; there are better ways.

DRAMA

It is likely that the beginnings of drama are already in our work. Possibly we use it in arithmetic with a shop in one corner of the room; better still, there may be four shops, adequately staffed and well supplied with customers. The elements of drama may surely lie here. The child cannot help using his imagination to some degree if he uses these shops to help him with his arithmetic. He buys things. He sells things. He is shopkeeper, handling money, pricing goods and making out bills. There is a considerable degree of freedom and drama can as well begin here as in the reading or English lesson.

Let the children improvise from the very beginning. Keep the class as a unit with all of them participating. To do this some consideration of available space is necessary, Use the school hall if possible. Avoid the stage. It is probably in use as a classroom anyhow and even if it is free it is one-sided and necessitates the use of too many tricks. Clear the classroom to obtain as big an acting space as possible. Call in the scene-shifters and get the maximum space in the middle or at one end of the room. If there is nowhere else to pile the furniture, put it in the middle and act round it!

Begin now with free movement, perhaps to music if it can be arranged, allowing the music to set the mood. Then be still, holding the same mood. Next, create improvised scenes involving groups of people – a crowded beach, a railway station, a crowd waiting for a bus. Let the teacher move about with the children, encouraging and helping. 'Let the children talk if they need to. Don't stop improvised speech because you can't put up with it or because you can't see the point. Don't be too critical. Try to get all involved and avoid showing-off by particular individuals.' It is unwise to let the situation persist for too long. Change the setting – a street scene (specified) and remember to bring the weather in.

This is the core of the work. Our drama should come from this; taking an incident or situation arising from the group-playing here suggested. Play a short scene involving one, two or three of a group, pieced together between the children and the teacher. Keep the scene brief; let it grow; let the speech be improvised; recast the same scene quickly; constant movement and change. While the main group is busy, play one or two short scenes within the main scene, as many as experience, conditions and expediency allow. They may even be prepared beforehand, but only to the extent of discussing the characters – no scripts at present.

Drama, thus envisaged, is a group effort – all are doing; the boy who lifts the chairs is as vital as the juvenile lead; and this co-operation is important to the slow learner. It will help to bring out the retiring and to quieten the noisy. From these early beginnings, plays will take shape which will have come from the children themselves. A script for each will be evolved – largely simple words and sentences to preserve the shape and outline of the piece. Here is legitimate motive for writing.

This "scripting" must not imprison the work in too tight a jacket and if this happens it is better to leave the script and come back to it later on. It is much better to encourage the children to write about 'what happens in our play' than to force the pace towards a scripted play, either their own or someone else's. While keeping the interests and ideas of the children in mind, it is probable that the taste and inclinations of the teacher will guide the work on individual lines.

All this is not meant to suggest that the classroom is all indiscriminate acting and no audience. Children enjoy watching one another perform and audience is as important as cast. From, and together with, the group work suggested earlier little playlets can be subtracted and developed to be performed within the rest of the class, i.e. with the rest of the class seated about the players. These playlets should be short; there can be several different groups doing the same playlet; several groups in action, one after another, using here any limited assistance they can get from a dressing-up box.

Simple miming is valuable and popular. It can be done by volunteers at first; soon, others not so keen to begin with, will want to try. Let these mimes be very simple and very brief – they serve very well as breaks between changes of work. 'Pick up a pin, pick up a sheet of paper', 'Open the door to a visitor', 'Put on an overcoat', These are individual mimes which could develop into duets or trios. Next, instructions to perform certain mimes may be written on cards. The child takes a card, reads his instructions and performs his mime which is guessed by the remainder and possibly, written down. Do not let this kind of thing continue for too long. Stop it and go on to something else while the group is still eager.

Clear speaking can be encouraged by telephone conversations

DRAMA

with a real instrument for preference. Simple conversations begin, such as asking the doctor to call or a telephone message to a shop, followed by some practice in the use of the telephone in connexion with the emergency services. Occasionally the tape-recorder could be introduced to record and play back the pupils' voices – a surprise and a treat.

The use of a real or simulated telephone will sometimes assist the shy child, as will the use of masks. These may be purchased but it is an exciting project in craft work to make the masks from a relief plasticine base upon which layers of damp paper are pasted. Painted and varnished, they form the basis for plenty of imaginative dramatic work. Success is more likely if a mask is made first.

Puppets can be made in a similar manner but this is a comparatively lengthy project and with the slow learner interest may very well evaporate long before the end. More immediate targets are advisable.

Under careful guidance there is available material for dramatic expression in almost everything the children do. Stories from the Bible, stories from reading books, stories and descriptions from history and geography all lend themselves to dramatic expression. In fact it may be sounder to 'show it' than to 'tell it'. However, a word of warning is necessary. The value lies in what the children are doing and not as to how far their work approaches a mature, adult level. Do not solve problems for them. Pick a group, give them the time to get something done. If they are all of a similar level in, say, reading, it will give the teacher the opportunity to do other much-needed coaching with the remainder. Let it be like teacher-guided charades rather than a teacher-driven exercise.

So much for the beginnings of dramatic work with the slow learning groups in the secondary modern school. As the subject develops higher up the school it will lead to the production of plays from scripts, but not until the reading level is adequate. Play these in the round, in the centre of the school hall and leave the use of the stage until last. Remember that if it is necessary to produce a play for public performance, it should arise from the work done in lesson time and in the classroom. Perfection means polishing, and polishing means repetition, and repetition means lack of spontaneity. Too often the curriculum is slaughtered to make a parents' holiday.

Choose a play with a large cast if a major production is to be attempted – not a three-act play – but major in the sense that it will be the most important thing the group has attempted. Try to avoid the star system. Aim at having plenty of small parts and few stage directions and if all these conditions are impossible, you must write the play yourself! Begin early; call in assistance and work as a team all the way through, keeping the group conversant with what is going on. Plan the project to the last detail so that everyone, not only the actors, is involved. Put the play into the arena; have your audience around you so that while they admire they may also participate completely.

Book List

CHORPENNY, CHARLOTTE, *21 Years with the Children's Theatre*, Children's Theatre Press, Anchorage, Kentucky.
COGGIN, PHILIP A., *Drama and Education*, Thames and Hudson.
COLLINS, FREDA, *Children in the Market Place*, U.L.P.
SLADE, PETER, *Child Drama*, U.L.P.
— *Introduction to Child Drama*, U.L.P.
WILLS, JOHN, and GARRARD, ALAN, *Leap to Life!* Chatto and Windus.

C. G. GOLDING

Chapter IX

HANDICRAFTS

It is not the intention of this section to encroach upon the domain of the fully qualified specialist in handicraft who teaches the subject, probably to a fairly high standard of technical skill and knowledge, to the majority of classes in the secondary modern school; rather is it meant to be an encouragement to the teachers of the C and D streams to supplement that teaching by giving opportunities for the boys to use their new-found skills by applying them to everyday problems that arise, in, and out of the classroom. This may be done by making models, carrying out minor repairs, exploring the possibilities of light crafts: in fact, in any way in which craft work readily lends itself to integration with the other subjects in the curriculum.

It may be that the teacher of a backward class will find that the time-table does not allow for any specialist instruction in handicraft for his boys and, if they are to get any practical instruction and experience at all, he will have to provide it. In most cases it is bootless to complain at this seemingly unfair treatment of the C and D children. The average secondary modern head teacher, coping, as he does, with over large numbers, coupled with shortage of staff, often conceives it as his first duty to provide specialist instruction for his abler pupils. Only after the requirements of his A and B streams have been met will he look to see if any periods remain on the time-table when the backward classes might be fitted into the handicraft room. Whatever arguments may be advanced decrying this policy, there are an equal number of quite valid ones that can be put forward in defence of it, so, for the purposes of this chapter, it is best to leave this meatless bone of staff room contention, and see how best to deal with the situation as it exists.

Few teachers who have experience of teaching dull children will deny that the handicraft period, properly handled, gives great satisfaction to this type of child, rivalled only, perhaps, by the P.E. and games lesson. This is because, in these lessons, a boy can satisfy his urge to imitate the older people he admires: workmen like his father, older brother or neighbour. The dull boy's hero is unlikely to be a person of academic bent: he seldom sees a grown-up writing an essay or learning history, but he frequently sees them doing carpentry, mending motor-cars and playing football. In the vast majority of cases he can also enjoy the satisfaction of moderate success in these practical fields that is denied him in academic subjects. The old fallacy that a compensatory factor could be assumed when working with backward children – that if they were poor at Three R's they were automatically clever with their hands – finds little following these days: but, as with most fallacies, this one contains a grain of truth in as far as a dull child may manifest a woeful inability to master basic subjects, but his failure may be less pronounced in handicrafts and he may even approach competence. The truth is that, on the whole, the child of average, or above average intelligence, shows a higher standard of skill at handicraft than his duller school-fellow. Should a pupil in a backward class show pronounced skill in craft work it would be wise to investigate his school history and home background to see if he has not been mistakenly dubbed 'backward'. On more than one occasion marked competence at handicraft has led the teacher to suspect, and later discover, some hitherto undetected but remediable cause of his apparent backwardness. Therefore the teacher of the backward who finds in his class a boy with marked ability at handwork should look carefully for some emotional factor or physical defect causing retardation rather than assume straight away that he is dull.

It does not fall within the scope of this chapter to give detailed accounts of techniques in the various handicrafts commonly practised in schools, for many excellent books on these subjects are readily available (as I have indicated in the list at the end), but it is hoped to show how craft work, realistically taught, will help to give a backward boy confidence and self-respect and, incidentally, accelerate his progress in other subjects by reviving his interest in school work generally. The main advantage from the teacher's point of view is that he can exploit a ready-made situation in which he does not first have to create an interest among his pupils. Almost all of them will be already anxious and eager for increased practical and creative experience in the classroom: in fact, this eagerness may already be showing itself in undesirable ways if a large proportion of practical work is not given: in unruly behaviour and inattention: restlessness during sessions of "chalk and talk": growing impatience with continuous failure in basic subjects. The only difficulty the average teacher should find in putting over handicraft will be in its organization or in keeping the enthusiasm of his pupils within bounds and profitably directed. It is in the hope of smoothing out any such difficulties that the following suggestions are offered.

The Organization of Handicraft in the Classroom
Tools and Equipment
In any classroom in which backward children are to be taught craft there should be, as basic equipment:

Sink, with water supply.
Two carpenters' benches with vices. It does not matter if these are dilapidated so long as they are steady and have the vices in working order.
One or two large working tables (where it doesn't matter if the surface gets stained or scratched).
One large, shallow cupboard in which to store tools.
Ample shelf space or racks for storing materials and displaying models.
A gas ring, or similar heating appliance.

If the room is too crowded with desks to allow the introduction of tables and benches, throw out the desks and let the children sit at the tables for conventional lessons.

The following list of tools should be sufficient for light handicraft with a class of about twenty-four pupils:

2 hammers	2 coping saws
2 14 in. tenon saws	1 nail punch
1 20 in. handsaw	6 assorted files and rasps
6 assorted chisels	2 bench hooks

1 Stanley drill
1 set bits $\frac{1}{16}$ in.–$\frac{1}{4}$ in.
1 pair pincers
1 No. 5 Stanley Steel Plane
1 mallet

1 screwdriver
2 trysquares
2 8 in. 'G' cramps
1 hacksaw
4 1 in. paint brushes

In addition to these items consumable stock such as nails, cold water glue, screws, sandpaper, varnish, paint, etc., will be necessary. Even at present day prices, tools and consumable stock can be purchased for well under £20.

The tool racks in the large, shallow wall cupboard, or fixed directly on to the wall, should have the outline of the tool drawn on the wall space behind where the tool is to hang. This can be done by drawing round the tool in chalk or charcoal and getting the children to fill in the outline with white paint. If, at the end of a session, any outline remains uncovered by its tool its absence is obvious at once: this saves time in checking. Label each outline with the name of the tool as a valuable aid to word recognition. What a lot of boys call pincers 'pinchers' – saws 'sores' and so on. It is also more workman-like to refer to tools by their correct names.

Two wooden boxes for scrap timber and odd pieces should be provided to keep the room tidy – a deep box for long pieces and a shallow one for short pieces.

Allow plenty of time at the end of the session for putting away tools, as this job, if rushed, can be dangerous and is not conducive to an orderly and deliberate routine.

Make each boy responsible for checking a small section of equipment: one for files, one for chisels, one for tidying scrap boxes, etc.

Periodically a session will be required for sharpening, oiling and maintaining tools. The woodwork master might show the boys how to do this, or it can be done by the local ironmonger. Tools should be kept at maximum sharpness and efficiency at all times: it is the *blunt* tool which is the *dangerous* one. It is also a useless one.

Models in course of construction should have each part labelled with its owner's name (pencilled lightly direct on to the wood) to avoid time waste and confusion at the beginning of a session.

HANDICRAFTS

Materials

A suitable, inexpensive and easily worked wood for some of the models described later is Parana pine. It is strong, straight grained, and has few knots. It should be ordered from the merchant planed on both sides (P.B.S.) as this provides a satisfying surface, after light sandpapering, and cuts down mess from shavings in the classroom – no small consideration if all subjects have to be taught in the same room. Some useful sizes are 1 in. × 1 in., 6 in. × ½ in., 9 in. × ¾ in. in lengths to order. The woodwork master will no doubt be able to help further in the matter of ordering timber from a merchant. It is inadvisable to order hardwoods such as oak or mahogany, except for specific purposes, since they are not easy for the novice to work, and are expensive.

A valuable source of supply is the local furniture factory. Most of these factories will supply to schools, free, or at a nominal charge, off-cuts of plywood and odd pieces which are very suitable for classroom use. If in doubt where to apply, ask the children; they usually know all the sources of supply of free firewood in the district! It might be diplomatic to make sure, in the first instance, that you are not encroaching upon some other teacher's source of supply, for many handicraft teachers supplement their timber stocks in this way.

Waste from old furniture can be used and adapted but watch out for the tiny holes bored by the wood beetle. No parent will thank you for a tea-pot stand which has been the means of introducing woodworm into the dining-room suite! Dismantling old furniture can be useful at times to show its manner of construction and often, useful screws, hinges and other fittings can be salvaged even if the timber is too warped or split to be of service.

The teacher should not be afraid of a certain amount of waste. Most L.E.A.s are generous in requiring only a certain percentage of the money initially spent on stock to be refunded through the Sales Book. Also, material spoiled is not necessarily material wasted, for the child may have learned much from his failures. Providing the reasons for his failures are pointed out on the spot, young Johnny's failure to make just what he had in mind may have taught him many things which we, as teachers, appreciate and take for granted. Merely handling and working with timber will teach him something of the relative resistance of various materials, their strength and fitness for purpose. For instance, he will learn that plywood is no good for making a scooter, heavy wood is necessary for book-ends: that one cannot plane across the grain without a shooting board, nor, for that matter, across nails or other resistant objects embedded in the wood, without damaging the blade. He will learn to recognize various woods by the grain, weight and hardness; to appreciate their relative costs (that oak is much dearer than deal) and realize that mistakes can be costly.

Backward children, especially, need these practical and self-evident experiences. A failure may teach a child much about his own limitations as well as his abilities, and, providing this is not allowed to discourage him from attempting a more suitable task, be a valuable experience.

Co-operation in School and at Home

In order that the boy may feel a sense of purpose in the work he is doing, everything he does must seem meaningful to him. The co-operation of a number of people and agencies can be enlisted to this end. Work, however crude, so long as it has been done to the best of the pupil's ability, should be praised and displayed. If the model is used to demonstrate some fault for the others to avoid, counter-balance its shortcomings by some reference to its merits, no matter how difficult any merit may be to discern: point out how hard the boy has been working at it: say what a good idea it was to try to make it, in the complete absence of any concrete praiseworthiness.

The first model a boy makes is usually to take home for his parents, and their praise and thanks for his small gift, however crudely it is made, will provide incentive for fresh efforts, However, sometimes a thoughtless or ignorant parent laughs or pours scorn upon the child's gift and this discouragement must be offset by the teacher. An example of this was provided by the boy who had worked hard to make a tea-tray. He was given a shilling to pay for the raw materials, and proudly took the finished article home. Imagine his feelings when his mother complained that the tray was not big enough for their large family, and made him return the tray to school with a badly spelled note demanding her shilling back! In this case the tray was bought by the teacher and used in the staff room so that the boy often had the satisfaction of seeing his handiwork in use.

HANDICRAFTS

The teacher will often find himself the recipient of the boy's next product, and any such present, displayed and used in the classroom will give this pupil, and the others, great satisfaction and encouragement. If other teachers can be persuaded to entrust small jobs to selected pupils – making articles of classroom equipment, repairing cupboards, replacing screws, etc., it will lend a sense of purpose to the work.

One of the most useful allies that the teacher of a backward class can cultivate is the school caretaker. If he can be persuaded to supply a weekly list of minor repairs which might be undertaken by the boys, a never-ending source of useful and practical work can be tapped. Repairing locks, replacing screws and windows, fixing shelves and coat racks, simple repairs to school furniture are a few of the jobs that constantly need doing about a school. Let the boys take full written instructions for any jobs undertaken outside the classroom – a valuable aid to comprehension – and yourself unobtrusively check any measurements and materials used to avoid undue waste. 'Unobtrusively' must be stressed, for, to build up the self-confidence of the boy, he must feel that he is becoming self-reliant in these matters.

If the primary school which feeds the senior school the boys now attend is near at hand, a number of opportunities for fostering continuity of education occur, and may help the junior and senior teachers of backward children to meet and compare notes and so improve the child's education generally. How proud the boys are who make a Wendy House for the infants' school; nesting boxes, rabbit and hamster hutches for the more backward juniors; table mats, letter-racks, ash-trays, teapot stands and door stoppers for the infant and junior school staff rooms. They will be proud to display their newly acquired skill to their old teachers, and the respect and admiration of the younger children will certainly do them no harm.

Suggestions for Crafts other than Woodwork
Paper and Cardboard Models
These are of use in the production of group projects on ports, railway stations, villages, farmyards, airfields, etc., and will give the teacher ample opportunity for teaching the use of ruler and compass. If a boy appreciates the necessity for accurate measurement, careful use of scissors and fine definition in pencil drawing he will the more

readily understand the need for adherence to reasonably fine limits in woodwork. Paper is usually available to the child at home so that he can easily practise this craft out of school.

Clay Modelling

This helps with the appreciation of the three-dimensional aspect of craft work. Often, a boy who has shown no aptitude for translating the three-dimensional world into the two-dimensional language of drawing will shine at modelling. The delight with which children discover the sheer satisfaction of handling and moulding a plastic material makes experiments in clay worth while. It is messy, and so, doubtful if the whole class should engage in this activity at one time: in any case it will not appeal to every child simultaneously, and a point to remember is that handicraft, to capture the child's full co-operation and enthusiasm, should be offered to him when, and where, he feels the urgent need for it. The absence of a kiln should not discourage the teacher; temporary, unfired work gives great satisfaction in the making. Alternatively, the art department might be encouraged to buy a kiln or to construct one. Another solution is to make contact with another school which possesses a kiln. It is not so good a plan to have pottery fired commercially, since the children do not actually see this important stage being done.

For the very slow or dull boy the children's craze for PLASTER MODELLING in rubber moulds might be exploited. This craft is of doubtful educational value in itself, but it can provide a jumping-off point for more instructive individual work later on. The boys certainly enjoy painting these models, and one backward class recently made all the Christmas decorations for Christmas cakes baked in the domestic science centre – an excellent example of co-operation between departments.

Needlework and Rugs

Many boys are not averse to learning embroidery – especially if the design is of a pictorial nature – and any teacher who possesses the ability might introduce this craft to his pupils. The more repetitive work involved in rug-making is of very doubtful value educationally, but many adults find great relaxation in following this repetitive occupation and it may well prove to have a relaxing effect upon an

HANDICRAFTS

especially turbulent or emotionally disturbed member of the class. Very beautiful results are obtained in this craft with very little skill, but it must be remembered that it is expensive and time-taking, and only the best quality materials are effective; cheap rug wool is a waste of money since it mats together, collects (and clings to) dirt, and looks unattractive after a very short while.

Metal-Work

A gas ring or open stove will allow soft soldering to be carried out. This can be used in making wire frames for lamp shades, wire work, toasting forks, etc. If noise is no object, beaten metal work produces beautiful results and is effective in fostering judgement of eye, muscular control, and restraint in the use of tools. These qualities, of course, are invaluable in all craft work.

Gardening

The possession of a school garden, no matter how modest, will offer many uses for the products of the handicraft lesson. Tool racks, repairs to handles, cold frames and seed boxes are in demand throughout the year. One of the early exercises in woodwork, years ago, was to produce a plant label, accurate in length, taper, and width and thickness to a small fraction of an inch: but such practices are useless with dull children (or with any other kind, for that matter) since it means that they labour for hours to produce an inferior article that can be bought for a fraction of a penny. One of the lessons that handicraft can teach is that ability to 'do it yourself' can save money – an idea that is attractive to most people and to children especially.

The possession of a school garden also gives the teacher the opportunity to 'thin out' – his class – not the plants. Half a dozen boys can usefully be employed in the garden on their own for periods up to half an hour, after training, while the teacher takes a smaller group for handicraft in the classroom. How lucky are those schools which have a garden immediately outside the classroom door or window – as many recently built schools have.

Basket-Work

This is a very beautiful craft, and easily learned by dull children. They must be very carefully instructed in the basic techniques and no stages (such as adequate soaking of the cane) omitted when they are left to work on their own, for the beauty and durability of the finished article is entirely dependent upon the precision with which each operation is carried out. It is also rather expensive.

Wood Turning
Although this can only be carried out in the woodwork room in which a lathe is available, the woodwork master will know that this craft is well within the capacity of a dull boy who has reasonably good muscular co-ordination and has been taught to use a lathe. Excellent and professional-looking results are produced which greatly encourage the older boy. Of course, it requires knowledge, skill and expert supervision on the part of the teacher, but those who aim to give a wide range of useful experience to the backward class must be prepared to achieve at least some of these simple skills for themselves.

Design Appreciation
An important aspect of craft work is awareness of design and fitness for purpose. Mrs Myers has already spoken of the need for a close link between art and crafts and it should be seen that any design for a model suggested to the boys is well proportioned and in good taste. Many of the models described in many so-called educational books and magazines on the subject are very questionable in this respect. We all know the monstrosities that were perpetrated when the craze for fretwork swept the country a few years back, and anyone still in doubt as to the kind of 'arty-craftyness' referred to cannot do better than listen to Miss Joyce Grenfell's devastating denunciation of this cult in her monologue on 'How to Make Useful Presents for Your Friends' from, among other unconsidered trifles, beech-nut husks. The suggestion that one might make a useful fur coat from the fluff which collects under the bed could not be more ludicrous.

Having made a conscious study of good taste and simplicity in design, let the teacher design things for the boys to make, and later train them to design things for themselves. It would be helpful if part of the wall space of the classroom could be used to display pictures of objects which are well designed, and if, occasionally, a little display

HANDICRAFTS

of small, well-designed examples of pottery, woodwork, basketry, etc., could be arranged, so much the better. It should not be necessary to say much to the boys about these displays – they will look at them and get the idea; think how quickly examples of *bad* taste catch on, simply because they are constantly thrust in front of the public eye. The forces of good taste are seldom so obtrusive in our furniture and hardware shops and other places where goods are displayed, and so it falls to the teacher to draw his pupil's attention to what is good, simple and useful. The immature taste of most children is naturally drawn to the fanciful, ostentatious and bizarre in design, and has to be guided gently into channels where simple beauty or utility (both, if possible) are the paramount virtues.

A good rule is to advise them to eschew anything which is deliberately designed to look like something else, and give as examples: tea-pots which look like Anne Hathaway's Cottage but which do not pour successfully: the table lamp which resembles (although not very accurately) a sailing ship, and which gives very little light, and that poorly directed; or go to the other end of the scale and point out the hideousness of the stockbroker's house with its imitation Tudor beams on the façade vying for attention with a tangle of twentieth-century exterior drain pipes and other plumbing. The mentality which, in Victorian times, thought up frills for voluptuously swelling piano legs, is still with us. Covers shaped like 'Crinoline Ladies' are still being sold to shroud telephones or as tea-pot cosies, and the thought of hiding a perfectly decent and well-designed telephone or tea-pot beneath a lady's skirts can only strike any mature judgement as in extremely questionable taste.

One method of gently imposing this pattern of good taste and judgement on the boys would be to design, in the first instance, about a dozen easily made models, and confine the boys' selection of things to make within this range. A list of suitable models might include:

Clothes horse	Table lamp	Folding camp stool
Letter rack	Book ends	Trinket box
Tea-pot stand	Book racks	Needlework box
Toys	Nesting box	Table mats
Boats	Bread board	Towel roller

Conclusion

In conclusion – one or two things to be borne in mind when considering teaching handicraft in the ordinary classroom. The teacher must resign himself to abandoning the idea of a permanently tidy environment. How untidy the room is at the end of the day will depend very much upon how much attention has been given to the organization of the period and the thoroughness with which the clearing up routine has been put into action. Any extra trouble taken in this direction will be easily offset by the wealth of practical experiences the boys will have gained in solving life's everyday problems. A problem in an arithmetic book, worked correctly or wrongly, will only result, for the child, in a tick or a cross. A problem in handicraft, tackled in the right or the wrong way, results in an obviously satisfying conclusion, or in practical and concrete evidence of faulty thinking or working demonstrable to even the meanest intelligence.

Give the boys the opportunity to do a wide variety of handicrafts, teach them simple techniques, praise and encourage at every opportunity, and the backward classes will become a real asset to the school. The contribution they make to the smooth running of the school community as a whole will give them that confidence and self-esteem which is the right of every boy as a reward for work well done.

Book List

CALTON, *ABC of Bookcraft*, Evans.
FITZRANDOLPH, M. (ed.), *30 Crafts*, Nat. Fed. Women's Institutes.
Dryad Handicrafts Instructional Leaflets, Dryad.
GLOVER, *New Teaching for a New Age*, Nelson.
GOODGER, *Woodwork and Metalwork*, Dryad.
HILS, KARL, *The Toy: its value, construction and use*, Ed. Ward.
MACEWAN, SHEILA (ed.), *Your Children's Crafts*, Sylvan Press.
PEACH, H. H. (ed.), *Craftsmen All*.

R. E. BEINDER

Chapter X

HOUSECRAFT

In this chapter an attempt is made to consider how far, if at all, the more backward children in our secondary schools are a problem to the housecraft teacher and whether it is in the interest of the children themselves to deviate from the normal patterns of housecraft teaching.

Every secondary school has some less able children, but the degree of backwardness varies considerably and while the comment that a child 'cannot read' means a fair lack of fluency in one school, in another it means complete inability. Where circumstances are suitable the real 'Special Class' or 'Backward Stream' is being catered for to an increasing extent. It is being staffed as far as possible by those who have a particular interest in the children. The range of ability in these special classes tends to be higher than in a Special School, but is still such that the approach to work is expected to be rather different from that in the normal classes and also rather more variation in behaviour is expected.

Much of what follows can apply to these special classes, though they have not been the chief consideration. There are in our secondary schools some children who do not qualify for a special class and yet are unable or clearly unwilling to benefit from the good opportunities provided in the school – those 'difficult Cs and Ds'. The problems discussed here and the examples used have all been drawn from such classes.

Some housecraft teachers take their share of D stream classes willingly enough but find the task discouraging, others enjoy the children and choose to teach them. Both will recognize these staff room comments.

They cannot remember anything.
They cannot read.

Their standards are so low, their work is so untidy.
They are so noisy and uncontrolled.
They never *do* anything.
Sometimes this is a quick judgement based on comparison with preconceived standards, sometimes it is a fair statement of fact and worth considering when planning for and teaching a slow class or outstandingly slow girl.

Memory

'They cannot remember' is often a perfectly fair criticism. Memories are much less reliable here than in the A classes and the memory of each child will tend to be very uneven, making some children unpredictable or unreliable. It is easy to expect too much from Sylvia with her willing manner and careful craft work. Sylvia is so obviously the one to select to serve the unexpected meal or cook on Open Day, yet when the occasion arises she flounders or panics to everyone's disappointment. Or perhaps she may be capable of making a very supreme effort and coping with the situation and while it is very nice to have someone in the class who can always be relied on to do these things, it is worth watching Sylvia sometimes and noticing how much strain and effort her reliability have cost her – and also how she manages to bridge gaps in her memory.

Remembering what to bring for a lesson depends only partly on interest. Often lack of memory hides other difficulties. The message which reaches home may have been oddly twisted, mother may be unwilling or unable to supply the exact articles. A child who often forgets or who is often in trouble because her efforts to remember are coloured by imagination can grow afraid of using her memory. Explanations may be difficult to express, while 'I forgot' is easy, and is expected of Mavis. The children come only once a week to housecraft and it is unwise to make a big issue if a week-old message has been freely interpreted. Perhaps it will not be so easy to make sure that they all cover the syllabus, but in this class it is often wisest to be really appreciative with those who remember and bring the right things, and to help others to make really good use of what they have brought, however unexpected it may be. Those few who arrive deliberately empty-handed may deserve the dull tasks allotted to them, though in some cases more is gained by providing them with a really interesting alternative. Rose and Queenie, a thoroughly difficult pair, could neither be persuaded, encouraged nor punished into remembering cookery money or dishes, but tension was relieved on all sides when they were 'abandoned' to the large dining alcove to clean, polish and make loose covers while the others cooked, an arrangement which made the morning profitable for all the class. Eileen, however, began to truant from the centre, for even when she remembered what to ask for, Mum saw no reason to provide it. Eileen became happier when she found that for her there was always a nice blouse or skirt in school to launder when others brought their own. It is hardly necessary to say that Eileen was a shy first year, while Rose and Queenie were lively 'fourth years'. Whether it be dishes or laundrywork, a quiet acceptance of something unexpected and a reserve of work for those who bring nothing often goes a long way towards building up a good response. A tiny notebook can help the little beginners who are backward, giving them a little careful writing each week (for a book to go home must look nice), and also ensuring that the right message goes home, for articles or money.

They cannot remember how to do things. A good sequence of work does help to impress methods, but sometimes inability to remember is due to conflict between the way things are done at school and at home. Also some girls, particularly those who are overanxious or whose homes set very high standards, become so afraid of doing the wrong thing that they cannot recall the right. Certainly all the usual teaching aids can assist these girls to remember methods, provided they have good help in the early stages of using cards, diagrams and recipe books. The sequence of work in making a mixture by the creaming method may be established by practice with a variety of cakes and puddings, with teaching aids provided for future reference. This is usual procedure. It is in the 'future use' that Carol shows her weakness of memory and where a rather different approach may help Carol and her friends to feel competent. Some have the ability to learn recipes if the incentive is strong – perhaps a lunch party when they have proved they can remember. Some are helped by a quick verbal revision of a recipe before they set to work. This confuses others, but after they have collected the ingredients or made their selection from the vegetable rack they can be 'triggered off' by a quiet reminder to 'get them nice and clean', or 'keep the pudding mixture soft'. Christine may not do either by the orthodox method she has 'been taught', but if she can begin to rely on herself to tackle practical problems her confidence will grow. For those who do not remember how, it does seem most important that they should be helped from the very earliest stages to try to do things for themselves, to concentrate on what they want to achieve and to think out how to achieve it. This approach does mean a wide variety of methods and even standards of work, and it takes courage at first to leave Christine to her own devices, but she will benefit.

They cannot remember quantities. It is not so difficult to provide quick reminders of quantities as of method. If Sheila can read the names of the ingredients and the quantities, a notebook or recipe book or card is the obvious choice and if it is her own notebook she may find pictures for matching the words and to remind her of finished dishes. (She will need guidance in the selection of pictures and may be unable to produce suitable ones from home.) Memory is not the only handicap here, though, and what appears to be lack of ability to remember quantities may be an incomplete understanding of weights and measures. If Sheila is always the very last at the store table and seems to be careless over quantities it is well worth finding out, by a test or game, whether she can (*a*) understand the quantities she hears or reads, (*b*) use them in practical weighing and measuring. For Sheila, too, basic proportions may be quite incomprehensible (to every ½-lb. flour use 4 oz. to 8 oz. fat, 4 oz. to 8 oz. sugar). Sheila is more likely to remember the exact quantities for a sponge sandwich in a certain recipe book and later be very proud when she finds that her 'cake' will steam or bake for puddings or turn into little buns or a big fruit cake. For Sheila and her friends it is worth working out the fewest possible definite recipe quantities instead of the more general 'basic proportions' even if this means work or use of terms not technically correct. At least confidence will improve and, with it, understanding.

Reading

Since housecraft is taught to children of secondary school age, a certain fluency in reading, writing and number is usually taken for granted, with the result that it sometimes seems quite impossible for certain children to cook a dinner, for they cannot yet read! We tend to forget that many adults run a home and family without being able to read or write. If they are successful home-makers – and many are – these adults do have a fundamental conception of practical number and even if vocabulary is limited they are capable of comprehension at a very practical level.

Backwardness in the basic subjects can mask a girl's general practical ability unfairly. It will be harder to teach these girls in the early stages of assignment work. Not only is reading a problem for them but also verbal expression. Certainly they 'do not listen', but very likely a verbal description is not really within their comprehension. Once it is accepted that a girl may honestly fail to comprehend a simple suggestion and may need explanations of simple things at her level of understanding, it is easier to tune in to her wavelength. The shy and the aggressive can be equally ashamed of their failure to distinguish teaspoons from tablespoons, and the sooner this shame can be broken down by the attitude that this is the sort of thing they have come to learn, the sooner they will relax and begin to make full use of their practical ability and the easier it will be to explain without 'talking down' to them.

A very few people have had training and experience in the teaching of both basic subjects and housecraft and are, of course, in a very strong position to help these children and understand their difficulties. It is very easy for others to feel helpless and discouraged when 2C examination papers come in for marking beside 2A's, but in many cases this is not a true picture of what 2C know or can do, but only of what they can express in words, an abstract exercise very difficult for them.

Doris's examination paper is a typical example. Aged 12 and in 2B (in a two-stream school), she was academically the most handicapped in her class. The single problem can sometimes prove even more difficult to help or handle than a whole class, similarly handicapped.

Mashed patts

you Bomhl the patts there you Mashed the putts Wome a fumre and Endy Sun bread Mashed it in two the patts and Emd meat to thery mashed the potts had.

(You boil the potatoes then you mash the potatoes with a fork and add some butter, mash it into the potatoes and add milk, too, then mash the potatoes hard.)

Throughout her paper she used 'bread' or 'butter', 'meat' or 'milk' indiscriminately. Abbreviations such as 'marg.' were normally permitted in notes, hence the use of 'patts', though the vowel has been elusive.

Now Doris was willing, capable and jolly. Perhaps her standard of finish would be rather more appreciated by her large and cheerful family than in a technical examination, but in the housecraft room she did not seem particularly hampered by her reading difficulties – because of Doris herself. She would watch and copy, experiment sensibly and ask if she did not know or understand. This practical 'attack' does occur, but not too frequently, and even Doris's practical ability can only be developed by verbal questions and answers or by seeing tasks prepared. She has comprehension and ability to use words verbally, but a particular weakness in reading and writing. Written messages and recipe books do not help her.

Yet Doris is not the problem that others are – her first few attempts at free written work disclose her difficulties, to see her at work is to recognize her strong points. Others may easily appear foolish, slack or lazy because of difficulties in comprehending and using what they can in fact read aloud. Unexpected gaps in simple basic knowledge can be at the root of much misunderstanding and aggressive, 'careless' or difficult behaviour.

There are several queries which arise from Doris's and similar examination papers, questions which must necessarily receive different answers or attempted solutions depending on people and circumstances.

(a) Could Doris go further if her reading improved?

(b) Are there difficult or slow children who are really just hampered by a problem of literacy?

(c) Should housecraft be entirely practical, providing a thorough course in which the girls can be successful and avoiding as far as possible all use of written or printed word?

(d) Might housecraft be one place where a reluctant reader can begin to realize the uses of reading and number, perhaps even to enjoy reading (even if only magazines)?

HOUSECRAFT

(e) Has the actual teaching of reading and number any place at all in the housecraft lesson?

(f) Can the housecraft teacher co-operate in any way with the teachers of English and mathematics?

The answer will be different in each case. Sometimes it is worth a great deal of trouble to teach number and reading to a girl or a class in housecraft, in other cases it is wiser to drop both, using display and discussions instead of note-taking. Sometimes carefully prepared books of recipes are valuable, giving practice in neat writing. These are even more valuable if girls can reach the stage of writing up in their own words and can use these books to cook from. Such a book is much more easily used if illustrated, but the one really backward girl in a more able class may not be able to use it, her difficulties in reading and poor writing may make it a waste of housecraft time. She can build up a useful scrapbook during this time but pictures do need to be purposeful and should be accompanied by written work (the child's or the teacher's). This may be just names or prices for identification, or the girl may write a passage 'freely' on paper, and stick it in beside the picture if satisfactory and useful. When abilities are very uneven in an older class, the one or two really backward girls can do quite constructive work while others are writing, if given a felt pen and labels to make for jars or notice-boards or for the display table.

Before deciding to drop reading and writing for one girl or a class it is worth considering whether this is fair to her, and how far she will need the skill as an adult. Magazines, newspapers, health forms, time-tables and grocers' lists may all confront her. It may well prove wise to drop reading and note-taking for Pamela in 2C or 3C, but in the fourth year she may be ready to look up bus times for a visit, make a grocer's list for the class party, even write an invitation or begin to enjoy 'looking at' magazines. With backward girls it is worth dropping even some work which seems fundamental and essential at times, but it is equally worth while to pick up the threads when opportunity occurs later.

Number is not so easily set aside even temporarily, but sometimes it is necessary to realize that our common terms mean little to a girl, our tools for measuring are foreign to her experience. 'Gill' may be a strange word; oz. and lb. may be confused; 'pint' means 'milk in a bottle' and may refer equally to a large quart or a ⅛-pint bottle for drinking – with disastrous results to the custard. Apart from the mechanics of using scales, there are not weights for 3 oz. or 5 oz. and if a recipe needs ½ lb. and the weight is labelled 8 oz. it may not be recognized. Homely measures may prove much more reliable – provided the dessertspoons are kept firmly in the dining-room. Doubling and halving recipes is very difficult for a slow learner, but the first stage is to weigh out twice or to share the ingredients between two and use one share.

Standards

Housecraft is very vulnerable, for every adult has favourite methods at home and is aware of standards of cleanliness and the value of methodical work in the kitchen, and the teacher of the C or D class often feels it is necessary to explain the position to a visitor either in self-defence or in defence of the children, even though they may be working hard and profitably. It is worth considering why this need is felt, and whether any difference is to be expected between the standards of the G.C.E. class and the C stream.

Methodical work and routine is more difficult to establish with a less able class. Some really do have poor memories, some have a habit of absenteeism, and in many cases critical faculties are less developed, things are genuinely 'not noticed', if seen they really do not register. There are two groups of children who will take quite a long time to become aware of what needs doing and it will be even longer before they will go one step further and take the initiative and put the offending saucepan on the rack without being asked – these are (1) the children who find the housecraft room standards unbelievably high and (2) the over-protected children who are shy of even opening cupboards and drawers for they are rarely allowed to do things at home and are always afraid of not achieving the standards set at home. Often a good deal of fear and diffidence must be overcome rather than the apparent laziness or listlessness, though these undesirable characteristics may easily develop if initiative is not encouraged.

As with any class, the younger they start and the longer they work together as a group the better. Routine such as preparation, keeping tables clear, clearing up, can be established by all the usual methods, but there will probably be a large number of girls in the class who have really got to learn how to work methodically, therefore the room may look less orderly during the morning. A slower child will take longer to remember which knife to use if the ones at home are different shapes and sizes, she will take longer to learn school methods which differ from those used at home, and it is often unnecessary to alter a perfectly good method, though the resulting variety may again give a less orderly appearance to the room.

There will be many who need training as well as good supervision in the many duties involved in 'clearing up'. Some of our children work like a much younger child and a tendency to drop the job when the interesting part is over, to do no more than thrust things out of the way if really pressed, even to claim fiercely 'I've done my share', can be due to this immaturity. Of course, they may just dislike clearing up, but often a little help and encouragement to finish off a job properly 'in a grown-up' or 'responsible' way does help to establish more thorough work and more stable attitudes.

In fact, there is no need to alter a good routine because this is a less able class but individual deviations from the usual methodical pattern are to be expected, some will need more help and encouragement than usual to grow methodical and thorough, and the growth will in some cases be slower than the average. More time must be allowed for preparation and clearing up for both are real learning situations.

While the lesson is in progress there may not appear to be the same orderliness and efficiency as in a G.C.E. class, but most certainly all food must be nicely served, the room and equipment really clean and tidy at the end of the lesson, laundrywork clean and looking fresh and ready for use.

Standard of craft does tend to be lower where high manipulative skills and accuracy of judgement are required. In some cases muscular co-ordination is below average. In some cases poor co-ordination of hand and eye mean that handling tools will be awkward even after watching a good demonstration and more individual help and teaching during the practice class will be necessary than with other classes. This lack of eye-hand co-ordination plus the tendency to use fist rather than fingers is at the root of much carelessness in washing up and laundrywork, and while not an excuse, is a point for supervision and training rather than punishment.

Speed (apart from the slapdash) is sometimes slower than usual either because manipulation is more awkward, or because hands have less strength (as for beating and cleaning really dirty things), or simply because Sheila is so enjoying mixing or making quite sure that each piece of dough is the same size that she continues with one stage much longer than is necessary, growing absorbed in it.

Where standards at school and home are different, slower children will have much more difficulty in bridging the gap. Sometimes the gap is very big indeed and simple fare, family-sized quantities and good but homely standards may be the best starting-point in these cases and requests from home can be a useful guide.

Most children produce better work if they can see the value of it and this applies even more to slower children. Simple work is not always the best choice for good results. At 11 or 12 Dorothy may have been promoted to cooking supper for her Father and brothers and may well make excellent fish cakes and meat patties at her first effort. Two or three years later a quickly-growing Dorothy may tire easily, or affect boredom because it is the fashion, and feel fish cakes are messy, but being more mature she may take a pride in making a simple rice pudding 'really nicely'. There are occasions when really good standards are finally achieved because a girl has been allowed to undertake quite a big piece of work at her own level, even if this is poor, and then has gradually improved her standard by practising the details – if she had worked on the more logical idea of acquiring skill in the details first she would have lost interest and felt a good deal was waste of time.

In worrying about maintaining our own standards of craft and of the housecraft room we are apt to forget that with these slow learners their standard of general practical ability is of the greatest importance. The girl who can size up a situation, tackle the job and see it through and can show in her way of working that she is able to consider other people, leaves school with a good foundation for adult life. In housecraft many need first to be encouraged and given confidence to do things themselves. Once this positive attitude is achieved much can be done to build up higher standards of cleanliness, of personal appearance, of manners, of working together as well as orderly work and good craft. Throughout the course there may well be a tug-of-war between building up a general competence and maintaining high standards. To concentrate only on the first may mean a great deal of slovenly work, to drive only for perfection is to reduce the value of this course to these children by half.

Many of the less academic children prove both useful and able in the school as hostesses, taking responsibility for floral decorations, cleaning of trophies, helping in the dining-room, and with staff teas. The housecraft teacher can help and encourage where the carrying out of these duties does help to build up a girl's confidence, or where she is helped by holding a responsible position in the school. It is also the housecraft department who will realize if any value to the girl has passed – for some duties become unconsciously a routine chore and just keep girls from their lessons.

PLANNING FOR THE SLOWER CLASSES

Lack of ability in one subject is rarely if ever compensated by brilliance in another, but many of these girls are less handicapped on the practical side than in the classroom. There are several possible reasons for this. It is necessary to keep this positive view of the children in mind as well as their limitations when planning their work.

Parallel Classes

If all streams follow exactly the same syllabus, how will the slower groups compare? Very unevenly. It is not really fair to the children to keep lessons exactly parallel. Occasionally, for reasons of organization or to give equal opportunity, a big department plans the same scheme for a whole year-group. The teacher can help herself and her children by suggesting not a week-by-week plan but a more general scheme with freedom for each class to cover the ground in the order most suitable. The occasion arises most with the younger classes but even here treatment of the subject will vary and one class of 1D suffered greatly from the scorn of 1A, for when each had prepared the same little meal one afternoon, the A form had discussed the nutritive value and the D form had discussed how to use knives and forks when eating the meal. A few weeks separating the two lessons would have led to little more than an assurance that friends had 'done the same cooking'.

Schemes of Work

A scheme built up for the particular class is usually more satisfactory than a simplified version of another scheme. The paritcular plan makes it possible to give girls the practice they need to progress a little each term and prevents forcing of work that is either too childish or requires a greater maturity than they show at present. It allows for liaison with the class teacher or specialists in English, geography and science as suggested, for instance, by Miss Cooper in Chapter XVI.

A general plan is the most useful, allowing freedom for one topic to be developed or another quickly dropped according to how valuable each proves in practice, a more fluid plan than for other classes.

Fundamentally the content of a good housecraft course has changed very little, however modern the presentation, and no course is complete without:

(a) good practice in cookery including choosing and cooking meals and entertaining.
(b) good experience in handling and laundering fabrics and awareness of modern trends.
(c) good standards of cleanliness and freshness in the home, including care of modern equipment and finishes.
(d) and particularly for the slow or backward children many opportunities for discussing, planning and managing time, money and stores.

During each term the girls should learn some new skills and practise those they have already learnt; they should add to their general knowledge relevant to home-making; they should have plenty of opportunity for exercising common sense and self-reliance in carrying out unaided work which requires initiative. Though theory (general knowledge, planning and managing) and practical work always overlap it is a great help to plan some lessons with a bias to one, some with a bias to the other, and so energies will be more firmly focused.

Much of this is the basis of sound planning for children of any ability. With slower children it is so easy to expect too much or too little that throughout every term it is wise to make close observation of the real value to the children of the work planned. Social maturity

HOUSECRAFT

is a better guide than chronological age in planning and on paper a well-adapted scheme for more backward classes is very likely to differ from others in two respects – the sequence may not appear to grow logically from well-laid foundations (as 'Dorothy' has already illustrated) and the quantity of work planned must be very much more fluid than usual.

To spend a whole morning doing one thing well is quite foreign to Irene. Every week she has to take the family wash to the Launderette and do all the ironing. The arrival of the bag-wash for ironing instead of 'one shirt of your father's' has been the nightmare of laundry lessons for generations. This is reality to Irene, however, and if these circumstances prevail in the group a great deal can be learnt if this forms part of the term's work. It seems more logical to learn first how to handle fabrics, gathers and collars, and increase quantity and speed of work, but in practice, provided the girls are taught and helped, and the work really well discussed, the big homely task that all understand can be a good beginning rather than end point. Such a beginning often resolves itself, girls begin to judge their own standards of work, then it no longer seems a waste of time spending an afternoon learning and practising to do a few things well. In the same way one group can cook and eat a dinner each week long before they can use a recipe book. It is possible to build up a number of good menus which do not even need a preliminary knowledge of foundation recipes. In the early stages of such a group of lessons general practical ability is considered, while the later lessons concentrate on good standards.

With the slower girls in the top classes it is often wise to give a very definite tone to the lessons. Some can include more advanced cookery, upholstery or other interesting things, just for the present enjoyment of creative work. Even if girls never make such things again these lessons can be justified in many ways. Other lessons should be definitely thinking towards the future. Obviously this will include the mothercraft course with the school nurse, and the planning and managing work in housecraft and all the work on modern equipment and fabrics. Other groups of lessons should consider the present and immediate future and include preparations for school journeys and for interviews and the first job, carefully prepared visits or films often by arrangement with the Youth Employment

Officer, and entertaining. Work planned round visits to local stores and markets including visits to canteens and cafeterias can provide observation and discussion material of even more practical use than some big outings.

In fact, during the whole course the ground covered may be very similar for all streams, but for the slower classes sequence may be different and the lack of examination syllabus permits experiments in making the work of more practical value. It also permits individual children to concentrate on cookery or needlework if they are contemplating such a post on leaving school, while others can be using housecraft as a basis for learning a good deal about modern trends or other 'general education'.

Planning Lessons
Routine is an excellent thing, particularly with an unstable class, but a rigid routine with slow children can become dull and lethargic and any emergency change in routine is apt to have lively repercussions. The familiar four sections are as useful with this class as with any other.

(1) Preparation.
(2) New work or practice.
(3) Clearing up.
(4) Discussion.

The preparation sets the tone for the rest of the lesson and some slow children do need plenty of time to prepare not only hands and aprons but thoughts. A rapid start to a lesson can leave the diffident and the dreamer far behind.

This class needs more time for clearing up and more help. So many can go through all the motions of drying a plate and still put away a damp smear.

Where memories are short the building up of good attitudes can in some measure compensate. The discussions of the morning's work are most valuable, though they may be difficult to establish at first. Whether the discussions are in small groups or the whole class, whether or not accompanied by note-taking, the value depends on skilful directing so that the girls contribute with genuine interest.

Within this regular framework of preparation, clearing up and display with discussion, slower children benefit from variety of presentation of lessons. Each term can usefully include some demonstration lessons, some assignment or group-work and two or three lessons for a 'centre of interest'. Slow and backward girls are capable of tackling all these types of lessons profitably.

New skills are best taught by demonstration and practice. In these lessons good standards of working are set by example and followed up by supervision.

Assignments and group work give opportunities for initiative and self-reliance. Even the most backward 11 year-olds can become accustomed to lighting and managing their own ovens and trying to solve their own problems on the days they 'pretend they are alone in the house' – provided help is available if really necessary. It would be cruelty not to be near Christine when she lights her oven for at first there is a very narrow margin between gaining confidence by doing the task unaided and growing more afraid of it. A blind eye is a help to the conscientious supervisor of such lessons, for the essential point is to give children an opportunity for achieving something 'on their own' and even the slowest members *will* achieve the result they want if left to their own devices, but some of their methods may be surprising.

Centres of interest usually take two or three lessons if girls are to collect their information and be given opportunities alone or in groups to explain it to the rest of the class and practical work will usually be revision but some may want to try out something new to support their information. The work is valuable if it increases understanding and encourages outward thinking. Ideally such a group of lessons should be centred round a single visit, e.g. to the local food market or the fabric hall of a big store or to a day nursery, but this may not be possible and it may be necessary to plan a block of work on modern equipment in the housecraft room or modern fabrics in the needlework store.

Such topics may sound dull for a teenager, nevertheless a short period of two or three lessons can make her more aware of a good deal that she should know of care, use and selection of things and the class can be justifiably proud of the information collected. Christmas term entertaining and summer term topics on use of freedom or leaving school will satisfy the present interests of the girls and balance those in which the real usefulness is less immediate and more adult.

The Children's own Planning

As adults many of these slower girls will find difficulty in managing – time, money, food. They are very young to appreciate this in school, but a few lessons concentrating on marketing or one-pot cookery can give another angle to their discussions, while in many cases opportunity to use real money for shopping or costing is often worth more than a good deal of pencil and paper costing.

Some of the class will find it very difficult to make a time-plan with pencil and paper in the orthodox way, or they may do a beautiful time-plan which is just a piece of carefully written work and in the child's own mind is set aside as soon as she starts the real work of cooking. For practical purposes (with the future housewife in mind) it may be more useful to discuss with individuals or let groups discuss what they will do next week, what they will need and to help them plan their morning in sections – what they can do before play, before the second bell – and note just a few landmarks such as when to start dishing up, when to start cooking a new dish or one not recently practised.

One Outstanding Child

Sometimes the whole class is fairly slow to learn and work can be planned accordingly. If others are average and only one girl is particularly slow it is necessary to give her a fair balance of private work suited to her ability but also to her age, and also a fair share of work with the class with unobtrusive help so that she is not unsuccessful and "stands apart" as little as possible. How far she is accepted as a person by the class depends to some extent on temperament and age, of course, but careful selection of work does help. The younger girl may happily work with a scrapbook or build up a pictorial dictionary or recipe book while others make notes, or she may work hard matching words and learning spellings. As the time for note-taking draws near, each lesson, the older girl can show signs of being awkward, and would be better employed setting out the display, writing price tickets or making posters. It is in this side of the work that a girl will be conscious of her limitations and will need help in overcoming or facing the deficiences. In practical work suitable selection is easier, for the observers (the other children) are less aware that Pauline has had a much simpler task if it is presented as nicely as the rest.

Behaviour

The really tough class found in some areas, where teachers are asked to work 'with a missionary spirit', is largely a social problem and much of the behaviour more suited to a book on maladjustment. School attainments are rarely up to average standards in this class even when potential abilities are really quite high and some of the behaviour patterns are directly due to low ability or unnecessary failure in school work. Standards are often very low, aggressiveness very high and language and behaviour calculated to shock. Underneath this façade much of this chapter does apply even to this class though presentation of really suitable work will have added difficulties and at first it may be necessary to select what girls *will* do rather than what they *should* be doing. In these classes such things as self-control and ability to work with others are of the first importance, housecraft being the vehicle only in the early stages. To know that the teacher sets certain standards and firmly maintains these gives the girls a sense of security, even though they test her strength at times. This firmness needs to be tempered with understanding. Much more is achieved in the long run by an acceptance of things as they are at first. The girls often respond well to a quiet voice and manner and respect, in their own way, a certain amount of dignity, but they also appreciate and respond to real enjoyment and enthusiasm, a sense of humour and evidence of a wide general knowledge.

Discipline can be a constant source of worry in these classes if there is a drive for a preconceived too formal standard. Once it becomes possible to accept – and like – the children as they are and to build from there, the fear of losing control of the class, or of 'being cheeked' diminishes, and if the class is a little noisier at times, looks a little less organized and needs three minutes instead of one to stop work and listen, the response is there and loyalty can be very firm even if sometimes rather strangely demonstrated.

The one 'dreadful child' in a class is fairly common in C and D classes. She has acquired a bad reputation and lives up to it. Her classwork is well below average. Her ability may or may not be truthfully revealed by the work she produces, her behaviour is more suited to the class just discussed. At first she may prove just as awkward in housecraft but, sooner or later, and often by chance, Annie will reveal a different side of her nature and quite often the classroom menace can be quite a different child in housecraft. Again the possible reasons are many, but having 'got through' to Annie the next thing is to help her build up a better reputation for herself in the school. This must be demonstrated and proved and have sure foundations or she may retain her bad name in the school though be recognized in the staff room as protected by the housecraft department, perhaps with the suggestion that she 'gets away with it' there.

Usual Behaviour Patterns among Slower Girls
The whole question of behaviour problems covers a wide field and is often relative to the general tone or attitude of the school – if bad behaviour is a *chronic* problem among the D children it is often a sign that the work they are expected to do is unsuitable. Apart from the extremely difficult and omnipresent children just mentioned, the backward children are often revealed by or hampered by one of two characteristic behaviour patterns in the housecraft room:

(*a*) The lively excitable children whose behaviour follows the pattern of a younger age group (noisy and uncontrolled).
(*b*) The withdrawn child whose lack of ability to smile, respond or enjoy can be distressing to watch or who can be a very real drag in a practical class (never *do* anything).

'They are so slow – and never listen.' Betty, with tousled curly hair and apron strings round her elbows, clattered happily through the afternoon, always one beat behind the others, confusing the advice they all gave her so readily and quite unaware of the mounting exasperation of the teacher, who knew that lessons were governed by bells. Betty, of course, was ready to put down her tools and talk to the visitor from a Special School, saying, 'I'm a little bit backward, too, but not here, not in this room, only in lessons, things like arithmetic and reading'. Not all can express so clearly what they feel, but there are so many Bettys in our classes who feel the same. Red crosses on a page of arithmetic so clearly show their limitations but they feel proud of their achievements in housecraft without realizing their shortcomings. When others in the class are more able, Betty, however nice a child, can be a constant worry because she does not keep up. If the whole class is slow, obviously less work can be planned, but if just a few are slower the others must not be kept back to their pace. Betty may actually be slightly deaf, in which case she probably never 'tunes in' at once to the words of advice given to the group, thus missing the first points and never quite grasping the rest. She may hear perfectly well but her rate of comprehension may be slower than the others, even with her full attention. Betty takes longer to switch her concentration from what she is doing to listening to instructions and her slowness to respond is less worrying if it can be accepted. She and others like her do need longer to 'stop work and listen'. It is not spoonfeeding to realize that she cannot take in several instructions at once and to remind her of the next stage in good time. It is often a help to stand near Betty when giving class instructions and sometimes it is possible to enlist the help of her neighbour if she is lagging behind, but Betty is capable of quite good practical work and will be quicker if she knows what to do.

Betty, of course, is typical of the first group. Slow to hear and comprehend, she enjoys cookery – and cleaning – as a primary school child would, playing with mixtures and arranging ornaments without thought for time. To watch Betty with this in mind is to understand her behaviour. To understand is the first stage towards helping her to grow up. It is unfair and unwise to expect a much more mature attitude from her just because she is twelve or thirteen and to force such behaviour will be unsuccessful, leading to childish fits of temper now and a sulky attitude when she is a little older. While Betty does need firm handling, there must be some acceptance of childish behaviour and remarks and a gradual building up of a more mature attitude and a sense of responsibility. Betty becomes a problem when childishness is regarded as naughtiness and rejected or punished. Talking quietly to Betty, about the way she is using her hands while she scrapes, about grown-up topics when she serves a coffee tray or while eating the dinner she has cooked, will make her feel more grown up and behave with more thought and stability. Betty is only one of a class, of course, and should not obviously receive more attention – or licence – than others.

The noisy, lively or aggressive children can upset the whole lesson and keep all attention away from the diffident and withdrawn – who deserve and need as much help. Both are commonly found in the C and D classes and some find the quiet ones more worrying than the wilder spirits. The little shadows who creep round the room and 'never do anything' can go unnoticed for some time. Pauline is a nice little girl in the classroom where she gives no trouble and no one has thought seriously of suggesting her for a Special School, but her ability is very borderline. The noise, bustle and clock watching in the housecraft room paralyse her, her too wet mixture is the last to reach the oven, and the shame and bewilderment of discovering that there seems to be something wrong and unsuccessful about using the floor of the oven for baking slows down still further a vague routine of clearing up. For people trained to appreciate and develop efficiency, organization and good timing, Pauline and her like can be a real worry and exasperation. However responsible the children may be, good organization is needed where ovens must be shared if twenty children are to be well occupied and produce good results within the lesson period and leave the room clean and tidy for the next class. Pauline is slow, she appears to dream until long after others have started, appears to wander vaguely even when standing still – in fact, she just never does anything. Her quality of good behaviour, which has kept her in the form room and the school, is not enough for her to be able to conform in housecraft. It is possible that she finds this colourless cloak useful in the classroom. It will take a long time and much patience and sympathy to gain Pauline's confidence and help her to come out of her shell a little. She must not be forgotten in the general activity and is better working among the quieter girls of the class. Pauline is so often overlooked and was pink with pleasure after a visitor to the class spoke to her, for, said Pauline, 'that lady talked *to me!*'

The withdrawn child often has very little real contact with the other children and at first is more likely to be drawn out of her shell by the help of an adult. It is important to talk to her, quietly, during supervision of practical work. It is necessary to stand by her to make sure she does not dodge such frightening things as picking up kettles of boiling water. At first a little judicious help such as guiding her hand, giving an extra long taper or turning on the tap for her helps to overcome fear when lighting gases. She must realize quite clearly that she is to do the job herself, but will appreciate such help in the early stages and must not feel she is being forced. For some time it will be necessary to be unobtrusively near her when she is about to do something new or frightening, to make sure she does not dawdle or dodge the task and to give a little, almost casual advice or help – or prodding – if necessary. Often her lack of contact with others means she cannot gain confidence by teaching another girl the difficult task she has learnt and so forget herself. It is not desirable that dependence on adults should last, of course, and the next stage can usually be either to choose carefully a more able girl who can help her or to make her one of a group whose practical results are of similar standards.

NEEDLEWORK

The slow learner is less shamefully outstanding in needlework classes now than she was in the days when every girl made the same garment. By June, Pauline would be pushing the reluctant elastic though the legs of the limp, bedraggled knickers she had started in September, while most of the class were turning up hems of the summer dress they had made to match. Now it is much more common to find the girls in any one class making a variety of things and there are so many 'teaching aids' to stimulate the girls' interests in all sorts of interesting things demanding a wide range of talent and imagination that Pauline's self-respect need not suffer so heavily.

It is not always easy to select just the right work for these slower learners, particularly in the early stages, and it may be necessary to take into consideration some of the following point.

Most of these girls work slowly yet benefit enormously from the achievement of finishing something. Some will select and finish quite quickly the small things that they see in an exhibition of finished work. For others it will be wiser to by-pass hand sewing, even embroidery, for a while and to concentrate on machining – first patterns, then skirts, aprons, cushions, repairs. This does mean that more material is used for those making fairly large things quite quickly on a machine, but it is worth it if Pauline begins to realize that she can make things (even though she may still say that she 'cannot do needlework'.)

Colour sense and imagination may be very limited but there is always the possibility that the slower child has realized that her ideas (often more childish) are not as acceptable as those of others in the class and has stopped trying. Opportunity to combine colours and texture in the making of pictures and patterns often helps the younger girls while full use of their interest in dress can encourage more confidence in their own judgement of colour and style among the older girls. Where taste and colour are concerned it is often necessary to balance very carefully the value to the child of (*a*) letting her carry on with her own immature or unconventional choice or (*b*) persuading her to adapt this to something which is 'good taste'.

Slowness and poor craft work (uneven, clumsy stitching, clumsy manipulation of material and of scissors) can be directly due to poor manipulative ability, and girls may need particular help in using their fingers, tools and eyes. Work may be poorly 'finished' and though this may be laziness or habit among those who have little pride in their work it sometimes happens because critical faculties need to be encouraged and because small points in even some quite simple process may not have been understood.

Pattern work will be harder if arithmetic is difficult and trade patterns of simple straightforward style may be best from the beginning in some cases.

Embroidery and decorative work may overlap with the art course, soft furnishings and mending quite often overlap with housecraft. The really slow girls who will not be capable of much dressmaking after leaving school, who may always need much help with setting sleeves, will need, as adults, to be able to shorten and lengthen hems and make other alterations. Real repairs, actual and necessary alterations of dresses they have been given or of a dress being passed on to a younger sister, are necessary to bring reality to work or mending.

It would seem to be important first that the child should have pleasure in making something herself (finishing it quite quickly) and that this soon develops into pride in making it well. Machine work and hand sewing are both important but in the secondary school there

HOUSECRAFT

may be some stages where there is very little hand work. The backward girl who leaves school feeling confident to make her own clothes also needs to be able to select patterns that she is capable of using and materials that she can handle. She deserves a wide course that will give her at least an introduction to colour, fabric, trends, equipment, as well as giving her an opportunity to learn how to make, care for, mend and decorate, but confidence to start must be balanced by awareness of her own limitations.

Reading References

Recent changes in the traditional approach to housecraft have taken place because of social changes. The present emphasis on home making and managing is well suited to the less able girls since this is the aspect of the work which they find so difficult.

The most helpful reading matter is that which reminds us (*a*) of the homes from which our girls come and which they in turn will build up and (*b*) how present trends affect home making. The following list indicates a variety of reading with the emphasis on the social side.

The books of Sir Cyril Burt.
    ,, ,, ,, Sir Basil Henriques.
COLLIS and POOLE, *These our Children.*
PACKARD, VANCE, *The Hidden Persuaders.*
Which and *Shoppers Guide.*

Good Housekeeping booklets and advertiser's pamphlets on packaged foods, frozen foods, etc.

Articles dealing with modern trends in equipment, commodities, fabrics and surfaces in magazines such as: *Home Economics, Housecraft, Good Housekeeping.*

HILARY DEVEREUX

Chapter XI

ENVIRONMENTAL STUDIES

> *The natural environment of the child, in his early years especially, is his home. But from the age of five upwards almost every child becomes aware of school as part of his surroundings, and at a later stage, of that wider environment of the community in which he lives. One of the chief aims of education is to make him, by the time he leaves school, ready to play an eager part in that community, and to lead a useful and satisfying life.*
> 'School and Life' (Ministry of Education, 1947), H.M.S.O.

The three factors bringing about our most effective learning are our interests, our experiences and our abilities. If we consider the duller children in our secondary modern schools it will be clear that they are unlikely to learn effectively from a curriculum that is but a slower, simpler version of a grammar school course, and to meet their needs we have to get away from the tradition of specialization and subject-teaching.

Paramount in our learning are our abilities and, in considering the education of dull children, we need to keep their limitations in mind constantly.

With careful guidance, however, these children can learn a great deal from experience, and it is our task to provide them with suitable experiences. I suggest this can most effectively be done through environmental studies in which the children are called upon to take an active part in observation, recording of first-hand experiences, and the performance of tasks entailed.

If children are to have experiences that will help them to 'lead a useful and satisfying life', the topics we choose to study must be carefully chosen to give first-hand knowledge. Topics that look impressive on paper will prove useless if they seek to give knowledge far divorced from the lives of our pupils, and at second-hand through the exclusive use of books.

ENVIRONMENTAL STUDIES

Within our environment we have to find topics to arouse the interests of our children, as well as being satisfying mentally and physically to them.

Properly organized, the study of environment involves all the usual subjects of the curriculum, but gives to each a place in the practical life of everyday affairs. If I make but little mention of subjects, such as history or geography, dear to the heart of specialist teachers, it is not because I wish to detract from the value of such subjects, but because I believe they are made more real by the personal study necessary to complete work on a topic.

Clearly, the suggestions I make here will have to be freely adapted to meet the needs of vastly differing organizational forms found in secondary modern schools. On one point, however, I must be dogmatic. In schools where there is complete specialization throughout all streams, environmental studies, as I see them, impose a degree of collaboration between members of staff that will be rare indeed! From every point of view such studies should be taken with one teacher who has wide interests and sympathy with slow learners. The paragon required has been fully described by Sir Cyril Burt.[1]

There can be no sharp division between subjects and we must be prepared to switch from topic to topic to meet the interests of individual children in the class.

It may justly be objected that since the children are in normal schools, they should be made part of those schools, and, less justly, be treated exactly the same as all other children within the school. A compromise that works reasonably well and which is worked out in detail later by Miss Cooper is for the children to take the obvious specialist subjects like woodwork, metal-work, domestic science, etc., but to spend about half their time with one teacher taking general subjects. The periods given to general subjects should be in blocks of two, three or four periods on the time-table so that children are not interrupted by a bell signalling changes of room, lesson and teacher when they are in the middle of an interest. This suggested blocking of periods is given additional weight by the fact that much of the work involved in environmental studies should be undertaken outside school on visits necessary to the study.

At the same time, we must also enlist the aids that are at our

[1] *Causes and Treatment of Backwardness*, p. 110-11.

disposal within the school and keep careful watch for suitable radio programmes, films, film-strips, books, wall-charts, visiting speakers, music, plays, etc. In short, we should make full use of all visual and aural aids we are fortunate enough to have.

The length of time spent on any particular topic and the detail in which it is studied will depend largely upon the ages and abilities of the children concerned, and, with some co-operation within the staff of a school, a topic studied soon after entry to the school might well be taken up in greater detail later in the school life of the children. Later and more detailed studies of the same topic could indeed be said to be essential consolidation of earlier teaching. Obvious examples of such consolidation would arise in studies of 'Homes and Home-making' and 'Our Town'. At an early age the studies of 'Homes' may be quite satisfactorily confined to children's exploration of their own homes, whereas they will show a later interest in 'Homes of the Past', 'Homes in Other Lands', 'How it is Made', 'Hygiene in the Home', and so on.

In a study of 'Our Town', children in their first year in a secondary modern school might need to become familiar with the main physical features of their town and would gain little from attendance at Council meetings which would benefit older children.

We must take care that the topics we choose are able to sustain interest, but I would emphasize the danger of following every aspect of every study before leaving it. The class must not become bored by our insistence on inquiry into all the minute details we feel they should know.

It is often a good idea to choose a theme and then subdivide the work into studies of about a week's duration. To illustrate this point I have appended an outline plan for the topic 'The World of Work'. The time spent on each 'chapter heading' should be adapted to the needs of the children. Doubtless, other aspects of this topic will suggest themselves to you, and the programme I suggest should not on any account be followed slavishly.

On all possible occasions children should be given opportunities for carrying out the processes described, and an expedition undertaken by the children will inspire more lively English and arithmetic than any textbook.

The teacher of a class working on the lines suggested will need to be on the best of terms with colleagues responsible for domestic science, gardening, woodwork, etc. Quite apart from the overlapping present in all studies, there will be value in practical work involved in such topics as 'Every Man a Gardener' or 'Woodwork in the Home'.

Depending upon the teacher's experience and skill, as well as the size and age-range of the class, there will be times when it will be possible to split the class into small groups and have each group working on a different aspect of the same study. This form of organization makes it possible to match the scope of the work with the ability of each child within the group, and it is clearly a valuable exercise in co-operative effort. As each group completes its section of the study the results can be pooled and information gained by one group becomes available to all. The major drawback of this form of organization is that much of the knowledge is gained at second-hand, but there are, nevertheless, topics that are best treated in this way. Certainly it avoids criticism that studies along one theme tend to stretch out and become boring; it also means that each individual child is likely to have a different task suited to his abilities. It will help if you examine the outline plan on the study 'World of Work', with your class in mind. Split your class into small groups to cover the chapter headings suggested and this will give you a practical exercise in organization that might help you to decide whether you are yet ready to tackle work in this way.

Whatever the form your study takes the least able children must be given responsible tasks that are within their ability to perform.

The study of environment should begin with topics with which the children are most familiar, about which they already know something, and can most readily gain first-hand experience and information. By choosing such a topic we can give children immediate confidence that here are tasks with which they are able to cope. Then it is the task of the teacher to widen the experience and knowledge of the children.

Clearly, any study based on 'Homes and Home-making' could be developed to any suitable degree according to the ages and abilities of individual children. Within their homes can be found an almost inexhaustible source of material suitable for investigation. The construction of the house, sources of raw materials and the manufacture of household goods present opportunities for worthwhile work to cover every subject of the formal curriculum.

English is very adequately covered by the reading and writing entailed in finding and presenting facts, writing letters for information and descriptions of household articles and manufacturing processes.

A great wealth of practical measurement and calculation is provided in a study of homes and, at the same time, we can impart important social training in the matter of domestic economy and budgeting. Domestic science, hygiene and mothercraft could clearly be introduced in such a study (detailed suggestions on these lines have been given by Miss Cooper, and her chapter should be read in close conjunction with this).

Illustrations and models may be used to develop artistic sense and there is clearly room for guidance in good taste in the discussion and choosing of furnishing materials, designs, colours, etc. The establishment of a school flat furnished and run by the children of the school is an obvious asset in this direction.

What estate agents call 'all main services' give plenty of scope for everyday science. In this field, too, there is opportunity for discussion and investigation of the qualities of materials purchased for our homes, particularly with the increasing use of man-made fibres.

The development of homes in this country could be valuable social history. Geography could be covered by our investigation into homes of other nations, as well as discovering the sources of raw materials used in the building of houses and the manufacture of household goods.

Although environmental studies will cover all subjects in the normal curriculum I can never see them as separate subjects. In studies such as I suggest a widespread educative method is used and there are no clear barriers between subjects. For example, a discussion of raw materials involves:

(a) History—development of the use of the materials.
(b) Geography—source of the materials.
(c) Science—its qualities and manufacturing processes.
(d) Arithmetic—costs and comparisons with similar and earlier materials.

(e) English—writing up information gained from reading, visits and letters.

All these subjects and others overlap at all stages of the study.

A study of 'Homes and Home-making' could well be started from a survey of the homes in which the children live now. The children's powers of observation could be helped by setting them tasks on the lines suggested in the task sheets appended.

Any course of environmental studies should involve knowledge of the work carried on within the community we share. The everyday work of local industries and trades should be part of the children's experience and this should mean visits to local factories, farms, shops and workshops, etc., as well as visits to school from people who earn their livings in a variety of jobs. Into such studies we have opportunities for introducing a great many social considerations.

When I carried out such a study with a fourth-year mixed class the B.B.C. was running a series entitled 'The World of Work', and this met some of my requirements extremely well.

On the question 'What is a good job?' we arrived, by heated discussions, at the stage where we could vote on the relative importance of these factors in considering employment:

THINGS TO THINK ABOUT

Security: Is there a job for life if I want to stay?
Prospects: Can I improve my position in this firm?
Holidays: How long? When? Convenient for family holidays?
Pay: Enough to live on? Fair for the work entailed?
Hours: Are they reasonable? Are they convenient? Any split duties? (e.g. 5 a.m. to 9 a.m. and then 6 p.m. to 10 p.m.)
Workmates: Are they a happy, helpful crowd?
Variety: Do I want a job where I keep doing work I know, so becoming quick at it? Or would I be happier to have a frequent change of task?

Our discussions revealed the ability of these children to think objectively, and their fairness in considering these points would have astonished those who hold the younger generation in poor esteem.

We did a great deal of arithmetic in working out weekly wages from various real-life hourly rates which the children provided from talks with their relatives and friends.

When we worked out the hours likely to be worked in various trades and professions we compiled exercises involving a good deal more learning than just arithmetic!

By the use of books, radio, films, visits, etc., the children gained knowledge of the main jobs of work being done in the community in which they live. Besides the more obvious jobs concerned with manufacture and distribution I included doctors, teachers, ministers of religion, probation officers, nurses, welfare workers, firemen, policemen, postmen, and so on. Too often the social agencies provided in our complex society are not fully used because people in need lack the knowledge of the existence and availability of such facilities.

Knowledge of their environment should also include the location of public buildings such as offices dealing with supplies of electricity, gas and water, the local government departments dealing with such matters as health, education, housing, welfare, refuse collection, rating, licensing, etc. In addition, a child should know the churches, museums, playgrounds, theatres, cinemas, libraries, fire stations, police stations, railway stations, bus stops and services, hospitals and like places in his area. Situations in which people are likely to need these services should be used as the basis for written, oral and dramatic work in the classroom.

Task sheets similar to those provided in the appendix can be set to encourage children to find out information for themselves.

Often these tasks will mean a great deal of work for the children, but the type of sheet that leaves blank spaces for the children to fill in an odd word or phrase is often subjected to criticism on the grounds that the children are given too little to do. Of course, the form of the task sheet depends upon the abilities of the children, but there are surely few secondary modern schools where the children in the lower streams would find it easy to:

(*a*) read the requirements,
(*b*) understand them,
(*c*) collect the information needed,
(*d*) complete the sentences by correctly filling the blank spaces.

ENVIRONMENTAL STUDIES

Anyway, the ability to complete a form correctly is clearly an asset nowadays.

All services in our community will provide opportunities, the degree of investigation varying according to the children carrying out the tasks.

We should try to give children some idea of the evolutionary pattern of our society. This necessitates a knowledge of our times, and of people who have helped to change society. Children are always keen to learn about colourful personalities and our history abounds in men and women whose lives are examples of courage and selflessness.

Wherever possible, children should be given experience in environments differing from their own, and this means that town children should be given chances to know the problems and opportunities of life in the country and vice versa. School visits and exchanges could be used to give this experience, as Mrs Sterry describes in detail in the next chapter, and so I will say nothing further on this.

The minimum requirements for a course of environmental studies should include for all children, irrespective of their immediate environment, opportunities to learn about life in towns, cities, centres of industry, villages, seaside resorts, ports and, eventually, this should include knowledge of life in countries other than their own.

A great deal of all that is natural must be included in any study, and there is ample scope for such study, whatever the immediate environment. Outings to the seaside and country are not the only ways to study nature and in the heart of any city we can learn plenty from the study of habits of plant and animal life. Nevertheless, an exploration of the seashore during a school camp can arouse a genuine sense of wonder in city-bred children. Observing and recording the growth and habits of life around them should be an essential part of any child's education. We should try to cover at least the following aspects of living things around us:

(1) *Care and Behaviour of Living Things*
   (a) Life cycles of animals and plants.
   (b) Physical needs of pets and farm animals, considering food and suitable shelter.
   (c) Wild animals; their behaviour, diet and shelters.

(2) *Plant Life*
Habitats; needs for growth; uses to man.
Seed dispersal and subsequent germination.
Plants used for medicines, dyes, clothing, food, building, furniture.

(3) *Local Surveys*
Plant and animal life in local gardens, fields, streams, rivers and streets.

(4) *Grasses*
Types; development of uses by man for food, clothing and shelter.

(5) *Birds*
Habitats; breedings; preservation; migration; uses to man and to nature.

(6) *Fishes* in local streams and rivers; the seas of Britain; tropical fish and their care.

(7) *Natural Phenomena*
   (a) Observation and recording of rain and rainfall; snow, fog, hail, sunshine, cloud, wind.
   (b) Seasons; day and night.
   (c) Heat, light, water, fire.

(8) *Trees*
Names, types, timber, leaves, fruits, uses.

(9) *Training for Leisure*
   (a) Stock-keeping.
   (b) Gardens and allotments.

(10) *Collections*
Identifying plants, trees, grasses, birds, fishes, animals, shells, stones, etc.

(11) *Clubs* for:
Observers, Animal Protectors, Wild-Life Preservation, Preservation of the Countryside, Rambling, Young Farmers, etc.

In interpreting the world around them to handicapped children we will realize their lesser ability to pick up knowledge of the things they see and we need to guide their interests. Our methods must be based on the low level of the children's ability to learn and we must aim at increasing their all-round interest in life.

Explanations must be in simple language if slow learners are to have understanding. Abstractions should be avoided and children should, with that essential guidance from teachers, experience and observe things for themselves, making full use of the concrete materials available in their immediate environment.

Much of the work I suggest here will have to be carried out in evenings and at weekends, and parents and friends will be involved. Where teachers take steps to establish a happy relationship with parents a great deal of interest and help is forthcoming.

Time will be spent in school writing up information gained largely out of school and in arranging this into book form with suitable illustrations. Personally, I provide quarto loose-leaf paper; ruled for written work and plain for illustrations. This paper lends itself well to the making of 'concertinas' for large diagrams and pictures, and if illustrations or charts spread over several sheets of paper they are easily joined by strips of adhesive tape on the back of the sheets.

I provide the basic plan for any study and aim at this as a minimum, but at the same time everything possible must be done to encourage extra individual effort by way of illustrations, models, exercises, and information. We must be prepared to allow individual children to follow their own lines as much as possible. On no account can we expect a uniform standard of work throughout a class. Unless you are uniquely fortunate you will find that your lower stream class has within it a range of intelligence and attainment far wider than in any other class in the school; your records should prove this to doubters!

Arrange your task sheets so that children gradually build up the knowledge they have into a logical sequence; let them see their 'book' growing.

My insistence on the necessity for first-hand experiences should not be taken to mean that I do not attach great importance to books in pursuing a study. It is essential that your class has a reasonable library to use and the list of books I have given for class use might be considered as a nucleus, remembering that a great many very useful publications cannot be included. Never fail to store illustrated magazines, pamphlets and catalogues that are likely to provide information and illustrations.

Above all, in studies of environment never forget the simplest of all methods of learning – one that frequently has more effect than elaborate recorders and projectors! I refer to knowledge passed by word of mouth and, at all levels, children must be allowed to discuss their studies with each other and with their teachers. Here is one teaching aid that is seldom in short supply, and from each other, and from our informal chats with them, children acquire a great deal of true education.

Effective and inexpensive, too, is spontaneous dramatization. To live the part of historical characters, or to be a modern workman building a house, might give considerable insight into the character or actions involved.

Speech and drama help us to sort out ideas and form a vital part of preparation for written work.

Frequently, teachers become convinced of the value of environmental studies, but hesitate to take the plunge because they are beset by fears that spelling, or arithmetic, or writing will suffer. Children must, of course, be taught the mechanics of the Three R's, and class lessons must sometimes be given. Consider frankly, however, the progress made by your class if you have stuck to formal class teaching of your slow learners. Has the improvement over a four-year course really been great? Are the children really competent in reading, writing and reckoning? Are they balanced boys and girls still deriving pleasure and satisfaction from school life?

Children are surely more likely to see the point of learning a rule or process if it is obviously helping them to write up a topic that really grips them. In practice, children will be found taking much greater care in the work for 'My Book of ——' than in a series of unrelated exercises on punctuation, capital letters, etc. Indeed, it is my experience that slow learners too often set themselves standards that are too high and care has to be taken by the teacher lest these children become discouraged by work that does not match up to the standards they set for themselves.

It is true, too, that some teachers feel the need of support from a carefully designed syllabus that tells them what to teach, when to teach it, and the books to use in the teaching of their subject. No such syllabus can match exactly the needs of *your* class, and it will be better to work out your own schemes rather than accept without question those provided by other people.

It is, therefore, with considerable misgivings that I have appended extracts from some of the task sheets I have set for children. These examples will certainly not provide you with a crib which you can use with assured success! They are meant rather to provoke you into original thought that will enable you to devise work suited to the needs of each child in your class. Always, you are the vital link and all the suggestions I have made are with the knowledge that you are constantly ready to help, advise and encourage. Only you know the children in your class sufficiently well to understand their limitations and needs, yet I hope that what I have written here will help you towards meeting those needs the better.

Appendix
'THE WORLD OF WORK' – *Some topics for discussion and investigation*

(1) *What is a Good Job?'*
Security – Prospects – Holidays – Pay – Hours – Companionship – Recreational Facilities – Variety of Tasks – Pensions – Training – Physical Conditions.

(2) *'How Many Hours do they Work?'*
Take typical examples of the hours worked by parents of the children and compare the weekly hours worked by such people as:

> Shop assistant – bus conductor – teacher – factory worker – farmhand – newsagent – greengrocer – butcher – policeman – postman – clerk – housewife – train driver – lorry driver – building workers, etc.

(3) *'How Much do they Earn?'*
From newspapers, Trade Union literature, etc., find the rates for a variety of jobs. Make simple calculations of weekly wages from hourly rates and vice versa.

(4) *'Learning the Job'*
Conditions for trainees in jobs investigated:

> Initial qualification requirements – length of training period – pay during training – processes to learn – knowledge to gain – apprenticeship schemes – H.M. Services – local schemes, etc.

(5) *'People Who Help Us'*
Which people help us to live happy lives? – To whom can we turn in times when we need help? – Who looks after our health? – Who makes our laws? – Which people help us to keep law and order? – Who cares specially for children? – Who is particularly interested in old people? – and so on.

(6) *'Building Homes'*
Trades used in house-building – training of tradesmen – part played by each tradesman – materials they use – costs of building (hours of work, materials, etc.).

(7) *'Workers for Education'*
Include the less obvious people such as caretakers, cleaning staff, school meals helpers, county supply department, education committee, education office staff, gardeners, groundsmen, builders who maintain building and decorations, etc.

(8) *'Transport Workers'*
Training of workers according to transportation methods – conditions of work, etc.

(9) *'Yes, Madam!'*
Qualities required for work in shops – differences in requirements according to goods sold – conditions of work, etc.

(10) *'The Nation's Health'*
People who work in hospitals, clinics, schools, etc. – Local government employees in refuse collection, water supply, drainage, etc. – Specialized services such as home-helps, midwifery, sanatoria, etc.

(11) *'National Insurance'*
  Prepare tables showing:
  (a) amounts paid by workers at various ages
  (b) amounts paid by employers
  Devise exercises based on the use of these tables.

Examples

A boy aged 16 years pays   s.   d. weekly if he works. When I leave school I shall have to pay   s.   d. weekly.

A factory owner employing twenty men all over 18 years old will have to pay £   s.   d. altogether for these men every week.

What do we get for this money? Family doctors – hospitals – dental treatment – pensions – sickness benefits, etc.

(12) *'Income Tax'*
Comparative amounts paid (concrete anonymous examples from a local firm?) – Who takes it? – How is it spent? – Is it worth it? – What do *I*

get out of it? – Effect on overtime pay ('If I earn an extra pound, *they* take two pounds from me!')

(13) *'Changing Jobs'*
Is it wise to change jobs? – Who will help me to find a new job? – How do I give notice to my present employer? – Why do I want to change?

(14) *'A Job for Me?'*
Which jobs in the local and national newspapers would suit me? – What do I want? – Can I do these jobs? – Would I like them?
    Encourage realistic assessment of abilities and limitations.

(15) *'Danger Ahead!'*
Jobs that involve personal risks:
    Fireman, steeplejack, racing driver, film stunt man, trapeze artist, lion tamer, bomb disposal, test pilot, leper doctor, etc.

(16) *'Enjoy Yourself!'*
Jobs that help in our leisure entertainment:
    Cinema projectionist, commissionaire, usherette.
    Theatre stagehands, actors, actresses.
    Holiday camps, hotels, cafés.
    Radio and television: manufacture, servicing, installing.
    Seaside: concert parties, Punch and Judy, swimming pools.
    Sports: football, cricket, cycling, tennis, etc. People who organize; people who make equipment.
    Stars: stage and screen, sport, 'pop' singers, musicians.

(17) *'Home Comforts'*
    'Our Food' – workers who grow and distribute it.
    'Clothing' – making, designing, distributing.

HOMES AND HOME-MAKING – *Where I Live Now*

(1) The address of my house is...
(2) It is a detached/semi-detached/terraced/house/maisonette/flat/shop/bungalow.
(3) It is owned by..
(4) The repairs to our house are paid for by...
(5) My house was built in the year..................., so it is .... years old.
(6) The total width of my house is .... feet .... inches.
(7) My front door together with its frame measures .... feet .... inches.

TEACHING THE SLOW LEARNER IN THE SECONDARY SCHOOL

(8) The height of the window in the ground floor front room of my house is .... feet .... inches.
(9) My parents tell me we pay .... every year for Rates.
(10) In my house we have .... reception rooms, ... kitchen, ... bedrooms, ... bathroom, ... W.C., and ....

HOMES AND HOME-MAKING – *My Home – Ten Things to Do*

(1) Draw a map of the streets around your house.
(2) Mark the position of your house on this map.
(3) Imagine you are telling a friend your exact route to school from home. Write exactly what you would say.
(4) A stranger knocks at your door and asks the way to the railway station. Write the exact directions as you would write them for the stranger.
(5) Make a list showing the names of the shops nearest your home selling these things:

Articles	*Nearest Shop*
Groceries	
Meat	
Fish and chips	
Fruit	
Fish	
Clothes for ladies	
Pots and pans, etc.	
Clothes for men	
Milk	
Newspapers	
Sweets	
Garden tools	

(6) Make a list of all the materials used in building your house. Here is a start for you:
 Bricks, sand, cement, glass, . . .
(7) Make a list of the times letters are collected from the post box nearest to your house.
(8) We are going to act some short scenes in class where a stranger asks you the way to certain places from your home. Think what you are going to say if you are asked the way to the park, the theatre, the cinema, the football ground, a church and the nearest bus stop.

ENVIRONMENTAL STUDIES

(9) Make a sketch of your house showing how it looks if you stand on the pavement opposite the front of the house.
(10) Can you suggest a reason for the name your street has been given?

THE ROOMS IN MY HOUSE

Measure every room in your house and give the main measurements like this:

Ground Floor: Sitting-room 17′ 6″ × 16′
               Dining room 15′ 9″ × 14′ 6″
               Kitchen 13′ 9″ × 8′ 6″

Here are some words to help:
attic basement bedroom cellar middle rear bathroom.

HOW IT IS MADE

(1) Make a list of all the things used in building your house.
(2) From books in the library find out how each of these things is made.
(3) Write a few sentences about the making of each material.

IS THIS YOUR HOUSE?

Terraced house, looking on to public gardens. Built 1805. Close to East Station and the bus station. Small gardens front and rear.

Ground Floor: Entrance Hall   Lounge
               Dining-room   Kitchen   Outside w.c.
First Floor: Front bedroom (french windows to wrought-iron balcony).
               Rear bedroom   Bathroom   Separate w.c.
Second Floor: Two attic bedrooms.
               Main water, gas, electricity and drainage.

(1) Whereabouts in town is this house?
(2) How many years ago was it built?
(3) Can you find out another important event that happened in the year this house was built?
(4) What is an 'attic bedroom'?
(5) Would you need a lot of stair carpet for this house? How do you know?
(6) If you travelled out of town to your work would this be a convenient house for you to live in? Why?
(7) Draw a rough map of the streets around the house you think is described here.

(8) Supposing you liked everything about this house, but found the gardens too small to grow enough vegetables for your family. How would you overcome this difficulty if you went to live in this house?
(9) Name those rooms which we sometimes call 'reception rooms'.
(10) Make sketches to show the difference between a terrace house and an end-terrace house.

HOUSES FOR SALE

Modern semi-detached house, with garage, on high ground, to south of town. Good front and rear gardens. Quiet cul-de-sac. Three double bedrooms, bathroom, separate w.c., dining-room, lounge, kitchen.

Detached timber-built bungalow near common. Very large gardens. Detached garage. Five good-sized rooms, bathroom, w.c. kitchen, garden sheds. Main gas and water. Modern cesspool drainage.

On main coast road. Semi-detached house, built at end of last century. Good gardens front and rear. Large rooms throughout. Lounge, dining-room, breakfast-room, kitchen, outside w.c., five bedrooms, bathroom, separate w.c., glass-covered side entrance. All main services. Rateable value £56.

(1) Make a sketch to show what is meant by cul-de-sac.
(2) Make drawings to show the difference between a detached and semi-detached house.
(3) Would it be a wise thing to buy a timber bungalow? Why?
(4) To what uses could you put a glass-covered side entrance?
(5) What is meant by 'all main services'?
(6) 'at the end of the last century'. In what year might this house have been built?
(7) What are french windows? Draw a picture to show your meaning.
(8) Where would you expect to find a house with cess-pool drainage? Why?
(9) Can you sketch a wrought-iron balcony?
(10) What is meant by 'Rateable value'?

FINDING A HOUSE

From the local newspaper, copy advertisements of houses that fit these descriptions:
(1) A house with four bedrooms costing less than £2,000.
(2) A terrace house with at least three bedrooms and costing less than £1,500.
(3) Any detached house, at any price, with a garage and a large garden.

ENVIRONMENTAL STUDIES

(4) A cottage suitable for a couple about to retire. It must be cheap and the garden must be small.
(5) Any house that seems suitable for making into two flats.

(Many similar tasks could be devised, account being taken, of course, of the different values of property in the area.)

SELLING A HOUSE

Write advertisements for your local paper, describing these houses as you would if you wanted to sell them:
(1) The house in which you live now.
(2) The house of your best friend in this town. If this happens to be a house similar to your own, choose the house of any other friend.
(3) A house you know well in a nearby town.
(4) A house at the seaside.
(5) A house in the country.

OTHER PEOPLE'S HOMES

People in other countries live in houses quite different from ours. Men in our country used to live in different houses too.

Find books in the library about these different houses and write a few sentences to describe the houses that fit these titles:

'An Eskimo Home', 'A House in a Swamp', 'A Desert Home', 'A House in the Trees', 'Houseboat on the Thames', 'Life in a Cave', 'Living in a Norman Castle', 'African Home', 'On a Tropical, Island', 'Chinese House', 'A Victorian Sitting-room', 'A Georgian Doorway'.

NEW ROOMS FOR OLD

(1) Imagine you have £100 to spend on refurnishing and redecorating your sitting-room at home.
(2) You are going to decorate the room yourself. Look in local shops and choose wallpaper or distemper and paint.
(3) Make a list, showing the prices, of all the materials you need to decorate the room.
(4) Spend the rest of the money on furniture and furnishings. Remember that items such as cushions, pictures, lamp-shades, etc., help to change the appearance of a room. Make notes of the furniture you choose, including the prices, like this:

From Smith and Jones Ltd.
Three-piece suite covered in green uncut moquette. Loose cushions to chairs and settee.   £50. 10s. 0d.

From Charles Brown and Sons
12 yards of red and gold damask at 7s. 6d. per yard = £4. 10s. 0d.

(5) You will not have enough money to buy all the things you would like, so think up ways of smartening furniture you have already.

Example
Our coffee table is badly scratched. I will remove all the old varnish with paint-stripper and put wax polish on the plain wood to make the table look lighter.

(6) Collect all the patterns, pictures and sketches you can. Look for coloured pictures in particular. Use the library books for ideas.

IS IT WORTH IT?

Sometimes it is wise to buy on Hire Purchase and sometimes it is very silly to do so.

It costs several thousand pounds to buy some houses and if we had to save that much money before we could have a house we should be old men and women before we married! So, many very sensible people buy their homes on 'Easy Payments'. Sometimes, however, people are tempted by advertisements of small items which cost about 15s. 0d. cash and yet are available on easy payments. For such cheap items it would be wiser to save the money and go to a local shop where you can examine the quality of the article before you buy it.

It costs more to buy things on H.P., but we sometimes buy things in this way rather than be inconvenienced while we save for them. It would be rather silly to go without cooked meals for about three years while we saved to buy a gas cooker, even though it is cheaper to pay cash for one.

Before we buy anything on H.P. we should ask ourselves these questions:

(1) Is the stated cash price fair for this article?
(2) How long would it take me to save the money for this?
(3) Can I manage without it until I save the cash for it?
(4) How much extra does it cost on H.P.?
(5) Can I spare the payments out of my housekeeping money?
(6) Do I really need it?

Firms must state the cash price for goods they sell on H.P., but some firms might charge more than others for the same article. Look in many

ENVIRONMENTAL STUDIES

shops before you buy anything and make sure the price is not higher than elsewhere.

(1) Make four columns on a sheet of paper and put the headings:

Article   Cash Price   Deposit   Payments

(2) From local shops fill these columns with details of cash prices and Easy Terms for the things you think you would need to start a home of your own.
(3) When you have found these prices, work out how much extra it costs to buy these things on H.P. Here is a way to set out your sums:

Electric Stove   £   s.   d.
Deposit   14   18   6
Payments: £4. 10s. 5d. × 16   72   7   6

                          Total Paid   =   87   6   0
Cash Price   74   10   0

Extra charge for payments   12   16   0

Suggestions for further investigation of **HOMES AND HOMEMAKING**
'Home Laundry', 'Home Upholstery', 'Woodwork in the House', 'Flowers in the House', 'Heating Homes', 'Food for Families', 'Table Manners', 'Family Holidays', 'Christmas at Home', 'Home First-aid', 'Rainy Days in the House', 'Party Dishes', 'Children's Party Games', 'Pets in the Home', 'Teenagers', 'Growing, cooking and Bottling Fruit', 'Our Gardens', 'Family Clothes', 'Spending the Money', 'Water in the Home', 'Read Me a Story', 'Children's Sleep', 'Books for Boys and Girls'.

OUR POST OFFICE – *Ten Things to Find Out*

Find the words that best fit the blank spaces.
Write the complete sentences.

(1) Our post office is in..
(2) There are .... public telephones inside the post office.
(3) There are .... public telephones just outside the post office.
(4) To reach London in time for delivery by the first post there, a letter must be posted from our town before ....
(5) To make a local telephone call from a public telephone we need .... pennies.

(6) To post a normal letter to France costs ....
(7) To buy a Postal Order for 2s. 6d. we have to pay .... s. .... d.
(8) The correct name for the extra money we have to pay for a postal order is ....
(9) Our post office is open from .... a.m. to .... p.m on weekdays and from .... am. to .... on Sundays.
(10) Letters are delivered to my house at about ....

OUR POST OFFICE – *The Cost of Posting*

(1) How much would it cost to post a letter of less than 1 oz. to another town in the United Kingdom?
(2) What would you expect to pay in postage for a parcel weighing 2½ lb. and being sent to London?
(3) If you wanted to send the local paper to a relative in Scotland how much would the postage cost?
(4) What is the heaviest weight that can be sent by parcel post?
(5) What stamps would you put on a letter addressed to a man abroad in the Army, if it weighed exactly one ounce?
(The list of Postal Rates available from Post Offices can be used to devise many similar exercises.)

OUR POST OFFICE – *Using a Telephone*

(1) Look in a public telephone box and copy the instructions given there for making a call to a local number.
(2) Draw a map showing the shortest route from your house to the nearest public telephone box.
(3) How would you make a call from this box to a town 200 miles away?
(4) You have just witnessed an accident in which a man has been injured. Write exactly what you would do and say when you telephoned for an ambulance.
(5) The post office is closed and you need to send an urgent telegram. How would you use the telephone to do this?
(6) You have dialled a number and, after waiting for a reply, you decide that your friend must be out. How would you get back the money you put into the box?
(7) How much does it cost to rent a private telephone for one year?
(8) Look in the local telephone directory and find the name, address and telephone number of:
  a baker you know
  the biggest store in this town
  a butcher

ENVIRONMENTAL STUDIES

your greengrocer
this school
a cinema
a neighbour of yours who has a telephone
your doctor
the town hall
the railway station

(9) In the local post office or the library you will find Telephone Directories for London; look in them for the telephone numbers of these firms:
Gamages Ltd., Holborn
W. H. Smith and Son Ltd. – Head Office
F. W. Woolworth and Co. Ltd. – Registered Office
Daily Mirror Newspapers Ltd.
British Lion Films Ltd., Wardour Street, W.1.
Marshall and Snelgrove Ltd.
Marks and Spencer Ltd. – Head Office
John Barker and Co. Ltd. – Kensington
Royal Society for the Prevention of Cruelty to Animals – Head Office
British Railways, Victoria Station (Passenger Inquiries)

(10) This advertisement is taken from the local paper:
Boy or girl wanted for light factory work.
Good wages and conditions – Telephone Plastic Products Ltd., before noon Saturday.
If you wanted this job, what would you do to try to get it? Write exactly what you would do and say.

MY PARISH CHURCH – *Ten Things to Find Out*

Find the words that fit best into the blank spaces. Write the complete sentences.

(1) My Parish Church is called..
(2) It was built in the year ...., so it is .... years old.
(3) The Vicar at my Parish Church is called Rev. ....
....
(4) The Church Wardens are .... and
....
(5) The organist is ....
(6) The altar is at the .... end of the church.
(7) The church is built mainly of ....
(8) The font of our church is used for................................

187

(9) The place from which our Vicar gives his sermon is called a ....

(10) The small room where the Vicar and the choir put on their robes is called a ....

MY PARISH CHURCH – *Ten Things to Do*

(1) Find a photograph of your parish church and mount it on a plain sheet of paper.
(2) Make a sketch of the font in your church.
(3) Find a very old tombstone in the churchyard and make a sketch of it.
(4) Carefully copy the exact words from the tombstone you have just sketched.
(5) Look at a stained glass window in the church. What is it about?
(6) Draw the outside of the church as you see it when you face the main door.
(7) Find out the story of one famous person who has been connected with your church. Write this story in your own words.
(8) What are some of the uses to which the vestry of the church is put?
(9) On a large sheet of paper make a copy of the notice-board outside your church.
(10) Draw a map of the route from your home to the church.

Similar task sheets could be devised for investigation of other aspects of OUR TOWN:

'Public Library', 'Open Spaces', 'Safety First', 'Buses and Trains', 'Our Schools', 'Shopping', 'Houses', 'Visitors' Guide', 'Sport', 'Where to Eat', 'Entertainment', 'Inside the Town Hall', etc.

Some Suggestions for Study Titles

'Aeroplanes and Flying', 'Arm of the Law', 'Birds and Nests', 'Boys' Outdoor Games', 'Breeds of Dogs', 'Bringing up a Family', 'British Explorers', 'British Farm Produce', 'British Railways', 'By Coach and Bus', 'Care of Babies', 'Children's Toys', 'Clothes Through the Ages', 'Coal', 'Cooking', 'Cotton', 'Cup of Tea', 'Dairy-farming', 'Domestic Animals', 'Embroidery', 'English Fruits', 'Famous Inventions', 'Farm Animals', 'Fish for Tea', 'Food and Drink', 'Foreign Tour', 'Garden Flowers', 'Gas in the Home', 'Girls' Outdoor Games', 'Glass', 'Great Cities of the World', 'Great Missionaries', 'Great Soldiers', 'Her Majesty's Forces', 'Holiday Resorts of Great Britain', 'Iron', 'Knitting', 'Local

ENVIRONMENTAL STUDIES

Playing-Fields', 'Milk for Energy', 'Motor-Cars', 'Mountains of the World', 'Needlecraft', 'National Health', 'Our County', 'Our Local Theatre', 'Our School', 'Our Town', 'Our Village', 'Pets and their Care', 'Ports of Britain', 'Postal Services', 'Pottery', 'Radio and Television', 'Rivers of England', 'Rubber', 'Ships and the Sea', 'Sports and Games of Great Britain', 'Staff of Life', 'Sugar', 'The Boy Scout Movement', 'The British Commonwealth', 'The Cinema', 'The Merchant Navy', 'The Stage', 'Timber', 'Transport through the Ages', 'Vegetable Gardening', 'Water Supplies', 'Weaving', 'Wild Animals of the World', 'Wild Flowers of England', 'Wonders of Electricity', 'Youth Clubs'.

W. C. BEAGLEY

Books for the Teacher

ARMSTRONG, J. M. A., *Projects and their Place in Education*, Pitman, 1950.
Board of Education, *Handbook of Suggestions for Teachers*, H.M.S.O., 1946.
ETHERINGTON, T. H., *In and Out of School*, Pitman, 1950.
GLOVER, A. H. T., *New Teaching in a New Age*, Nelson, 1946.
Ministry of Education, *School and Life*, H.M.S.O., 1947.

Books for Class Reference

ANDERSON, JOHN, *Adventures in Work* (series – varied titles), Oxford University Press, 1950.
BIG CHIEF I-SPY, *I-Spy Books* (series – varied titles), *Daily Mail and News Chronicle*. Various dates.
BOUMPHREY, GEOFFREY, *Our Everyday World* (series – varied titles), Oxford University Press, 1950.
BRUCE-MILNE, M., *The Book for the Home* (Five volumes), Caxton Publishing Co., 1956.
BURMAN, W., PLEYDELL-BOUVERIE, M., and URQUHART, M. I., *Housecraft*, Macmillan, 1957.
CANDY, R. J., *Things We All Know* (Books 1, 2 and 3), Macmillan, 1958.
CARTER, BRUCE, *Men of Speed* Series, Newnes, 1955.
CLARK, DENNIS, *Man's Achievement* (three titles), Longmans.
CROOK, W. G. S., *They Work for Us* (series – varied titles), E. J. Arnold and Son.

CROSS, GWEN, *Tropical Library* (series – many titles), Longmans, 1957.

CROSSLAND, JOHN R. (ed.), *The Modern Marvels Encyclopedia*, Collins.

— (ed.), *The New Illustrated Encyclopedia*, Collins.

DEMPSTER, J. J. B., *Your World* (Books 1, 2, and 3), Odhams Press Ltd.

FISHER, A. S. T., *The Story of Life* (several booklets), Basil Blackwell.

GARNETT, EMMELINE, *Makers of History* (series – varied titles), A. and C. Black.

HARKER, PHYLLIS, *The Beginner Housewife*, The World's Work (1913) Ltd., 1956.

HERDMAN, T., *Longman's Colour Geographies* (twenty booklets arranged in four main groups), Longmans, 1957.

HURST, MARION, *The 1-2-3 of Homemaking*, The World's Work (1913) Ltd., 1949.

LAMONT, J. C., *Health and the Home*, E. J. Arnold and Son.

LEIGH, M. CORDELIA E., *Nature's Playground* (Books i, ii, iii and iv), Collins, 1956.

MCNICOL, HARRY, *Stories of Industry* (series of eleven titles), Fredk. Warne and Co.

MOORE, MARY F., *Macmillan's Social Series* (several titles), Macmillan. Various dates.

PARKER, MARY and NOYLE, GEORGE, *Glimpses of Family Life* (series of six booklets), Macmillan, 1954.

PIDGEON, RAYMOND, *My Home*, Thos. Nelson and Sons, 1952.

PUMPHREY, GEORGE H., *Good Manners*, Pitman, 1954.

— *Look After Yourself*, E. J. Arnold and Son.

SMITH, THYRA, *The Story of Measurement*, Basil Blackwell.

TAYLOR, BOSWELL, *They Served Mankind* (series – varied titles), Macmillan. Various dates.

THOMAS, M. W., *Britain Past and Present* (Books 1, 2 and 3), Thos. Nelson and Sons. Various dates.

VARIOUS, *Get to Know* (series – many titles), Methuen. Various dates.

— *The Golden Circle Reader* (series – varied titles), Cassell and Co. Various dates.

ENVIRONMENTAL STUDIES

Great Endeavour (series – several titles), Blackie and Son. Various dates.
— 'Evans Headway Readers': *The Book of the Town, The Book of the Country, The Book of the Air, The Book of the Sea, The Book of the Cinema, The Book of Football*, Evans Brothers Ltd.
— *Information Books* (varied series – many titles), E.S.A. Ltd. Various dates.
— *Know the Game* (varied titles – sports and games), Educational Productions Ltd. Various dates.
— *Man's Heritage* (series of seven titles), Longmans, 1957.
— *Men and Women at Work* (series – many titles), Longmans, 1950–8.
— *Open your Eyes* Series: *Look at the Past* (three books), *Man's Forward March* (three books), *The World and You* (three books), *Come and See* (three books), *Out of Doors* (three books), *Living Things* (three books), Chatto and Windus Ltd.
— *Parrish Colour Books* (varied series – many titles), Max Parrish.
— *Picture Pageant* (series – varied titles), Macmillan. Various dates.
— *Practical Work Books* (series – several titles), Thos. Nelson and Sons.
— *Project Studies of Everyday Things* (series – varied titles), A. Wheaton and Co. Various dates.
— *Puffin Picture Books* (series – many titles), Penguin Books Ltd. Various dates.
— *Understanding the Modern World*, George Allen and Unwin Ltd. Various dates.
— *Women of Devotion and Courage* (series – many titles), Cassell and Co.

WALTER, L. EDNA, *Ranks of the Valiant* (series – four titles), Newnes, 1955.

WHATLEY, W. E., *I Must be Healthy*, McDougalls.

Chapter XII

SCHOOL JOURNEYS

How often have parents said to me 'I would very much like —— to go with the school when they go away on holiday'. Let us get this point quite clear, before we go any further, that a school journey is not a holiday for either children or staff. Although the conditions are pleasant as on a holiday, it is a study period on a selected spot with material at first hand, and is a special case of the Environmental Studies discussed in the previous chapter.

The subject will be dealt with as if a school journey were in the process of planning and carrying through. I shall take for granted that the educational principles considered by Mr Beagley have also been considered by the reader.

Initial Preparation

My first piece of advice is to join the School Journey Association. Write to them at: 23 Southampton Place, London, W.C.1. Fill in the forms which will be sent to you, pay your subscription and then you can call on them for aid, whether you decide to spend your school journey in the homeland or abroad.

(1) *Letter to parents.* In order to ascertain those who wish to take part in the school journey, first circulate the whole group from whom the candidates are to be selected, with a letter in general terms, i.e., 'A school journey is being arranged. If you would like your child to go, will you please sign below and return the form to me as soon as possible'.

(2) *Headquarters.* Whilst awaiting replies from parents, consider the location of a headquarters, bearing in mind:

(*a*) A district offering enough scope for types of study to be undertaken, i.e. historical centres of interest, geography, geology, biological interest, etc.

(*b*) Reasonable access to a space for recreational activities, i.e. field for games, beach for bathing or swimming and, particularly for backward children, play to discover the properties of sand and water, to write, draw, design and build in sand. The *School Journey Association Book* will be invaluable at this juncture. It offers many suggestions for headquarters. There are addresses of places all over the British Isles, together with the numbers they can accommodate and the cost per head. It can be useful, when considering a particular headquarters, to turn to the end of the book. There is a list of the previous year's school journeys and the headquarters to which they went. A telephone conversation with the leader will give you an idea of what is to be expected at the address that may be under consideration. Having made up your mind, book the accommodation provisionally, pending a visit to inspect for yourself.

(*c*) Cost must be considered very carefully, bearing in mind the children's means. A certain headquarters may be attractive but the cost may be far beyond the means of some of the children. Under some authorities, there are schemes for assisting necessitous cases. Under authorities where no such facilities are offered, means must be found of raising money, to enable you to take children who would otherwise be deprived because they cannot afford to pay the full cost. In many districts there are committees who are willing, even anxious, to help with donations, but the best source is the school itself. There are many ways in which money can be raised, i.e. school functions such as plays, entertainments, jumble sales, proceeds of sales of work made in a hobby class, etc.

(*d*) When making your selection of members of the group to go with the school journey, be warned to keep an eye on numbers. If your group is too large you will find it unwieldy and you will lose the personal touch. A smaller group makes it easier to establish and maintain a family atmosphere.

Visit of Inspection
Previous reference was made to the telephone conversation with someone who has used the accommodation before, but it is still necessary to make a personal inspection with the following points in mind.

(1) *Accommodation.* First inquire the type of accommodation

available and to what use it will be put. You will want to know the size of the rooms, the number of beds per room, which are the rooms reserved for staff, how these are situated and whether they are in a convenient position to provide adequate supervision. Referring to the beds for the children you should, whenever possible, request the use of single beds. Toilet facilities and their convenient siting are very important. It is imperative that you inquire fully into *fire escape arrangements*.

(2) *Times of Meals*. On inquiry, it will be found that those times arranged for summer visitors are not always suitable for school journey. A discussion and a little adjustment will usually bring this into line. At the same time make provisional arrangements for packed lunches when visits mean being out all day.

(3) *Schoolroom*. For morning and evening assemblies and for school activities in the evening and on wet days, it is very useful to have a large room at your disposal. In my experience, I have found that proprietors have been very co-operative in allowing us to use the large dining-room for this purpose. At the end of the evening meal, the children have, in a few minutes, converted the dining-room into a very effective schoolroom. Before going to bed, they have left the room ready for dining purposes. If it is at all possible obtain the use of a piano, which will be invaluable for assemblies and amusement on wet days. Ascertain whether there is a toilet which the children can use when occupying this room. This will save unnecessary running up and down stairs and facilitate supervision.

(4) *School Milk*. Whilst on school journey, children are entitled to school milk on five days. Make a note of the name and address of the dairy which supplies milk to the premises.

(5) *Guide Book*. If you have not already obtained one by post, now is the time to buy a guide book. It is a mine of information.

(6) *Churches*. You have no doubt already ascertained the religions of the children who are going on the school journey. Find out the nearest churches to which the children can go on Sunday. This information can be obtained from the guide book. It gives a list of churches and a map of the district on which they can be located.

(7) *Transport Facilities*. Most districts are served by several coach lines and bus services. Whilst on the spot it should be easy to make

a note of the headquarters of each of these in preparation for any transport you may need for your visits.

Initial Correspondence

There are a number of letters which must be written well in advance to ensure that all arrangements are cut and dried. You will find this expedient both for efficiency and for the saving of money.

(1) *Insurance*. Membership of the School Journey Association entitles you to make use of their schemes for insuring the children whilst they are under your care. Obtain from the association forms of application for several different schemes of insurance from which you can choose according to your needs. On receipt of these forms, complete and return them in good time for the commencement of the school journey. The certificate of insurance should be in your hands before you set off.

(2) *School Milk*. Write to your local authority for the permit to obtain school milk whilst you are away. You have already noted the name and address of the supplier, so fill in the form and send it to the education authority for the district to which you are going.

A permit will be sent, either to you for handing to the milkman, or direct to the dairy, authorizing the supply of free milk.

(3) *Visits to Historical Buildings, etc.* Buildings or places of interest under the administration of the Ministry of Works can be visited either free of charge or at a reduced rate, by writing to the Ministry of Works, Department for Ancient Monuments and Historical Buildings. Arrangements must be made well in advance or you will find that you will have to pay full admission fees. Some authorities make a grant for the cost of educational visits, but they will not allow a charge on this grant, if permission to visit free could have been obtained beforehand. You may wish to include in your itinerary places which are privately owned. Party tickets at reduced rates can sometimes be arranged if a prior booking is made.

(4) *Equipment on Loan*. Some authorities maintain a stock of equipment, i.e. mackintoshes, groundsheets, rubber sheets, haversacks, first-aid boxes, etc., which are loaned for the duration of the school journey. Send a requisition for the equipment required and

give dates of the period when you need it. The articles will be delivered to the school a few days before your departure and will be collected again shortly after your return.

(5) *Transport*. Preparations must be made beforehand for transport to and from the headquarters, and for educational visits during the school journey.

If the centre chosen is within reasonable distance of the school, some authorities will provide transport to and from the headquarters. When long distances or boat trips are involved, railways are most helpful and co-operative. As much notice as possible must be given. A representative usually calls in response to your request. If you tell him what your requirements are, he will advise you and tell you all the facilities that the railway has to offer, including the reduced rates for party tickets.

Now is the time to write to the coach or bus companies whose addresses you obtained when on your visit of inspection. Ask for estimates to cover the visits you propose to make. Compare these and select according to the money you have allotted for your transport and you should be able to budget economically. Some authorities will not only provide transport to and from the headquarters but allow the group on school journey to retain the use of the transport for duration of stay.

(6) *Guide Books and Pamphlets*. If you have not already obtained your guide book to the district you intend exploring, write now for one. Pamphlets and guide books to the places of interest you are going to see are easily purchased from Her Majesty's Stationery Office or through your local newsagent, at a small cost.

(7) *Churches*. I have always made a practice of writing to the churches to which I propose to take or send the children. Courtesy demands that they be forewarned. Members of the congregation so often have their own favourite seats. To accommodate a large group suddenly, members must be consulted and small rearrangements of seating made. I have found the utmost co-operation when I have made contact beforehand. I have been granted a special interview to discuss the means of fitting into the church plans and in the case of backward children, a short talk has been inserted into the service. The group has been welcomed and made to feel quite at home.

Scheme of Work

The scheme of work should take the form of a textbook and enough copies duplicated so that each person taking part can have a copy for reference at all times. As it is to be the textbook, it should include all the material required for the duration of the journey. In compiling it, special attention should be paid to the following points.

Print. If the typewriter is to be used, make sure that the print does not become a compact mass which is, to say the least, uninteresting. I have found that the more interesting method of presentation for backward children is to use script writing. It can be varied in size and spacing at will.

Phrasing and Vocabulary. If the textbook is to assist the backward reader, then care and attention must be given to both phrasing and vocabulary. Bear in mind the average reading age of the group for whom the work is being prepared.

Illustration. The material in the textbook must appeal to the children however backward they are, so there must be illustration. With very little effort, pictures can be found and reproduced.

Material for the Textbook

Preface. A few general facts about the school journey which cannot be included anywhere else in the book, will make a good introduction, unless a special feature is to be included about the journey to the headquarters. There is also room here for a few timely remarks on behaviour, co-operation and a family atmosphere.

Daily Time-table. Copies of the daily time-table, giving meal times and the times of other activities, could be put up at vantage points for the children to consult, but in practice I have found that it is much more satisfactory for each child to have a copy included in the textbook. It makes for confidence in the child, a saving of time and smoother running.

Programme of Work. I did not include a programme covering the whole period in my first school journey textbook. Consequently, I was snowed under with queries, such as, 'When are we going to do so and so?', 'Where are we going today?' etc. The child's own copy of the programme obviated this difficulty. I also found that the children, on consulting their books to find out what the next day's activities were to be, began, with the help of reference books, pamphlets, etc., to prepare for the next day's work on their own, thus providing exceedingly good training.

When planning the programme of work, it is advisable to space out visits to places of interest in order to allow days between for local activities, shopping, relaxation, etc.

Maps. I have found it useful to include two maps.

(1) A map in as large a scale as possible, covering the journey from home to the headquarters and the vicinity showing the places of interest to which visits will be made. Some of the older children have shown great interest in plotting the routes taken on different days, especially if a different colour is used for each excursion.

(2) A map, in larger scale, of the district around the headquarters helps the children to find their way about. They can identify shopping centres, churches, the way to the beach, the way to the park or recreation ground, etc.

Religious Education. It is possible that some schools will prefer to take the school hymn-book for use at morning and evening assemblies. I have found that, as far as backward children are concerned, this means another book to remember but also, alas, to forget. If a few selected hymns and prayers are included in the textbook, which is the child's constant companion, it simplifies matters considerably. If required, bible references for daily readings can be included as a basis for religious studies.

Letter Writing. Next in my textbook I put what I call my letter-writing page. Every child wants to write its own letter to its parents. So often the backward child is baulked by its inability to spell and to put sentences together. This page has a series of prefabricated phrases with a choice of words to insert where needed. With a little imagination and thought, a comprehensive and useful list can be compiled. This idea can be used at the discretion of the teacher who will know the ability of the group he is leading.

Specific Visits. In your initial planning, you will have decided which places and things of interest in the district you are going to visit. A separate page or pages on each of these must be given in the book. The pamphlets and guide books which you have obtained will be most useful. I also find that a visit to the local public library is a good jumping off point. I am sure that in different sections of the library, you will be able to find books giving you all the subject matter you need. The public library has always been most helpful in allowing me, through the school organization, to borrow these books for the duration of the school journey. Having used these books for your own purpose of selection, they will be invaluable as reference books for the more able children whilst they are away. At this point I would refer you back to the paragraph on illustration. Somewhere in these books, I am sure you will find the pictures you need.

Biology, Geology, etc. Enough information should be given to point the lines the local study should take, i.e. for geology, diagrams of geological formations will show the children for what, and where, to look. Nature study, especially for backward children, must be carefully illustrated. A diagram of a flower without colour could be very misleading. On the other hand, even for a backward child, the subject matter should be such that it leads to research on the child's part.

School Curriculum

In the excitement of all these special studies, let us not forget the other subjects of the curriculum. The high lights have been dealt with up to this point, but what of the other subjects that spell school? There is enough incentive in all that we are doing to give ample motivation for many of them. The following do not appear in the textbook but they must not be neglected.

Reading. For the very poor readers, there is much in the school journey textbook that they can tackle, For the better reader, there are the reference books. On a number of occasions, children have surprised me with the amount of knowledge they have gained, when their reading ability has been suspect.

Written Work. During our school journeys, the children have always kept daily diaries. No dry as dust material here; only anxiety to get down on paper all the exciting things they have done during the day.

Letter writing is a strong incentive for producing written work. Of course, with backward children, there is always the one who cannot cope. May I refer you back to the page on letter writing. The thrill of accomplishment, be it with aids, is a joy to see.

Number. The backward child needs all the practice he can get in managing money. Shopping with his own money, remembering the price he has paid for his purchases, checking his change and generally accounting for his pocket-money is a grand opportunity for practical number. Also, in other activities, there will be numerous opportunities for the practice of number, e.g. building and construction of sand castles, designs in the sand, pacing the sands to the sea for incoming and ebbing tides, scoring for games, etc. An experiment with tide times proved to be very valuable as an exercise in time telling. Except when the tide played tricks, the children became adept at judging high tide the following day, especially when bathing on an incoming tide was the incentive.

Physical Education. As near as possible to the amount of time devoted to physical activities in the school curriculum, periods should be arranged, either in the local park, or on a stretch of sandy beach, when the children can take part in games which they have organized themselves, but, of course, under supervision.

Handwork. Given basic equipment such as paste, glue, gum, scissors, etc., much can be done with local materials. Models can be made from chalk, soft stone or wood. Beautiful designs can be produced from seaweeds. Shells can be used in numerous ways. A modelling medium has often produced quite good models of the subjects of interest that have been studied. Quite successful plans in relief have been made in papier-mâché, and models or pictures added: this piece of work is a valuable aid to the very difficult problem of map producing and reading, with backward children.

Art. Even those children who are loth to show what they can do when it comes to making pictures have been encouraged, by the wealth of material during school journey, to paint, draw or sketch something that has interested them. Even after they have returned to normal school routine, things they have seen during school journey appear in their work in the art class. Brass rubbings and leaf rubbings encourage an interest in and understanding of art forms. Church windows are a feast in colour. In studying them we have discovered interesting details about the change in design and the method of producing the coloured glass.

Singing. Children will sing at any time, suitable or otherwise, if they are happy. The difficulty, as a rule, is to stop them singing at inconvenient times. Inclement weather or in the evenings when their other work is done are times to organize community singing or solo items of individual talent. There are those who frown upon singing in the coach when travelling. Of course, it depends upon the singing. Properly done, not raucous and loud, in fact, not the sort of singing that turns the heads of the people on the pavement, singing in the coach can not only be enjoyable but useful. It can cease at a moment's notice if there is something to observe. Between times, it takes their minds off the fact that they are sitting for quite a spell, also, such things as stopping the coach for toilet purposes and it has even been known to make those who are inclined to be travel sick forget their discomfort.

Literature, Poetry, etc. There are very few places in England or abroad which have not some association with a poet or writer. Discussion will naturally turn to an interest in their works.

Final Preparations

Letter to parents. A few weeks before the actual date of the school journey, the final letter to the parents should be sent. To avoid any question of the parents not being fully informed, it should include the following items.

(*a*) Actual dates of school journey departure and return. Times should also be included when possible.

(*b*) Full address, including the name of your hosts, will ensure that the parents have the particulars always to hand.

(*c*) Children's personal requirements. For parents' guidance, a list of the child's *minimum* needs should be given in the letter. To some, this may seem superfluous, but when preparing for my first school journey, I was shocked to find how little understanding a few parents had shown in packing a child's case. This applies more to backward children, but even in some cases of normal children, guidance may be needed. All clothes should be marked with the child's name and when the cases are brought to school, it saves time and confusion if the case bears a label as well.

(*d*) Following this list, I have found it expedient to include a little instruction about pocket-money. During my first school journey, I learnt to my sorrow, and all too late, how essential this direction is. There were children who left school with as little as two and sixpence and others who started with as much as two pounds and had more sent on in the form of postal orders. I wasted much valuable time at the post office changing them into cash for the children to spend. This did not matter half so much as the reaction of some children to this money problem. The had-nots suffered from a feeling of injustice. I determined from that moment, that this should never happen again. I have now set a limit, which I feel is sufficient for those who would have plenty, and not beyond the reach of those in poorer circumstances. This, of course, could vary, but I feel that if the leader gives careful thought, he will be able to determine for himself a suitable sum. Even then, there will be some children who cannot afford this amount. When planning the distribution of the money raised for school journey, I have always set aside some of it, so that I can supplement the pocket-money of those unable to reach the standard set. All the children can then start on equal terms. When subsidizing the children care, and sometimes secrecy, must be exercised to avoid embarrassment.

(e) At the bottom of this letter, prepare a form which can be detached and returned to school. I have used this for obtaining a written sanction for children to be allowed to bathe or paddle. Again, some people may think this unnecessary. I know that we are supposed to have, in school, a full medical record of each child, but I have also discovered that odd ailments, e.g. trouble with ears and nose, have come to light when the question of bathing has been raised. This form will make sure that no over-adventurous child, disregarding possible dangers unknown to the teacher, does not bathe without parental consent.

Checking Cases. Despite the fact that a list of the child's minimum requirements has been sent home, and that a parent should know what a child requires, it is necessary to check the cases when they arrive in school. The procedure I have adopted and found most satisfactory is to have all cases brought to school the day before departure. They are then checked and locked away until the next morning. If anything is missing, there is still one day to rectify the mistake. A further advantage is that on the morning of departure the child's only concern is to arrive on time with no luggage to worry about. Also, transport usually arrives before the time arranged, and loading can begin at once if all luggage is to hand.

SCHOOL JOURNEYS

Dormitory Lists. You ascertained the layout of the dormitories when you made your visit of inspection. You will save time if you have made up your lists for the different rooms before leaving school. Unless there is some combination which might mean a behaviour problem, the children like to make up their own groups and they usually prove very satisfactory.

Learning to Make Beds. It has been my experience that making beds is not one of the things which all parents have taught their children. At some places to which we have been, there has been a shortage of staff, due to the fact that we go out of the season. One of the jobs that we have taken on is making our own beds. We have lessons in bed making at school and we are prepared for the emergency.

Arrival Cards. Getting ourselves sorted out, unpacked and generally settled in at headquarters is quite enough to cope with at the time. There is also an urge to get out and explore. In fact, writing a card to let Mother know that you have arrived safely is considered a nuisance. So, before leaving school, preferably on the last day, we sit down and write a card saying 'Dear Mum, I have arrived safely. I will write a letter later. Love ——.' When we go to explore, we drop the prepared cards into the nearest post box. Incidentally, whilst on the subject of postcards to parents; at the end of the school journey, each parent is informed of date and time of the arrival back at school, with a request for the child to be met.

Equipment. In school we are used to having everything to hand. Once you are away, there is no stock cupboard to which you can run. It is a good idea, therefore, if beforehand, you compile a list of the things which you think you will need, adding items as you think of them. When you are ready to pack, it is so much easier, as you gather the things from the stock room, to check them against your list. Do not forget to place 'library' on your list. There are the books you have borrowed from the public library, and a selection from your school library which should include some books for recreational reading. In the evenings when school work is complete, on wet days and sometimes, when we have arrived a little too early for a meal, a book to hand is a very useful stop-gap.

Illness. Did I hear you say 'I hope not'? I could not agree with you more. Nevertheless, there is always the odd chance. Children do the most unaccountable things at times. Just in case, arm yourself with a list of names, addresses, dates of birth and the names of the children's private doctors. These particulars will be needed for National Health purposes if you are called upon to deal with accident or illness.

Getting Installed

The first twenty-four hours are the test. It is now that you reap the benefit of careful planning.

Dormitories. Your lists have been prepared. With a little supervision, the children will sort themselves out into their appointed places quite quickly.

Fire Drill. The novelty of settling in will keep the children fully occupied for a while. Go over the fire escape arrangements again with the proprietor. As soon as the children are settled, call them together. Tell them what the fire signal will be. Then do fire drill straight away. It is an urgent matter.

Use of Bathrooms. There are conflicting ideas when it comes to the bathing of children on school journey. Some people prefer to set aside one evening for all hair washing and bathing. I have found that it is better to spread these activities over the whole week, dividing the number of children by five or six and sending that number to be bathed each evening. When dividing by five, the sixth evening can be used for hair washing, or if dividing by six, hair washing and bathing can be done at the same time. This can all be worked in quite smoothly during the period in the evening when school work is in progress, but someone should be on duty.

Routine. For efficiency, a routine must be followed. There may be a few extra items to include, but generally speaking, having given times, etc., in the textbook, everyone is conversant with arrangements.

Rules. The fewer the rules made, the fewer rules there are to disobey. The spirit of the communal life of school journey is, at all times, to be helpful. It may be necessary to emphasize one or two don'ts, but the fewer the better.

Staff. Extraneous duties are part of school journey. Take care that this does not result in a twenty-four hour day. Staff duties carefully planned avoid overwork for any one member of staff.

SCHOOL JOURNEYS

The Social Side of School Journey

We have discussed at great length all the preparations made to ensure that nothing shall mar the search after knowledge. But what of experience?

School journey widens the child's horizon academically but, in another way, the social value is far-reaching. Group behaviour improves rapidly as the children learn to live together and give and take for the happiness of the group. Our aim has always been to create a family atmosphere. Mutual help is the keynote rather than jealousy and quarrelling. To get the best out of our children we must learn to know them. We find out more about them and draw closer to them whilst we are living with them than we are ever likely to do in school. They grow in confidence in response to the methodical life that we planned so carefully.

There are children who have never before been away from home without the protection of their parents. Never yet have I embarked on a school journey without a small misgiving that one of these children may be homesick. I must help to bridge the gap and show that independence can be an adventure. Many parents of backward children are inclined to do too much for them. During school journey they must, of necessity, do a great a deal for themselves and those lacking in self-confidence gain much.

Many of our children live very restricted lives. They have very little opportunity to move in new environments and to mix with others in circumstances which can teach them correct behaviour, good table manners, etc. Here is a golden opportunity to help them to move with dignity and confidence in strange surroundings. Good habits in personal hygiene are easily learnt from the group. Supervision and a little kindly advice from the teacher on duty can make for great improvement where there is slackness at home.

I have stated that school journey is not a holiday, but, for those children who, without this opportunity, would not see the sea or the countryside or benefit from fresh, clean air, it is a holiday. I have seen pale cheeks become pictures of health and dull eyes grow bright.

I would like, at this point, to mention a group of children who are so often debarred from pleasures enjoyed by the majority – enuretics. I have never refused to include them in my group. Precautions can be taken to prevent damage being done. Then, with tolerance, understanding and kindly treatment we can claim to have cured children who, at the beginning of school journey, were regular offenders. The joy and gratitude on their faces when, for the first time, they wake with a dry bed is worth any effort you may make.

One of the values of school journey by which I set great store is the contact with parents. There are parents who would never take a personal interest in the life of the school. In many families, both parents go out to work and have no time for school functions, but when school journey time comes round, they will even get time off from work to come and see the children off and meet them on their return. A few timely words can create a contact which otherwise would have been lost.

The Follow Up

Returning to school gives rise to mixed feelings. The thrill of school journey is almost over. The children are glad to be reunited with their families and the school welcomes the wanderers with open arms and all agog for news of what they have been doing. With the excitement over, next could come an anticlimax. Is that where all the work we have been doing ceases? If so, then half the value is gone. There must be a follow-up. I cannot begin to suggest the many ways in which this can be done. Much will depend on the school organization, and the distribution of the group when it is again absorbed into the school stream. Is there a period on the time-table which could be used for a reunion, so that work begun on school journey can be rounded off or made the basis for further studies? Failing this could an evening club be formed? Can an exhibition of work be arranged? If the matter is broached whilst you are still away, the children will enjoy discussing it and offering ideas. If they are their own they will be most anxious to put them into operation. The enthusiasm, which created and carried through the school journey, will find a way.

After all, we knew that our venture was not to be just a holiday. Used to the fullest advantage, school journey is a golden opportunity from which both staff and children will derive lasting benefit.

E. G. W. STERRY

Chapter XIII

THE KEEPING OF RECORDS

Record keeping in one form or another has long been an integral part of most teachers' work. When presented colourfully and simply in the form of easily read charts displayed on classroom walls, they prove to be appealing to the children and a useful stimulant to further efforts. However, there exists among certain sections of the teaching profession, a profound distrust of the more detailed forms of record keeping. Their compilation has been objected to as a so-called waste of time and energy and their findings valueless. Indeed, such criticism may have some justification if unsound tests are used and if such a mass of assessments and figures are involved that the personality and individuality of the child are completely swamped and all that emerges from the records is a series of numbers. However, if the keeping of concise records is seen in true perspective with the integrated development of the child as he progresses through his school life, it will be realized that it has a real and vital place in the special class teacher's work and that the work involved is fully justified by the deeper understanding which is gained of the child, his needs and difficulties and the benefits to him which accrue.

Broadly speaking, records can be divided into two groups (a) those accessible to the class and usually on display on the class room walls and (b) those of a far more specialized, individual and confidential nature, which are intended to be available only to those who can use their findings in such a way that the child's progress educationally and socially will derive benefit.

I propose to start by dealing briefly with the first category. The keeping of records in the form of classroom display charts is familiar to all teachers. There is no denying that they are popular with children, particularly if they are large enough to be easily seen, are colourful, simply set out and hung at eye-level. A useful basic form is a large sheet of coloured paper on which the subject is clearly printed. Down the left-hand side should be printed all the pupils' names in alphabetical order. Columns fill the rest of the paper but it is wiser to restrict the number of columns to six or less. Too many are discouraging and the impact of the data set out is weakened. The charts should be renewed at monthly or even fortnightly intervals rather than having one chart to cover a wide range of work and involving a lengthy time span.

Work in arithmetic and reading lends itself to such displays. For example in arithmetic with a first year special class in a secondary modern school, two charts could be made recording the attainment in knowledge of tables ($\times 1, 2, 3, 10, 5, 0$ on one chart, and the remaining more difficult ones on another), a third for addition and subtraction to the third column of figures, a fourth for multiplication and division and so on.

In reading, the recording would cover attainment in diagnostic reading, comprehension work, books read both in and out of school and so on. Children should be shown how to enter their own results on the charts but care must be taken that a competitive spirit is not engendered. The object of this public display of records is for each child to see his own progress visually and to stimulate him to increased efforts to improve subjects in which his backwardness is serious. The teacher must show that she, too, takes an active interest in these progress charts by giving timely words of praise and encouragement, and should keep her own duplicate copy for reference.

The ladder type of chart interests younger children and for this each can adopt a symbol to represent himself, e.g. a flower, a bird, a plane, etc. The ingenuity and originality of the teacher will suggest uses to which this type of recording can be put, always, however, being careful to avoid over-elaboration. Finally, it is important to remember that all displayed material should be frequently changed. Nothing is more valueless and depressing than a mass of dog-eared papers curling and yellowing on schoolroom walls.

The second type of record keeping, i.e. the kind intended to be private and confidential, needs care and accuracy in its preparation and must have clearly understood aims to which its findings are to be put. There exists a certain school of thought which maintains

THE KEEPING OF RECORDS

that records of attainment, ability, personality, details of home background, etc., which may be handed on from school to school, can be misleading, biased, malinformed and savour too much of 'snooping'. Supporters of this theory claim that the child should start with a clean sheet. Experience, however, has proved without a doubt that data appertaining to home environment, medical history, previous academic attainments, etc., are essential knowledge for the successful teaching of backward children. It is obvious that the teacher's primary aim must be to diagnose the causes of such backwardness before she can make any effective start in tackling the problems of treatment.

It is essential that when confronted with a new class of backward children in a secondary modern school, the teacher should make herself thoroughly conversant with the size of the problem. To do this, she must begin with a clear picture of the educational attainments of each child seen in relationship with his chronological and mental ages. If I.Q.s are submitted by the primary school from which the child has come, the type of test used should be known. For example, if a verbal group test had been used, the result for a child with a reading disability could be quite misleading. It is a sound check if the teacher gives her own choice of I.Q. test and compares findings with those of the previous school. Experience has proved that a non-verbal test given to a backward class can give a more accurate result. At this stage, it should be remembered that too rigid fixing of the I.Q. result should be avoided, as it is liable to fluctuations subject to the effect of many other factors such as emotional instability, personality trends, temperament, etc.

Attainment tests to assess mechanical and comprehension reading ages, spelling ages and arithmetic ages should all be given. I will not give a list of tests, as there are so many and new ones are constantly coming on to the market: for an up-to-date appraisal it is best to consult the National Foundation for Educational Research, 79 Wimpole Street, London, W.1. Having collected all this data, which should be done soon after the start of the school year, allowing of course for a day or two of adjustment to the strangeness of a new environment, the next step is the recording of individual results. This is done by building up a histogram or educational profile of each child (see diagram).

HISTOGRAM OF J.B. (C.A.11)

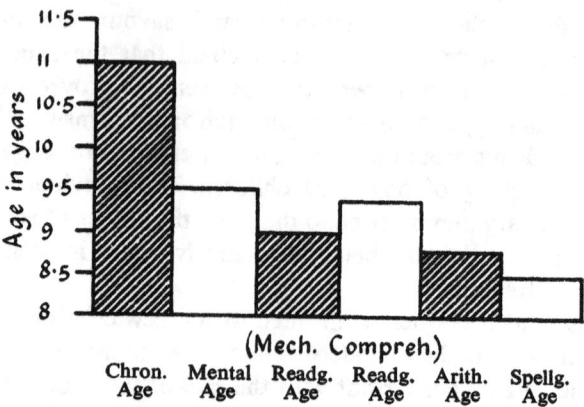

Thus at a glance, the amount of retardation in each of the tested subjects can be clearly read.

This histogram should be reviewed at the end of six months and after re-testing improvements should be superimposed on the original outlines.

From the data on the histograms, the educational quotient of each child can be calculated by using the formula:

$$E.Q. = \frac{E.A.}{C.A.} \times 100$$

Then to obtain the overall picture of the educational attainment of the class in relationship to the mental ages the one set of results should be superimposed on the other (see diagram below).

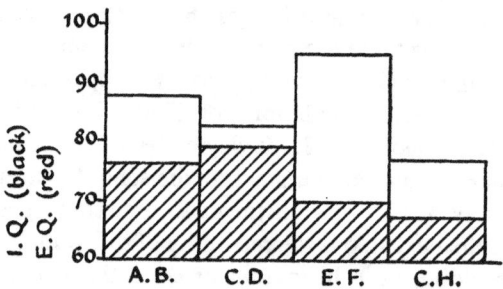

THE KEEPING OF RECORDS

THE KEEPING OF RECORDS

This type of graph shows the class range of attainment as well as giving the amount of individual ability and showing the children who are working up to or below their mental ability however limited it may be.

So far, I have discussed methods of recording measurable abilities when assessment can be made with reasonable accuracy by the aid of reliable tests. But to these recordings must be added other relevant data appertaining to the child's physical health, medical history, social background and behaviour attitudes towards contemporaries and to adults. Perhaps one could go so far as to say that this is really the core of the recording, for much backwardness can often be explained and treated in the light of findings which emerge from such information.

It is essential that a close and friendly co-operation is obtained with the previous schools, the medical department, the child guidance clinic, the home. It cannot be too much emphasized that the purpose of collecting all relevant information from these varied sources is to serve the best interests of the child. Tact and the ability to select and act upon significant facts are needed. At no time should the teacher press for information but should glean it as and when she can, using her powers of observation and training herself to make a mental note of useful facts. Neither is it wise to jump to conclusions, particularly at the start of a new school year when the child's reactions to his new environment may temporarily alter his attitudes. For example the change from the upper part of a primary school, to the lowest part of a secondary school is a difficult adjustment for some children. It often leads to instability, a difficulty in grasping new standards of behaviour and an inability to fit into a humbler place in the larger and older school community.

A great deal of often unsuspected material may be gathered from watching the child's behaviour during the break time or lunch hour when he is relaxed and as far as he knows quite unobserved by 'teacher'. From these observations one can often detect the bully, the easily led, the born leader, the lonely child, etc., traits which the climate of the classroom might tend to suppress.

These unobtrusive observations, which should be dated, throw useful light on personality and temperament which no form of testing can justly measure. For example the docile, solitary backward child, in the classroom, is rarely brought to notice so that usually there appears to be nothing one can comment upon. Yet often this seemingly negative personality has difficulties which may urgently need help. By observing him when is away from the classroom, one can see how far he seeks but is rejected by the group, how he passes his play break and what forms of activity he indulges in. A child's behaviour in relation to his contemporaries is very revealing. One should note the age of the child he tends to associate with, e.g. the boy who seeks the company of much older children even though they scarcely tolerate him and to whom he makes himself useful in devious ways, or the girl who is always found in the company of much younger children whom she likes to mother, and so on.

In addition, notes should be made of the reactions of the child towards the other members of the staff with whom he comes into contact. In a secondary modern school a special class, though mainly with one teacher, may go to other specialist teachers, e.g. for P.E. or music or practical subjects. The class teacher can glean interesting facets of the child's personality as revealed by the comments made by other members of the staff, e.g. in P.E. a child may reveal courage or lack of team co-operation, in art, originality, a sense of humour and so on. In a mixed school, the reactions of a boy to a woman teacher, or a girl to a man teacher can often throw a significant light on a child's emotional problems.

And so from these varied sources a composite picture can be fairly drawn up of the child's strengths and weaknesses which must be understood in conjunction with his more obvious difficulties in academic subjects. As with the educational progress, conclusions about personality and behaviour attitudes should be reviewed particularly at the approach of puberty.

All this data should be noted in a simplified booklet. Various forms of record books have been published but the one which has most practical value is the booklet compiled by the teacher herself, confined to essentials and with plenty of space for additional amendments at later periods.

I suggest a booklet made up of four sheets of paper (10 in. × 8 in.) stapled together and with plenty of blank space for additional notes.

THE KEEPING OF RECORDS

Page 1 would include details of name, address, date of birth, family history. Page 2 deals with physical data, defects of vision, hearing, speech, left handedness, etc. Page 3 covers all educational data with notes on special aptitudes, and page 4 has the observations on behaviour in and out of school, personality trends, attitudes to contemporaries and to adults, leisure time occupations, hobbies, special interests and dislikes, etc.

As with the histograms referred to above, necessary amendments should be made at six-monthly intervals or special entries as circumstances arise. Dating is essential for all entries. If possible a small photograph of the child could be included. The contents of the booklet are quite private and confidential but should be available for reference by the head teacher, or other teachers with whom the child comes into contact.

In conclusion, testing, assessing and the keeping of confidential reports are most valuable in special class teaching, but it must be remembered that they are ancillary to the main work of a teacher—which is teaching. Once this has been realized, they will not be dismissed as a waste of time, neither will their purpose be overemphasized. The true art lies not so much in compiling the records, but in knowing how to act on the information they reveal in such a way that the child will benefit.

MINNA SMITH

Chapter XIV

BACKWARD LADS IN APPROVED SCHOOLS

Remedial education has played a very important part in the treatment of the young offender within the last few years, and despite the problems which are 'peculiar' to such a school, satisfactory progress has been made in this field. It is often believed by teachers in ordinary schools that education in the widest sense plays a small part within Approved Schools, and that emphasis is laid on strict disciplinary treatment. This is by no means the case. The Approved School lends itself in many cases advantageously to the attack on backwardness, and on the other hand presents great difficulties which are not met in ordinary educational establishments.

It is not the function of this chapter to establish or analyse the causes of delinquency, which are manifold. However let it be said here that educational backwardness, which prevents pride in achievement, contributes in no small measure to the behaviour problems encountered in the Approved Schools. Before we can hope to commence the attack on backwardness, many factors must be considered, and the background of each individual must be studied carefully and sympathetically. Fortunately today, the teacher in the Approved School is supplied with a very comprehensive history of each lad, a history which includes psychological, psychiatric, social and family background, which taken together present an excellent picture on which one can prepare the attempts to help him.

Mention here must be made of the classifying School, which was given recognition by the Children's and Young Persons Act in 1952. Prior to his coming to an Approved School, the lad spends about a fortnight at this school, where he is examined before the treatment begins at the receiving school. A careful first-hand observation of the lad is made, and a diagnosis as comprehensive and accurate as possible, made of his condition. The Classifying School has intimate knowledge of the various kinds of treatment available, and of the Approved School staffs supplying the treatment. In brief, it is a case of placing the lad who is known, in the best place which is known. Examination and Assessment are the key words.

The greatest stress is placed on the lad's home background and family relationships. For this a four-point scale is used to denote how much case work the receiving school need do in trying to assist in this important aspect of the lad's rehabilitation. The Classifying School supplies us with a pen picture of the lad, his physical factors, medical history, previous history, home circumstances, family attitudes and religious background. On the educational side the lad's intelligence level is ascertained by means of cognitive testing. The Wechsler Bellevue Scale is used, and we are provided with the Varbel, Performance and Full I.Q. Burt's Graded Vocabulary Tests, and Schonell's Mechanical Arithmetic Tests are used for attainment purposes. A personality assessment is made by the psychiatrist, and general observations and recommendations are made. Thus it is that the teacher is given an excellent start in his attempt to help the lad.

Our school is an intermediate Approved School, with an intake age range of from 13½ to 15. We have seventy-five lads, most of whom are of inferior ability, as our school specializes in less able boys. The average retardation in reading is about four years, and that in number about five years. About a fifth of our lads have been to E.S.N. schools, or have been offered places therein. Two-thirds of our lads are described as being one of the following, 'insecure', 'immature', 'withdrawn' or 'aggressive'. In brief, emotional development has not taken place. At 15 the lad begins his vocational training. At the moment he has the choice of the following trades: painting and decorating; farming; gardening; maintenance; carpentry and bricklaying.

Our purpose is to give the lads a 'Happy purposeful life in a Christian Community, which develops understanding of, and respect for moral values'. It is our aim to repair the defects of character and personality and help to encourage new attitudes towards society. I feel that this can only be achieved by giving each lad a secure environment and above all by avoiding emotional isolation. The efforts of all our staff, male and female, are directed towards helping to understand the lad and his problems.

We can help the lad only by becoming emotionally necessary to him and by devoting as much time as possible to each individual. It is vital, I feel, that every member of staff knows each case history. Then everyone can help the lad to be understood. We all try to accept him as he is and thereby help him to understand himself and the circumstances of his being anti-social.

This we feel cannot be achieved without an individual treatment for each lad. The keeping of a cumulative record is vital. An important aspect of our efforts is the weekly case review meeting, at which each lad is in turn discussed. The staff are called upon to contribute any relevant information. Every lad needs a confidant in the school. He needs someone to whom he can go and unburden his troubles, someone who understands him and who is prepared to stand by him. Our ultimate aim is to try to transfer this relationship to someone outside the school.

I feel convinced that the classroom is a good starting-point in the rehabilitation of the lad. Here a good foundation can be laid for the promotion of emotional health and social adequacy. The newcomer to the class invariably looks sullen, apathetic or assertive. Prolonged failure and frustration have bewildered and depressed him. Very often he is unresponsive and dour. Obviously the first thing he needs is understanding and not teaching. Extra instruction has probably been given to him for years. He needs the conviction that he can do something and that he can learn. He must have self-respect and self-confidence restored. An upbuilding of confidence is the tonic he needs, and this can only be obtained through pride in achievement, which in the past has eluded him.

Thus it is that I try to create an emotional atmosphere of acceptance for every lad in the class. Each lad is accepted in spite of his lack of ability or his behaviour problems. I feel that a permissive atmosphere is essential, for every lad must feel that he belongs in the group. In addition he must feel that he is an important member of it. Competition is out from the start, the only competition which the lad has, is against himself, trying to improve his own standards. I firmly believe that learning should be thought of 'in terms of activity and experience'. Learning in concrete situations helps the lad to realize that what he is doing is real and related to everyday life. From the start the lad must be a willing partner, and should always be able to see the purpose of what he has to do. By working independently and in small groups, and in an atmosphere where self-respect and self-discipline is encouraged, the development of self-reliance, independence and personal initiative is fostered. It was that great pioneer of the Approved School, Mary Carpenter, who said, 'We must not try to break the will, but help it to govern itself wisely'.

As my groups are very small (the number of periods the lad being brought into class depending on his needs), I must try to be a student of every pupil in my group. Moreover, I must try to make myself emotionally necessary to each and every lad. A good personal relationship is essential. I firmly believe in the keeping of records in my class. The work of every lad in the basic subjects is carefully recorded after each session, a careful note being made of all the difficulties met with. As far as possible an individual plan is made for each lad, and recording is essential if any revision is needed in the programme. In addition notes are kept regarding the lad's personal appearance, his attitude to the schoolroom, his attitude towards his peers, his hobbies and recreational interests and, lastly, his general behaviour.

In number I feel that my primary task is to give each lad a good grounding in the four rules. Three main principles are borne in mind. Firstly, that the work carried out is within the lad's powers, making sure that he will meet with success. Care, however, is taken to make sure that the lad has to exert himself. The introduction of new work must be gradually done, with sufficient spacing of difficulties. Secondly, as already mentioned, every opportunity must be given for activity and experience. As our lads find abstract thinking difficult, and are helped by thinking in concrete situations, much of their efforts must take the form of practical activities. Thirdly, wherever necessary, our work in the basic skills is simplified.

Our tables as far as possible are introduced by practical work, the exercises being done in close accord with the needs and practices of daily life. By means of working hand-in-hand with the trade departments and basing our class work on the lad's daily work, we can try to make our arithmetic programme interesting and stimulating. As in many backward classes apparatus and games play an important part in trying to make the learning more interesting and real. Playing-cards are found useful for learning number combinations. Use is made of the spinning-wheel, dart-board, large dice made of wood, lotto, rings, jigsaw puzzles, used stamps and bus tickets, to help the lad in his number work.

Money is a real, everyday necessity, and will play an important aspect in the lad's later life. The lad must be able to deal with his money problems when he leaves us. He must be able to count and give change, assess and count his pay packet, deal with his stoppages, balance his budget and try to contend with hire-purchase transactions. Our sums take the form of the lad working out his bank balance, his pocket-money and deducting any fines. He works out his stamp bill for the month and finds out the cost of the daily newspapers and weekly magazines which we take. In addition we deal with the cost of such articles as clothing and personal requisites. Carefully graded pictorial cards are used in the form of simple problems. Such topics as, 'My Tobacconist', 'My School Leaving Outfit', 'My Sports Shop', 'My Book Shop, and 'My Tool Shop' are dealt with, and pictorially illustrated by means of making use of catalogues and advertisements.

I like to feel that reality is brought to our teaching of number. Our lads work in small groups and learn by really measuring, really weighing, really telling the time and really measuring liquids. Coloured, stoutly made foot and yard rulers are made by the lads, and tape measures are available around the classroom. The brightly coloured wall scale is used for individual and class measuring of height. Everything possible in the class is measured, and then we proceed to the dormitory, tennis-courts and football pitch. The preparation for the annual sports provide an excellent opportunity for dealing with measure. Such problems as making a right-angle, finding the circumference of the semi-circle, the concept of a furlong, quarter, half and mile can be brought home in concrete terms. Practice with scales is invaluable in the teaching of weight. Use is made of the school weighing-machine, on which the lad can weigh himself and his pals. We get our conception of smaller weights by making up our ounce, quarter, half and pound bags. We weigh made-up parcels, beans, sweets, nails and marbles. Each department lends itself handsomely to providing us with concrete examples in weight and in other aspects of number. Much of the produce and materials used give us the opportunity to work with and get the conception of heavier weights. The farm lad deals with and handles the hundredweight of meal, of corn and potatoes. The lad on the maintenance department is used to dealing with coal and coke in hundredweights and tons. Clocks made out of cardboard are made to help the lad unable to tell the time and much use is made of local bus and train time-tables. In capacity differently coloured half and pint, quart and gallon bottles are used in conjunction with a coloured wall chart. In addition petrol tins, paint drums and milk churns are made use of for practical work.

In English one of our main tasks is to help the lad to speak clearly and confidently. Speaking comes in all our lessons and can be taught unobtrusively at all times. However, there is I feel a danger of leaving speech to be learned incidentally. I spend about a quarter of an hour daily in reading a poem, having a debate, a class discussion or getting the lads to make a speech. The approach in our reading for the very backward and non-readers is based on individual work, the lad's interest being the main consideration. In the main the lad makes up his own reading book or magazine. I then write down what the lad wants to say underneath and then he copies his own words. Some lads take an instant liking to our books for 'backward readers'. This interest in a certain book can start the lad off. Whatever the approach, initial success is vital for the lad, and being able to learn or memorize the first few lines can spur him on to further effort. Great variety of simple matter is provided, the lad himself writing wall posters, a diary, a wall newspaper and accounts of visits. All are used in conjunction with cut-out pictures, drawings and paintings. The lad is encouraged to read the newspaper headlines, labels and advertisements. A home-made book containing the letters of the alphabet, with each letter pictorially illustrated, is used by each lad. He enters any difficult word in the appropriate page. This gives him an insight into the method of using a dictionary which is so important. The increasing of the lad's vocabulary is essential, and this can only be brought about effectively by getting to know about things. Stories are read to the lad, he makes models, takes part in nature walks and visits, all are made use of to enlarge his imaginative understanding of the world around him. In the main the sentence method is mostly used. However, as some method of word analysis must be used, the phonic and look and say approach play their part. Word games, puzzles, jokes from match-boxes, self-corrective cards, flash cards and sentences are used. In addition pictorially illustrated phonic lists, and word and picture matching exercises are also used in conjunction with the topic or work in hand. The method of attack in order to give the lad the greatest help is based upon careful study of his errors.

Our better readers work individually or in small groups, having a wide choice of books from which to read. The dominant factors in our choice of reading material are interest appeal, illustration, print, vocabulary control and age suitability. Our readers in the main consist of thriller stories, detective stories and hero adventure books. Books which can be used for reference are also very important. The classic books such as *Gulliver's Travels*, *Black Beauty* and *Treasure Island* have a great appeal to our lads. They are in pictorial form with the captions underneath, or in the form of a stamp which has to be stuck on the appropriate page. In addition much use is made of the daily paper, the better type of comic and the weekly magazines to interest our lads in their reading. The school and public library also help in our goal to enable our lads to read for pleasure, seek out facts and to comprehend. The short class play put on for the benefit of other classes, the play which the class makes up itself and the puppet theatre, all help in the teaching of English. Great pride is taken in the latter, as the theatre was made entirely by the boys. They chose the wood from the carpentry department, made the plan and the design. They also made the scenery, did the decorating and made the puppets. 'We made it', was the cry, and the staff were pleased to encourage and guide.

I like to feel that our written work comes naturally from our other work, from interest and need. Letter-writing plays an important part in the lad's life. The all-important letter home, to friends, to former teachers and probation officers, form an integral part of his everyday needs. I also place great stress on the ability of the lad to fill in a form. It is useful for him to be able to fill in the telegraph form, the money order form, to be able to make an application for a driving licence, and for a driving-test. With the co-operation of the local postmaster we have a fine array of forms, most of which are used in our daily lives. In addition our written work tells about personal experiences, describes hobbies, involves the keeping of a diary and the writing of short stories. Personal and group assignments are done on such topics as, 'What I found out'. The school magazine plays an important part in our written work. Every lad is given a part to play, however small, in its production. The contribution of information, fact finding, research, editing and selling aspects are all covered by the boys.

Collaboration is close between the instructors and teachers in trying to make our work interesting, stimulating and as real as possible for each lad. By this means the lad can bring his real problems encountered in concrete situations, and deal with them in class. The farm lad can base his number work on finding out the cost of feeding-stuffs, the cost of seeds, and the prices of eggs and milk. The lad on bricklaying can work out the sums involved in the cost of tools, the cost of bricks, sand and cement. He can learn to estimate the cost of simple jobs, and make simple plans of the work in hand. Each lad can record his daily tasks, seek out information about his department, and learn much about that which interests him, and is important to him.

Project work plays an important part in the education of our backward lads. The worth-while project, in an informal, friendly atmosphere can help in our attempt to adjust the lad to a healthy social group. The lad is encouraged to play his part in the group, to give as well as receive from it. An interesting project attempted by our lads was the erection and stocking of our pets' corner. About twelve lads got together and rebuilt an old shed. By devious methods (known only to approved school lads) they obtained the wood, borrowed the tools and made use of old bricks. The carpenters among them repaired the roof and made the door, as well as the hutches. The bricklayers repaired the walls and cemented the fish pond. The garden lads cleared the surrounding plot, got the turf, and planted the flowers. The painters put in the windows, decorated the shed and painted the signs needed. Next came the stocking of the pets' corner and this was done by a pooling of resources. Prices were compared, quotations sent for, and information regarding feeding habits and general care of the pets was hastily sought from the reference books. In addition the lads soon realized the necessity for writing letters, keeping records and accounts. The animals bought and begged from kind friends included tame mice, rats, rabbits, guinea-pigs and pigeons. As the young appeared they were sold to the lads and staff. The proceeds were used to replenish the stock and pay for feeding-stuff. The staff were seldom bothered except for technical advice. I have seen far better pets' corners made and equipped by grown ups, but none which aroused such interest and real enthusiasm. The lads had a continuous activity in which they were very interested for its own sake; real problems occurred, which demanded, and gave stimulus to, much thought, their ideas had to be tested and proved, and they had to work as a team.

Another project was carried out by three football enthusiasts. They decided to follow the fortunes of their favourite teams in the first division of the football league. They firstly made their map of England and plotted on it twenty-two teams. The large map was placed on the wall and by means of coloured wool the towns involved were marked. Space was provided for the industries, populations and interesting data of each town to be placed on the map. A league table was then made of stout cardboard on which the league placings could be changed each week. Reference books on football were then used to find out interesting information about the teams, their history, the names of the grounds, the teams' colours, etc. The newspaper accounts of the matches were pasted on cards and questions on number and comprehension asked. The number of goals scored, the number of spectators, the F.A. Cup receipts, and the distances travelled by the teams, all helped in the working out of an interesting number programme. The lads found out whilst computing their league table that a knowledge of averages, decimals and percentages was desirable. The question of population variations and differing industries was discussed. An Automobile Association book was very useful in working out travelling routes, working out distances and finding out the number of inhabitants.

A third interesting and successful project was undertaken by the farm lads. Here, about a dozen lads split themselves into groups of three and covered the following aspects regarding our farm. The first group dealt with the nature of the land; the kind of soil and the layout of the fields. They also found out the names and acreages of the fields and the layout of the buildings and their uses. The second group dealt with the work done on the farm; the crops grown and the yields. They also found out the breeds and numbers of livestock; the purchase of seeds, feeding-stuff and fertilizers and the amount of farming equipment we have. The last group obtained information regarding farming in other parts of the country, the dairy farm in Devon, and the fruit farm in Kent.

Nature study plays an important part in our school and recreational studies. Living in the country, we have ample opportunity to study actual objects and living specimens. We can study them first-hand in their natural setting. Here, again, we try to link our efforts with the daily experiences of the lads. The hobby plots help to give the lad a good insight into the things that grow in the ground. The various ways of producing plants and flowers are practised. By means of simple experiments the lad can see how the bulb differs from the corm. The method of producing, by breaking away some of the rhizomes can be experimented with, as also producing from runners, tubers and by layering. The lad learns about the various kinds of produce, those for food and those for ornament. He learns when and how plants should be planted, the best treatment for success and the times of the year when they are fit for eating. With the use of wall charts, the identification of all common trees is studied. Specimens are collected in spring, summer and autumn. A questionnaire is prepared asking questions regarding the shape, bark, lenticles, buds, foliage, leaves and flowers of the trees. The lads work in pairs, each pair dealing with a specific tree. The information is kept in a nature diary and the specimens exhibited on our nature corner table. The lads estimate the height of the tree and find out its circumference about four feet from the ground. They make bark rubbings and make plaster cast moulds of the leaves. The tree outline is drawn in summer and winter and drawings are made of the opening buds, leaves, fruit and flowers. Common flowers are collected, preserved and tabulated. The animals and their habits in our pets' corner are studied. We make special note and records of their breeding, hygiene and feeding habits. An interesting study carried out is the examining of a small area of ground. Simple experiments are carried out to find out the type of soil, whether it will hold water and to see if it may turn out to be heavy. The types of plants and weeds growing in it are studied, as are the insects and small creatures. The lads look after the aquarium, collecting the specimens, feeding them and studying their habits.

It is hoped that through our efforts the lad will learn to observe carefully. We attempt to help him to learn to appreciate nature and to acquire a humane attitude towards living things. Our final goal is to help the lad to follow a worth while leisure pursuit. It is hoped that the habit of neatness and orderliness will develop from the arranging of the nature specimens in the nature corner. Through looking after the animals and plants we hope that the habit of accepting responsibility will develop.

Another important aspect in our trying to help the backward lad is through our efforts in trying to give him success and pleasure in craft work. Here, again, we try not to divorce it from the everyday needs of the lad. In craft we do simple bookbinding (the folders and book covers being used to cover the diaries, note books and personal folders). The lads make up their own designs by the use of lino prints, potato prints, marbling and stencilling. Papier-mâché is used in conjunction with models and projects. In addition we do light woodwork, leather work, make lamp shades, cardboard modelling and basket-work. We are lucky we can make and design our own models from scratch. The wood is bought in large sizes, the lads cut and shape it themselves. Again a co-operative system is used. Some of the group prepare the bases, others make the designs and others do the actual basket-making. We make plant pots for our own plants, table mats for the dining-room and a wide variety of useful articles. We try to make our hobby self-supporting by selling the products.

An important aspect of our work in an intermediate Approved School is the preparation of the lad for a new and independent life. That is, his going to work. For every schoolboy this major change presents many difficulties. We may have prepared the lad as best we can educationally and vocationally. However, there are other vital aspects in our helping to prepare him to face the outside world. We must help him to prepare emotionally, socially and personally to face this revolution. If the right emotional and social climate has been established in the classroom, there is every chance of its following through to the lad's department.

In choosing a department for the lad, these factors are given the main consideration; the lad's own choice; his parents' wishes; his aptitudes and the type of employment he is most likely to obtain in his home town. Under a fully qualified instructor and within a group of not more than twelve, the lad starts an important phase in his life. For many of our lads the vocational training will be but a part of our overall plan for him. These lads will, at the most, be successful in the unskilled and semi-skilled types of job. For these lads it is vital that by good habit formation we inculcate the great need for punctuality on the job. Stress is also laid on the great need for neat appearance and clean habits. A sense of responsibility is necessary, the concept of a good day's work and above all, the vital attribute of getting on with their fellows. This question of 'human relationships' is more important than ever and plays a very great part in the individual's work and leisure.

As in the classroom the lad can derive the important feeling of achievement and belonging in his department. He needs praise for being on time, for being clean and tidy and for working well within the group. He should be encouraged for applying himself conscientiously to his job. Any help that can be given to enable the lad to have a feeling of achievement and security augurs well for his general rehabilitation. From the start the lad is working as a member of a team. As a result he is able to see and learn the value of teamwork and interdependence. The vocational training department plays an important part in the boy's life, in as much as he can see the result of his labours. The building lads can look with pride at the completion of the new flats, the new farm buildings and the new stores. They also learn to value and appreciate the work of their peers in other departments. They realize that without the aid of the carpenters, the painters and the plumbers the job could not have been finished. The great worth of co-operation and a concerted team effort is brought home to them and they learn to appreciate and respect the efforts of others.

Another important job in our efforts to help our lads is to guide them into worth-while use of leisure time activities. Recreation and hobbies play an important part in our efforts to combat boredom and apathy among the lads. Our difficulty is that in the main, it is the same lads who wish to participate in almost every hobby and form of recreation. The tragic case is where the lad has had nothing but failure and ridicule in class and out of doors. The aggressive and bullying type is seldom the lad who is competent at any activity. He needs sympathy and guidance to direct him towards self-respect and personal pride through achievement. The Oxley Tests in athletics are a wonderful help for the erstwhile failure. Very wisely competition against others does not take place. The lad has to achieve a certain moderate standard in a limited number of events. With encouragement and individual attention he can usually reach the level of attainment needed. Success brings the reward of a certificate. This initial success often gives him the confidence to strive for more ambitious efforts.

In our physical education we encourage the lad who seems unsure of himself. The only standards set are personal ones. The boy who is teased for not being able to throw a ball and the lad who is laughed at in the gymnasium for his mannerisms and showing of fear, is catered for. He is encouraged in a group where effort and progress can be praised by one and all. He belongs to a group where one and all can understand the difficulties of the other. On the football field and running track too, much progress can be made by a sympathetic and understanding attitude towards the slower and more awkward brethren. This, coupled with careful segregation regarding age and ability, is the key to helping to give the lad a feeling of taking part in a worth while and healthy recreation.

As far as possible team games are encouraged, where the lad can contribute his bit towards a united effort. Games are encouraged which give scope for plenty of activity and an emotional outlet. The boys play other schools at football and cricket. We give physical education displays and our cross-country team competes against other teams, as does the boxing team. In this way our lads are able to share happy social experiences with the community at large. We also like to think that our lads value the honour of being a member of a team, representing the school and upholding its good name. As much stress as possible is placed on leisure activities which enable the boys to mix freely with the people of the district. Our Young Farmers Club invite different speakers every week and themselves visit other such bodies. These speakers come from all walks of life and speak on such topics as, 'Keeping Pigeons', 'Local Folk Lore', 'Animal Health' and 'Judging Cattle'. The school mixed youth club invites local boys and girls. They have their own committee and organize their own programme. The girls have taken part in the annual pantomime and plays. The local old age pensioners are invited to our productions and they reciprocate by inviting our lads to a social evening. The cadet force have outside instructors and the lads attend outside parades and courses. This force is run on the lines of a youth club, with hobbies, recreation and practical schemes forming its basis. With the help of a friend in the district, our canoe club have built four canoes. Much pleasure is gained from this healthy activity on the local canal. Again, contact with the community is made by our lads attending the village craft club. Our aim is to hope that they will put into practice the common courtesies and good behaviour which we have tried to teach them. The lads also play a part in the village life by helping in the church choir.

Great efforts are made to help the town lad to appreciate the value of the countryside by the work of the wayfarers group. Here, an attempt is made to give the lad an insight to a happy recreational pursuit. Much pleasure can be obtained from learning to appreciate the simple wonders of nature and to learn something of the life of his counterpart living in the country. The wayfarers set off weekly to visit local beauty spots and places of historical interest. Here, again, all can take an active and worth-while part. The more able lad can plot the route on the map and take charge of the compass. Other lads can take charge of the food, whilst others prepare the fires for the brew. The lad who has a bent for drawing can draw and sketch things of interest on the trip. By following a healthy worth-while pastime, it is hoped that the lad will be helped in his physical well-being. Much pleasure can also be gained from belonging to a healthy social group. We hope that by experience the lad will learn the code of the countryside. This can be done by carrying out common courtesies such as fastening all gates, not leaving litter about, not walking over crops and respecting the property of others.

Thus it is that we like to feel that the vital social training, although not found on the time-table, is going on all day and every day. This is done in class, in department, on the playing-field and in our clubs. By example and training the whole staff try to help the boy to form habits and attitudes which will continue to operate as his life goes on. Great stress is placed in the training of health habits, which bring physical comfort and hygienic living. There are many opportunities for self-dependence and reliability – the making of beds, cleaning the dormitory and helping in the daily chores. Social participation is taking place all day, in the dormitory, in the dining-hall, in class and at work. The lads are making adjustments by working together in small and larger groups. They are sharing their tasks, taking turns and co-operating with their peers.

The test of our training comes when the lad enters the hostel. This generally takes place about two months before his leaving the school. Here, he has much more personal freedom. He has the opportunity to prove whether or not he seems fit to take his place and play his part in the community. We have to try to make sure that he is capable of adjusting himself personally, occupationally and socially to the outside world. He is left unsupervised and is trusted. He gets much more leave than the other boys and consequently more temptations beset him.

During this period a concentrated effort is made by the headmaster, the Youth Employment Officer and the boy's welfare agent to find a suitable job for the lad. Each lad is dealt with individually. His job is found in relation to his vocational training, his mental and physical state, school attainment, personality and interest. With careful and well-studied guidance these backward and erstwhile misfits can take their place in society. What is more, they can often play their part as important and productive members of society. The main consideration is that the lad finds security and happiness in his job. We hope to have contributed to this by helping him to have become a reliable, steady and responsible worker. The blind alley job has no place in the future of our lads. By means of placing a round peg in a round hole, the reward is often personal, social and occupational adequacy.

In many cases the school has to try to make up for the lack of moral training in the upbringing of our lads. Here, a great onus is placed on the staff. It is essential that we all try to act as models in trying to carry out the Christian ideals. By these I mean the real practising of tolerance, kindness, forgiveness, cheerfulness and good manners, amongst ourselves and with every lad. The religious instruction in class, the daily corporate act of worship and the Sunday services all play their part. It is our constant endeavour to develop trustworthiness and honesty by example, in an effort to influence the conduct of the boy.

I like to think that our discipline is based on self-discipline and that our lads realize that they can be happy and enjoy freedom within certain bounds. The lads are helped to understand that the only rules employed are for the good of the community. We try to help them to realize that conformity to them is essential in a well run social group. Stress is placed more on praise for effort, rather than on what is achieved.

In conclusion I can but hope that our programme helps our backward lads in the promotion of their physical and mental health, that it gives them a good grounding in the tool subjects and that it helps towards better group and communal living. It is also hoped that it helps to provide for the better use of leisure time and also the furtherance of desirable working habits and attitudes.

RALPH S. TAYLOR

Chapter XV

TEACHING BACKWARD ADULTS

In classes for adult illiterates which I have taken I have met the following types and causes:

Some have had no previous schooling, for example, gypsies, fair and small-circus folk who always seem to have been on the move. They settle down to a town life and find that they are looked down upon, because of their illiteracy, by town people.

A pupil sometimes comes from the heart of the country to take a job in a town. Perhaps his job necessitates reading or a better reading ability, more often it is because his illiteracy draws more attention in a town than in a country community.

There are some who are courting literate girls and who are afraid that they will find out about their illiteracy. Others have married literate wives or have been shamed by their children and have the courage to do something about it. Sometimes a man has to work away from home and needs to correspond with his family.

Some men have failed to learn through constant illness during childhood or suffered from physical defects, untreated speech defects, defects of sight and hearing; and with individual care and understanding can overcome the effects of these even now. Their failure may lie in the fact that they were cruelly scorned by other children in their childhood. Their teachers, too, probably overworked and perhaps unsympathetic, played their part by shining a light on the child's infirmity instead of helping him.

The cause in some cases is due to bad, inconsistent teaching. Some pupils were just lazy in childhood and allowed to get away with it. I am sure that Army discipline and the fact that they have to do what they are told in an 'Army School of Preliminary Education' helps a great deal in achieving success there.

Another reason may be the pupil's insecurity during childhood caused, perhaps, by the mother putting her work before the care of her child. It is good that a child helps in a house but some are overworked and do the household cleaning and shopping before and after school, often coming to school late and tired.

Some have been in trouble with the police and have spent much time truanting and in Remand Homes, and out of a normal school routine.

There are those now in mental deficiency hospitals who have passed through special E.S.N. schools and secondary modern schools and still cannot read. Some will never learn to read, others will do so now, often through better emotional and social conditions. Young men in institutions, psychopathic cases and genuine feeble-minded, attend because they are sent, or like coming, or want to get out and hold a job.

There are men in institutions and prisons who attend because they are bored and have nothing better to do with their time. Some come for the laughs if they can get away with it and with no intention or desire to do any work.

Workers from Jamaica, West Africa, Hungary and many other nationalities who can barely make themselves understood when they arrive in this country are keen, and eager to take advantage of classes for adult illiterates.

Whatever the reason for their attendance the wide range of pupils makes individual work essential. The fewer pupils you have to take the more individual time for each pupil. Rarely have I in civilian life taken a class of less than twelve, often of twenty. Army classes for illiterates do not, in my experience, exceed ten.

There is no simple rule for the teaching of adult illiterates. I have simply tried to find individual and general interests, and to use their present knowledge as a foundation for work on their illiteracy, not in a haphazard way but trying all the while to adopt a systematic, sensible approach where progress can be seen and appreciated by pupils and acquaintances. The teacher will need to be sympathetic and understanding, sincere and firm. He must be resilient and persevering and be prepared to try many different approaches. It is necessary to sum up your pupil, and to use technique and matter appropriate to his capabilities and needs. I have used the following methods and found them successful.

You can teach a young child with an introductory reader but there is nothing less interesting to a young adult or a bigger blow to his pride than to be presented with 'Here We Go', 'Happy Venture Introductory', etc. Some low grade patients in mental hospitals will read these quite happily but they are exceptions. An infant reader is not inspiring to an adult illiterate, but you can with success use the vocabulary list found, for example at the end of 'Here We Go' in an adult way.

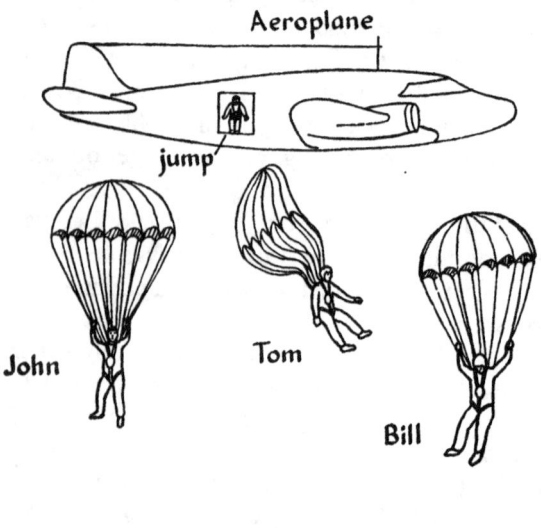

(1) Bill is a paratrooper.
(2) Bill can go up in the aeroplane.
(3) Bill can jump from my aeroplane.
(4) Bill can come down by parachute.
(5) Bill has two friends.
(6) One is John, one is Tom.
(7) John can jump from the aeroplane.
(8) Tom can jump from the aeroplane.
(9) The three friends can jump from the aeroplane.

TEACHING BACKWARD ADULTS

I have used in these few simple sentences and picture thirteen words from the twenty-seven used in 'Here We Go'. I would teach them in the following way:

(1) Discuss the picture, the aeroplane, paratroops, parachute, how it opens, what it is made of, how it packs, how it is fastened to the body, the quick release mechanism, how the parachute is controlled by the descending parachutist, etc.
(2) Draw the picture and write the words.
(3) (i) Read the first sentence.
   Draw a paratrooper.
   Copy the first sentence beneath the picture.
   (ii) Read the second sentence.
   Draw an aeroplane, etc. (and similarly with the others).

The above instructions can be given orally or written in card form.

Sometimes reading and copying the sentences will be sufficient after the oral work, sometimes more work will be needed before the words are known. There is no reason why two or three sentences only should be used, according to the ability of the pupil. The same applies to the number of new words introduced and the difficulty of the questions asked.

When the pupil knows the words contained in the book he will not, in my experience, show resentment when asked to read 'Here We Go' from the text, preferably to someone who cannot read at all.

He will perhaps ask to take it home to read to a child.

A simple mechanical reading test will tell you at which book to start a pupil. I always start with an easier book when possible to give confidence. Let us, therefore, use these words in an interesting and adult way, retaining the vocabulary control, repetition of new words used, etc., which a good series contains.

I have found a list of essential words very useful (see, for instance, the list given by Gagg and Gagg on p. 59 of *Teaching Children to Read*). It is easy to duplicate and I simply cross out the words known by a pupil and carry on from there, teaching those not known, in the way previously described.

I have found sentence cards using essential words useful for copying and illustrating,

> e.g. I like my dinner.
> I like my tea.
> I like my supper.
> .... etc.
> Here is a bicycle.
> .... a horse.
> .... an aeroplane, etc.

The easiest way to get pupils of this kind to use new words and to write them is by cultivating their interests, things that they have confidence in and sometimes know more about than you do. The following are interests I have encountered and developed:

The fairground boxer which spread from beginnings like:

> Come and see John the boxer.
> I can see one boxer.
> two boxers.
> three boxers, etc., to

Weights, fly, bantam, feather, etc., with list of appropriate weights: 8 stone, 8 stone 6 pounds, 9 stone respectively. The difference between them, etc.
Training exercises, general advice to boxers, types of punch, etc.
Number work – weights – stones and pounds.
> gloves – ounces.
> ring – 12–16 ft. square
> posts – 4–5 ft., etc.

Butchery. Names of joints, weights, price per pound, etc.
Electrical apparatus—mending an electric fuse, fire, etc., diagrams, names of parts, simple repairing instructions.
Getting married and all that it entails: the wedding speech, duties of best man, 'thank you' letter for presents, etc. Preparing for the reception.
Preparing for car-driving, moped test, etc. Reading and answering

questions on the Highway Code. Two copies of code made into matching cards were excellent exercises for interested persons. General preparation for practical and oral parts of the test.

Making toys for nephews and nieces, etc. I have a series of duplicated cards giving instructions and plans for making simple models —windmill, bus, etc. One is quickly constructed and a story is then written about it to be read to the child. I have found this to be a very popular exercise.

Making gardening pamphlets containing information including when to sow seeds, depth, distance apart, etc.

Woodwork joints and useful articles to be made in the home with simple instructions on how to make them.

The prime interest of some is to get in touch with their family. I have known cases who have corresponded with their families after lapses of as many as five years, starting as an educational exercise and ending happily with a successful reunion.

The illiterate soldier is taught by English Parade books 1 and 2, both dealing simply with the everyday life of a soldier in the British Army.

Some are interested in helping others and many pupils learn a great deal by preparing work for teaching others who know less than themselves. They take great pride in the improvement made by their pupil and will write for brochures and material for his further teaching.

The coal-miner is a favourite interest with many young adult illiterates. The dogs, the horses, the pools – everyone is interested in something. At a military prison where I once worked the men were not allowed out at all, some for years, and interests were hard to find. Scraping the barrel I read the history of the prison and we compared prison life at present to what it was like in the days when prisons were built. We visited the old punishment cells and the remains of the old treadmill, and created sufficient interest to do some successful work. With pupils following a normal everyday outside existence interests can readily be found, but for those in prisons and institutions who are not allowed out at all, it is much more difficult and interests must be brought in to them, e.g. an old sword, or gun, local Roman remains, a box with a secret drawer, my new moped bicycle taken into the classroom, map work (very successful) letters for brochures to far off romantic countries to dream about, or using the present-day news appropriate to the pupils concerned. A class notice-board helps a great deal, and newspaper cuttings are always encouraged. Ours is just a painted flat cardboard box, both large and serviceable.

The teacher of adult illiterates need not be an expert at anything but should be resilient and prepared to 'Have a go'. After all there is nothing to lose and much to gain, both educationally and socially.

Sometimes one finds an interest applicable to a class as a whole, e.g. a current TV film or wireless programme. The success of a discussion held on these depends on the teacher conducting it. Everyone has something to say if you ask a pertinent question within his scope of thought and speech. I have found the use of a microphone in another room very useful in overcoming shyness and lack of confidence. I would never try to force anyone to participate in this way. A pupil with a speech defect, magnified over a loud-speaker and laughed at upon his return to a group could be seriously hurt.

A great help, particularly in teaching adult foreigners speaking little English, is the medium of puppetry. Marionettes are much more successful than glove puppets at this age. The writing of the play involves valuable practical English presented in an interesting way. Tape recordings are invaluable, and after every 'play-back' the characters are changed. Speech is greatly improved, difficulties in pronunciation are overcome. During the production of the play two adults work closely together, one manipulating the puppet and the other speaking the dialogue into a microphone. This method is extremely useful in a class of mixed abilities. The better speaker is responsible for the dialogue, the manipulator working with him learns pronunciation and increases his vocabulary until he in turn becomes the voice for one less adept to copy.

A useful method I have used often to introduce a class interest in a piece of news, is the mixed word board which is composed of any number of boards hooked on to a large piece of soft board and used in the following way:

TEACHING BACKWARD ADULTS

Illustration 1

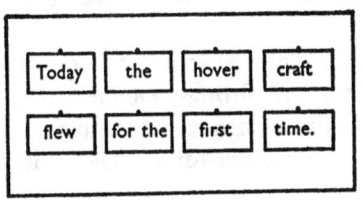

(1) Read, talked about, read again.
(2) Various pupils read.
(3) More advanced pupils can spell the words with boards turned over, in this way: Look at the word. Spell it with board turned. Then turn board to correct side. Was it right?

Illustration 2

(1) Jumble the board.
(2) Reassemble words in correct order (very popular).
(3) Unhook the words and give to various pupils who say or spell word, according to ability, before returning to correct hook on board.

These sentences can be copied in joined script, another copy can be made in any other style of writing, e.g. copperplate, Marion Richardson, Italic. The pupils then commence writing their own sentences.

I encourage the use of word cards and dictionaries from the beginning. The word card is a 12 in. ×8 in. piece of cardboard marked in rectangles 2 in. × ¾ in. with a picture sometimes of the appropriate interest in the top left-hand corner.

(1) Any word required by the pupil is written on the card by the teacher.
(2) If there is an old typewriter available the pupil types the word on a long communal sheet of paper.
(3) He then writes it in his sentence.

Everyone writes something in this way. Those who find it easier can write more sentences in the free writing part of the lesson.

In the same way I use Margaret McKinder's list of phonetic and phonogram words. Philip and Tacey's wall charts of digraph words are very useful to me.

Draw a picture of the words, write the word, write a sentence about or containing the word.

Use sets of boxes containing objects of interest to adults: screws, nuts and bolts, parts of electric plugs and fittings, engine parts, wireless parts, car shafts, pistons, etc., with names securely attached. This helps with vocabulary, and gives a motive for sentence construction.

Use, too, boxes containing jigsaw puzzle cards based on traffic signs, woodwork tools, engine parts, gardening tools, home structure, parts of body, etc., in this way:

(1) Fit the word to the picture.
(2) Draw a picture, write the word.
(3) Write a sentence using the word or combination of words.
(4) Ask the teacher for any word not known.
(5) He will write them as before on the word card.
(6) The pupil then follows same procedure as previously described.

There are some excellent colour illustrations found on many front covers of magazines which cater for a wide range of age and taste. I stick thin strips of white Sellotape on to the pictures, writing on them the appropriate key words. Sentences can then be constructed using these as before. I find these cards useful, too, for pupils to talk about over the microphone.

When the pupil's reading age improves set simple questions based on these pictures and their interests, wireless programmes, films, newspaper stories, etc. For example, read a piece on the life of

Stanley Matthews, answer the questions written below. Similarly use extracts from Dickens and other stories.

Comprehension work can of course be set at different levels.

    e.g. (1) Story read orally by teacher.
        (2) Discussed.
        (3) Oral questions and answers.

    or (1) Story read orally by teacher.
        (2) Discussed.
        (3) Written questions and answers.

Graded crossword puzzles starting with three-letter words are always popular. I duplicate individual question and answer sheets quickly and easily. It is a popular class activity if taken occasionally.

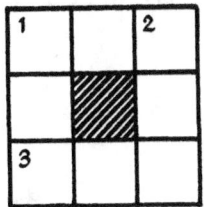

    e.g. *Across*
        1. A powerful engine.
        3. Reach for your..........

    Down.
        1. An Irish dance.
        2. Twenty hundredweights

When teaching writing I have found some who can write over my writing, some who can use cut out templates with success, others who can write below my writing, others who can copy from the blackboard and some who can write in a simple way from dictation.

I always need new cards written for labels and games and many do useful work using cut out templates, at the same time practising their writing, reading and spelling.

I encourage letter writing as soon as possible. At whatever stage of writing the pupil is, letter writing for brochures and catalogues, related to their interests is very popular. A reply to a letter sent is a tremendous boost to someone who is perhaps, receiving a letter for the first time in his life. A good exercise in writing for more advanced pupils is for them to make materials for those who need it; (picture word dictionaries, reading games, scrap-books, etc.).

In my experience many adult illiterates think that the answer to learning to read is a knowledge of phonic sounds. Invariably those taught at all were taught strictly phonically and even though they failed to read by it they still think that it is how they should be taught. This is something you can teach in an adult way using a completely new approach – what I call the morse method. Chanting a for apple, b for bat, c for cat does not get one very far with the type of adult I have had to deal with, but if you install a simple morse tapper powered by a 4·5 volt battery you can teach adults phonics in an adult way.

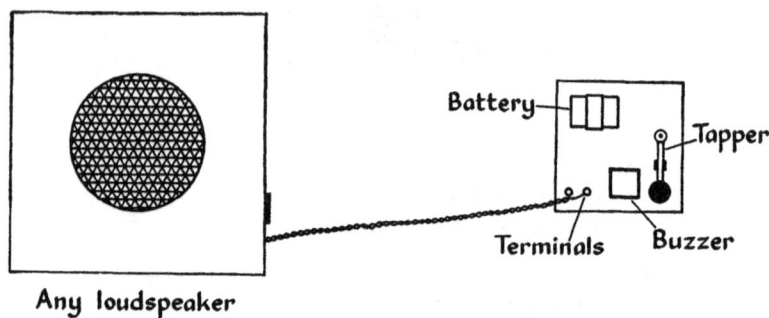

Any loudspeaker

An introduction to this could run thus: Wireless operators find it easier to call letters by their phonic names, a, b, c, etc., giving phonic sounds:

```
a will be sent as  . _
b                  _ . . .
c                  _ . _ .
d                  _ . .
e                  .
```

TEACHING BACKWARD ADULTS

(1) Put down as dots and dashes what I will send now .. _
(2) Look at the blackboard and find out what these dots and dashes represent: .— a. Give the sound of the letter.
(3) After practice at using these five letters join three letters together and send out: _... /.. _/_ ..
(4) Change to: _.../_./_..
           b a d

Sound the word. b - a - d
What does it say? bad.

Many words can be made with just these few letters, enough to give the class an idea of what it is all about and sufficient to create interest and confidence, e.g. (bad, dab, cab, bed, deb, cad) (bead, bade, dead), etc., at a later stage.

New letters can then be introduced.

When the morse alphabet has been completely introduced it can be used to change words in the first reading lists already mentioned into morse and the morse into words, e.g. what does this code say?

.___/___/..../_.
J   o   h   n, etc.

Other class uses can be recapitulation of:

(1) Words used for sentence writing.
(2) Daily spelling words.
(3) Words found difficult to read.
(4) Used in conjunction with picture and word work.

Draw a simple picture, e.g. boat sailing on the sea, with clouds in the sky. Write the morse equivalent on to the various parts of the picture. 1. Change the morse into words.
    2. Change these words into morse.

       e.g. 1. _.../..../___/.../...
               c   l   o   u   d   s
          2. s k   y
             .../_._/_.__

Again use the list of essential words now in the following way:

MORSE CODE

A	._	J	.___	S	...
B	_...	K	_._	T	_
C	_._.	L	._..	U	.._
D	_..	M	__	V	..._
E	.	N	_.	W	.__
F	.._.	O	___	X	_.._
G	__.	P	.__.	Y	_.__
H	....	Q	__._	Z	__..
I	..	R	._.		

Find out what these words say and change them into MORSE, e.g.

a	was
A	W A S
and	all
A N D	A L L

Substituting a pair of earphones for the loudspeaker you have an excellent individual activity, one pupil composing the message and sending to the other who is taking it down. It is useful for pupils of roughly the same ability or otherwise.

Finally, the bead, bade, dead words encountered form a good introduction by drawing attention to digraphs.

The best individual method I have tried with adult illiterates is the Fernald-Keller remedial method. Briefly: The pupil chooses what he wants to write about. Any word not known by him will be written down by me on a card in cursive writing. Use a card size 10 in. × 4 in. to begin with. This seems expensive, but I have always found waste card suitable. He will finger trace the card before attempting to write the word on scrap paper from memory. When he is able to write it successfully he can write it in his story, again without copying. He can, if he wishes, draw a picture illustrating his story. An indexed filing system will be kept by the pupil for future recapitulation and reference; (these are also useful as tests). I agree with Mrs Stopa (see Chapter IV) that the method is most valuable with individuals, but I have also used it with a group in this way:

(1) Individual pupils choose topic and start writing story.

TEACHING BACKWARD ADULTS

(2) If they want a word they come to the teacher who writes it on a card.
(3) They finger trace the card, leave it on his desk and return to theirs where they attempt to write it from memory on their sheet of scrap paper.
(4) They show it to the teacher and if successful write it in their story.
(5) When this is done they return to teacher for card and keep it in indexed filing system.

Stories written by other pupils form more suitable libraries for adult illiterates than printed books in the early stages.

I have taught many adults with no reading age but a good knowledge of number, particularly quick addition and subtraction of money; for example, fair-ground folk. I have also worked with adult pupils with a reading age of 8 + and very little number knowledge.

Some do not know that 1 represents . or 2 .. Duplicated cards containing large numbers marked like jigsaw puzzles are useful. The figure 5 marked in five parts can be cut up and counted and pieced together again.

A straightforward application of this would be:

```
              1 .
              2 ..
              3 ...
              4 ....
              5 .....
```

(1) Add these .. =
                 . =
                ... =
              ...... =
               .... =

(2) After practice without the key.
(3) Progress then to ten.

The next stage would be 2 + 3 =
                         .. ...

Use the pools. How many wins, losses, draws, etc? From the

newspaper, how many goals scored in the First Division this week? Second, Third, Fourth Division, etc.

Work cards can be easily and cheaply made, for instance:

'How many horses ran in the 3.30 p.m. race at Epsom?'

'How many ('and's), etc., are there in this story (newspaper cutting).'

I find 'Counting pictures' particularly useful as an interesting exercise in learning to count and recognize numbers.

Puzzle pictures can be drawn by joining the numbers together in numerical order. I have duplicated a graduated series, which start using only numbers from 1 to 10.

Another useful exercise for number recognition and manipulation can be based on a row of coins dated, for example, 1901, 1908, 1928, 1948, 1950, 1956, 1958.

We can use these numbers at various levels.

 e.g. (1) Add the first four figures: 1 and 9 and 0 and 1.
 (2) Add the first two numbers: 1901 and 1908.
 (3) Put the coins in their correct order.
 (4) Which is the oldest coin?
 (5) Which is the most recent?
 (6) How many years older is the 1928 coin than the 1950 one?, etc.

Some have no knowledge of money and money values, among them foreign members of the class.

Cards. A straightforward approach to begin with.

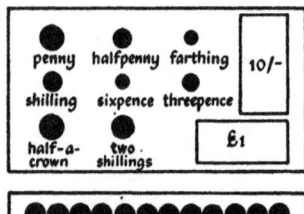

(1) Match money on money.
(2) Match names to names.
(3) Put correct coin on the X.

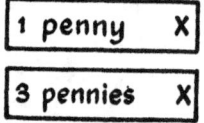

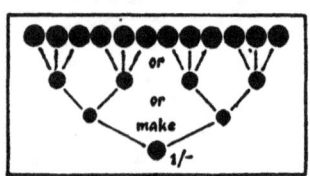

How many pennies make 1s.
How many threepences?
How many sixpences?
How many threepences in sixpence?, etc.

TEACHING BACKWARD ADULTS

I am sure that you will think of many other cards and exercises.

Shopwork using money to buy and sell is quite easy to arrange. Firms are nowadays usually pleased to send what you want with up-to-date price lists included.

We use tobacco and cigarette kiosks, ice-creams, sweets and chocolate, tinned foods, etc., – in fact anything that they will need to buy.

I try to give exercises with a reason, if I want someone to measure in ½-inches, inches, etc., I have prepared cards, the measurements of which can be copied and the whole made into a presentable model which can always be given to someone, e.g. boats, racing-cars, doll's furniture, etc.

Again you can ask: 'Cut me eight pieces of card 12 in. × 8 in. for duplicating, etc.

Or: 'I am going to Bradford next weekend, find me the distance from London to Bradford.' Using a map and mapmeter is a fascinating way of learning. Compare a mile as shown on a map to a local example. How many yards, feet, etc., does this represent, etc. Again, use their interests.

Cost of a young man's meals, cost of a meal worked out, e.g. Breakfast:

1 egg	4d.
1 rasher of bacon	8d.
Coffee made with ½-pint milk	4d.
Bread and butter	5d.
Total cost	1s. 9d.

Same approach to cost of other meals, cost per week, etc. An interesting exercise and an 'eye opener' too.

	£ s. d.
Again, Smoking 20 Cigarettes per day costs	....
Cost per week	....
Cost per month	....
Cost per year	....
Cost per lifetime	....

The young man about to be married is concerned with rents, mortgage payments, hire purchase, etc.

How much would it cost to run a 150-watt bulb for one evening? (six hours), etc. How much to run a TV set, 17-inch screen, for the same period?

Gas, coal, coke bills, reading a gas and electricity meter.
How much per bucket?
How many buckets used every day?
   ,, ,, ,, ,, ,, week, etc.
How far will one hundredweight go?
How many hundredweights would a 3-ton truck carry?, etc.
Again, a barrel of beer holds 36 gallons.
How many pints does it hold?
How many pints are there in 1 gallon?
How much does 1 gallon cost?
  ,,   ,,   ,, 4 pints ,,
  ,,   ,,   ,, 1 quart ,,
  ,,   ,,   ,, ½-gallon ,,
  ,,   ,,   ,, 7 pints ,, etc.

How much profit would the landlord make if the barrel cost £13 and he sold beer at 1*s*. a pint?

How much would I win if 'Dark-eyed Susie' won at 10 to 1 if I backed her 1*s*. to win
          2*s*. to win, etc.

Written questions such as these illustrated will encourage the adult illiterate who is good at number work to read.

How much would these essential household articles cost?

bucket	tables	crockery	linen	repairs
mop	chairs	cutlery,	bedclothes	paints,
brushes	sideboard,	etc.	curtains,	etc.
coal hod,	etc.		etc.	
etc.				

Add together the cost of a series of articles:

e.g. (1) How much would a bucket and a scrubbing-brush cost?
     (2) If you had saved £10 and bought a table for £3 and two chairs for £4. How much would you have left?
     (3) If a blanket costs £1 5*s*. how much would 3 cost?
     (4) If 4 chairs cost £6, how much would 1 cost?

TEACHING BACKWARD ADULTS

The young father to be would be interested in how much it costs to prepare for the baby's arrival.

pram £16
cot £4
nappies 2s. 10d. each.
bath £3
High chair £4, etc.

With much useful work based on this.

The young gardener (and I find many adult illiterates are interested in gardening) would again use his interests to promote reading, writing and number work.

Examples of using gardening to teach the adult illiterates.

(1) *Planting booklets* – show method of planting, e.g. depth, distance apart, cultural hints, etc.

(2) *Seed and sowing booklets*, e.g.

Broad bean	Sow Nov.-April	20 foot row	½-pint
Runner bean	,, March-July	50 foot row	½-pint
Peas	,, March onward	90 foot row	1 pint
Beetroot	,, March-July	45 foot row	½-ounce

(3) *Pest and disease booklets*, e.g.

Vegetables			Fruit and flowers		
Crop	Pest	Treatment	Crop	Pest	Treatment
Broad bean	Black fly	Derris	Apples	Aphids	Lime Sulphur
Cabbage	Caterpillar	D.D.T.	Roses	Black Spot	Bordeaux mixture

Concrete mixer for garden work, e.g. pools, steps, paths, etc.

	Cement (loose buckets)	Mixed ballast (buckets)	Water to add (buckets)
Foundation	1	6	¾
Pools, steps	1	4	½
Crazy paving	1	3	½

I have duplicated a series of ready reckoners including farthings and halfpennies. I have often been requested to teach these although the utilitarian value of teaching farthings is doubtful. The series also includes ready reckoners and exercises based on a multiplication table square, ft., in., galls., pts., lb., oz., and tons, cwt.

For those who cannot or who are not sure how to tell the time I use the key times in their day as props on which to base further understanding.

In a prison it would run:

6.0 a.m.   At 6 o'clock I get up.
7.0 a.m.   At 7 o'clock I have my breakfast.
8.0 a.m.   At 8 o'clock I start work.
10.0 a.m. At 10 o'clock I have a break.
12.0 a.m. At 12 o'clock I stop work, etc.

Jigsaw cards fitting the clock face to a picture of the particular time are useful.

So are cards fitting the clock face to the time. Also question cards based on this, for example:

When do you start work?
At what time do you get up?, etc.

The times at which TV programmes start are very helpful to the teacher of backward adults. A card could comprise:

(1) The pasted sheet of radio programmes from the *TV and Radio Times*.
(2) Beneath a series of questions, e.g. At what time did Gun Law start?

The use of quizzes can cater for all necessities in a popular and valuable way.

There are so many examples at a different attainment level that can be presented in a mature way to incorporate a variety of interests.

Finally, I feel that if a pupil works hard he deserves some recognition of work well done. A popular feature of classes of adult illiterates which I have taken has been the introduction of three-monthly reports which consists of a week by week summary of what the pupil has done and ending with a brief progress statement.

These reports provide motivation in varying degrees for better work during the next term.

TEACHING BACKWARD ADULTS

This chapter has not meant to give one cut and dried method for teaching backward adults. The methods which I have described are those which I have used and found successful for me.

Look upon them, if you like, as a list of suggestions for your own experiments in this field, with my sincere good wishes for their success.

D. H. J. PHILLIPS

Chapter XVI

A UNIFIED CURRICULUM

The general pattern of organization in the secondary modern school during the decade and a half of its existence has been that of full specialist teaching. With the present pressure on it to provide opportunity for children with sufficient ability to take recognized examinations, it is likely to remain so. But is it, in fact, the most suitable for the slow learning child? It is striking how many of the contributors to this book have, from their different points of view, had a little grumble about specialization in passing. In this final chapter, I will try to consider how best the dull child's education can be integrated.

Under specialization the child may be taught by as many as five, possibly six, different teachers in the course of one day, entailing adaptation to as many personalities and individual methods of approach. To the slow child this presents real difficulty. We must remember his mental age is well below his chronological age. We do not consider specialist teaching suitable for a child of 9, yet in fact there is little difference in mental power between a dull child of 12 and an ordinary 9-year-old.

These children are slow in all their reactions. They work at a slow pace and a very real feeling of pressure is engendered by the knowledge, possibly also the reminder, that the bell will ring. When it does terminate the lesson, not only are the children frustrated at not having finished, but they must then think quickly what they need, collect the necessary equipment, get themselves to the next place on time, and be ready to adapt to the different personality and approach. Their inability to cope with the situation brings disapproval all round.

They need individual work at their own level and pace in basic subjects, with time allocation to suit their individual needs in order

A UNIFIED CURRICULUM

that the work attempted may, by its completion, bring a sense of achievement.

Their inability to integrate knowledge without specific help is well known by those experienced in teaching them. The impossibility of integration of work under full specialization results in such knowledge as they acquire remaining in watertight compartments, and they are unable to apply it to everyday use. It is, therefore, quickly forgotten.

Specialization puts emphasis on the subject and in general on written work, which for these children is putting the cart before the horse. Their need is for experience and practice in oral expression and practical work. How can they express in writing what they are incapable of stating orally? In fact how often will they need to write? Since the amount of knowledge they are able to acquire is restricted by limited mental ability, should we not first consider carefully their needs for adult life, and then direct all their learning towards meeting those needs?

If we do this honestly, we shall see they will need to ask, as clearly and concisely as possible, for information and help in connexion with their job and running a home; to listen carefully to instructions and messages; to write a friendly letter and sometimes, though less often, a simple business one; to deal practically with money, simple measuring, and possibly weighing. They need the practical skills necessary for running a home, some training in personal hygiene and grooming, and a knowledge of the services available to them for the promotion of good health and prevention of ill health.

Schemes of work designed to meet these needs can be broadened or narrowed to suit individual ability, but they will always need to be unified if they are to be of the greatest value to the slow learning child.

The majority of teachers are not aware of the slow child's great limitations in both experience and vocabulary. Twice recently this has been forcibly brought home to me. First, at an education conference during a lecture on the teaching of arithmetic to the slow learner. The point was made that material used must be within the child's experience, an example of unsuitable material being given as that of finding the area of a lawn, to a child, living in a block of flats in an industrial town, who had never seen a lawn. The mathematics

TEACHING THE SLOW LEARNER IN THE SECONDARY SCHOOL

teacher at my side murmured, 'Good heavens! that's never struck me before.' On the second occasion, having told a child to put three and a half spoons of tea into the pot, and seen her hesitate, I asked, 'Do you know what I mean by half a spoonful?' She replied, 'No', so I showed her. My colleague who was present remarked, 'It would never have dawned on me that a girl of that age wouldn't know what half a spoonful was.'

It is only when one is able to deal with them individually and see them all round that the extent of their limitations becomes apparent.

Social training is an essential part of our education, but a much greater emphasis on it is necessary for slow children: it was no accident that this was the first topic taken up in this book. Their lack of social graces and ignorance of accepted behaviour patterns are frequently behind people's misjudgement of them, both in and out of school. They are dubbed rude when they have no intention of being so. They need to have put before them in this field aims within their capacity, and frequent opportunities to achieve them, and in addition much patient personal help. For instance, however slow a class may be, it could be given such aims as being the best behaved, most polite, most helpful class in the school, where everyone works to the best of his ability. Such aims are well within the children's capacity for achievement, but repeated opportunities must be provided and directly pointed, much help must be given and success recognized, before such a pattern of behaviour becomes habitual in the child. It entails the children's being in the care of one teacher for a large proportion of the time and is not possible under full specialization.

One of the major problems facing us if we advocate non-specialization is the lack of sufficient teachers who are able and willing to spend the greater part of their time with slow children. I use the word 'able' in terms of interest and understanding of the slow child's limitations and needs. The majority of teachers prefer teaching bright children and it is only when there is a deep concern for the slow child that interest develops into understanding. In a school where there is no one specially interested it may be best for both staff and children that all take a share in such work, rather than put the weight of class teaching on one or two resentful conscripts.

A UNIFIED CURRICULUM

We have probably all experienced clashes of personality between teacher and taught. They can create real difficulties on both sides, which are enhanced when those taught are adolescent. Perhaps the strongest reason for specialization is the relief afforded where such a clash occurs.

Two arguments are frequently used in support of full specialization.

The first is the need for adaptation to other personalities in adult life. In the world of work such adaptation is much more circumscribed than is usually thought. True, they must be able to work with their colleagues, just as they had to co-operate with other members of their class. But in such jobs as they are likely to do adaptation to superiors is usually much more limited than is supposed. It usually involves only foreman or departmental head, and providing there are no clashes of personality, this and the narrow sphere of work involved provides the stable, limited environment which is needed.

The second is based on the children's need to be as little different from the others as possible, but the operative words 'as possible' are seldom recognized or stressed. So the argument develops on the lines of 'We don't want them to feel different' so they all do homework, French, geometry, etc., without regard for whether these subjects are of value to the children, or merely, in the long run, have the effect of teaching them that they cannot learn them and in that respect are, in fact, different from the others.

If we study the children's needs we see they can best be met by the compromise of partial specialization. Within the stable environment of one teacher and one room for the majority of the work, opportunities may be given for individual work at the child's own level and pace, where a sense of achievement may be experienced, social training given emphasis, and integration of knowledge aided; in addition, through specialist teaching in such subjects as domestic science, handicrafts, art, music, and physical education, practice is given in adaptation to a limited number of personalities and approaches, and the children are enabled to feel as much like the others as possible.

Under such partial specialization, assuming the class teacher to be responsible for the core subjects, i.e. English, arithmetic, social studies, and religious education, what emphasis shall the work have?

Here I am considering the needs of girls, but what is said can be adapted for boys, if the reader considers the underlying principles of an integrated approach to school work. Reference should also be made to what Mr Beagley and Mr Taylor have advocated for boys.

These girls are the potential mothers of the next generation, most probably, though not always, in the lower income group, who, generally speaking, tend to marry younger than the brighter girls.[1] They are then faced with the problem of being a wife, running a home, raising a family, jobs difficult for anyone to do well but doubly so for those with very limited intelligence. What help can we give at school to these somewhat handicapped 'adults in the making'?

Their interests seem always to lie among the more practical subjects, domestic science, needlework, etc., so the work may well have this slant with emphasis on the practical work and integration of basic and domestic subjects as our aim.

Immediately we begin to consider integrated schemes of work we are faced with the questions – where shall it be done and who is to do it? It is obviously uneconomic to provide a fully equipped domestic science room for each such class, for in any large secondary modern school the number of slow learners needing this help will be such as to necessitate there being several backward classes. Neither do dual trained teachers, specially interested in or even willing to teach these slow children, at present exist.

The basic subjects work must, therefore, be done by the class teacher in the ordinary classroom. Once the children's need for such an approach is realized and the decision made to try it, the difficulties can be surmounted by co-operative planning and discussion on the part of teachers of domestic science and those in charge of special classes. What is chiefly needed by the class teacher is a knowledge of the general pattern of domestic science teaching, the problems met with when teaching the subject to slow learners, and co-operation from the domestic science teacher over assignments and the type of work being tackled at any particular time.

Let us look at the general pattern of domestic science work.[2]

[1] Collman, R. D., and Newlyn, D., 'Leisure Activities of Educationally Subnormal and Other Ex-pupils in England', *American Journal of Mental Deficiency*, Vol. 62, No. 3, November 1957.

[2] E. L. McIntosh, *Suggestions for planning a scheme of work in Housecraft.*

A UNIFIED CURRICULUM

Year I The Pupil Herself

The work covers personal hygiene – Preparation and serving beverages and snacks – Washing up – Laundering cloths.

Year II The Pupil and the Home

The work covers the basic processes of housecraft, e.g. basic cake mixtures, short crust pastry, simple salads, simple laundry work, and basic cleaning processes. Assignment use for revision.

Year III The Home and the Family

Basic processes are continued and topics have a bias towards planning and carrying out the normal work of the house. This work leads up to meal planning with consideration of food values, balance, variety, and cost. A freer use of assignments is made including group assignments to promote co-operation. Dinners, breakfasts, teas and suppers may be included.

Year IV The Family and the Community

The aim is to give opportunity for organizing and carrying out the work of the house, to encourage the development of initiative, resource, and a critical attitude to one's own efforts, and to widen the child's interest. It will include topics such as:

Salvage – dealing with household refuse.
Thrift – apportioning the weekly wage, savings, insurance, thrift in the use of fuel, etc.
Young Children – feeding, amusing, and general care.

From discussions I have had with teachers of domestic science in a number of schools, and from the points made by Miss Devereux in Chapter X there appears to be general agreement on the difficulties met with in teaching the subject to the slow children. First, of course, is the slowness itself which limits the amount of work that can be given and makes individual assignment work difficult. Added to this is the inability to read and comprehend an ordinary assignment card and to organize the work set in terms of both order and time, as a result of which instructions must be given orally and much of the work done as class work. There is also the children's limited knowledge of weights, measures, and money, and their inability to use them accurately. Examples given were that they do not appear to realize that four ounces and quarter of a pound are the same thing, that a gill is quarter of a pint, nor are they able to halve or double quantities in a given recipe and work out costs per meal and per head. In some cases they cannot even bring change correctly when sent shopping. Lack of both memory in the child and co-operation over money in the home are both sources of irritation. Both vocabulary and reading limitations, reinforced by limited experience of foods themselves, make the teaching of food values and its application in planning balanced meals very difficult indeed.

The object of assignments is to give training in planning, organization, and timing of work, which is so essential before the skills learned can be put to efficient use when running a home.

It was generally agreed that the child could probably work from them if the reading and organizing preparation could be done in the ordinary classroom before the lesson took place, leaving all the time in the domestic science room for practical work. It was also agreed that the study of foods and materials used, where they come from, comparative costs, and nutritional value, if done as classroom work, could be of immense help, especially if given at an appropriate time.

It is obvious that the general domestic science scheme as previously outlined could be extended into units of work in the ordinary classroom, with the child's interest in the subject and her growing interest in the adult world as the driving force to learning.

Below are typical examples of such units which have been worked with slow children.

First Year

Dairy foods: milk, butter, cheese, all of which the girls will be using in preparing beverages and snacks in their domestic science lessons.

A visit to a dairy farm – in cities this could be to a milk bottling depot – was followed by a study of milk from farm to doorstep, the history of milk, its food value.

Butter manufacture and the use of butter-milk for pig feeding and production was extended to a simple study of life in Denmark.

English cheese manufacture provided opportunity for a simple

A UNIFIED CURRICULUM

study of the dairy counties and sending letters asking for information. It was extended to look at life in Holland and Switzerland, with their contrasts.

At this stage the work can be recorded as simple sentences forming captions to the children's own illustrations – either free hand or traced. Suitable recipes can be used to start the cookery section of homecraft books, short letters of thanks written in respect of the visit, the best of which is posted; a simple vote of thanks taught and used on the occasion of the visit. The inviting, welcoming and entertaining of guests, together with thanks for hospitality form an excellent basis for speech work and social training.

Arithmetic work included capacity and cost, quantities and cost, both for a given number of people and per head, fares and very simple time-table calculations, as well as realistic shopping and making of bills.

The girls become vitally aware of the fact that the work of many people lies behind their simple meal of cocoa and sandwiches, and the unit leads on naturally to another one on beverages.

Second Year
I. *Flour*
   (a) A visit to a downland farm. Wheat, oats, barley, from seed to table and the uses we make of them.
   (b) A prairie farm in Canada. Homes, clothes, work. Wheat transport to England. Milling and its effect on food value.

II. *Sugar*
   Sugar cane growing and harvesting in the W. Indies. Clothes, homes, and work of the people. Manufacture of sugar. Typical songs.

III. *Cotton* – In connexion with their laundry work
   Life on a cotton plantation in America.
   The story of the discovery of America. The trek west, which was done by reading to the children, H. Morrow's *The Splendid Journey*. The girls' interest in films and film stars was used, and they found the state from which each came. Some plantation songs were taught in music lessons. Transport and importing of cotton led to its manufacture, costs, and uses. A little was done

on the Industrial Revolution, and the work of Lord Shaftesbury was taken in scripture. Mill workers today and where they spend their holidays led to the question, 'What does our town (which is a seaside resort) offer of interest to holiday makers?' – and to some environmental studies and visits.

Third Year

The domestic science work for this year includes meal planning and the girls can now tackle knitting themselves jumpers and cardigans or making such articles for toddlers. Therefore suitable units of work are on

> I. *Meat and Fruit* – studying life on a farm in New Zealand. Life on a ship. The uses and care of leather.
>
> II. *Wool and Fruit*
> Life on both sheep and fruit farm in Australia.
> Sea routes, air routes. Time. Fares.
> The story of the Flying Doctor.
> Australia as a penal colony through the story *Sarah Dane* which, with a little careful pruning, can be read to the girls.
> The story of Elizabeth Fry's work in connexion with prisons. The function of the police force today with a talk by a local police officer.
> The work was extended to include the manufacture of wool in England, and Agnes Furlong's *Elizabeth Leaves School*, was read to them.
> It is sometimes of great value to enlist the aid of the music teacher.
> In the unit referred to above the girls were taught 'Waltzing Matilda', and, through gramophone records, something of the work of Australian singers and musicians whom they may see and hear on television and sound radio.
>
> III. *Dried Fruits* – (in connexion with Christmas cakes which they will be making this year).
> Mediterranean lands where they grow – how they grow, are harvested, and dried.
> National costume and dances.

Fourth Year

Whenever we are facing a change in our way of life we begin to project our thoughts towards the unknown before us, and, as it were, brace ourselves to meet it.

At this stage of their school life the girls are feeling towards the world of work in which they will soon find themselves.

I suggest, therefore, that we can best help them by treating the period as one of transition from school to work, during which we try to give them as much understanding as possible of the society in which they will take their places as young adults. See, too, the sugtions made by Mr Beagley in this connexion, in the appendix to his chapter.

Examples of units of work intended to help the girls towards such understanding, which have been tried out with fourth year dull girls, and have proved of interest to them, as are follows:

I. *Setting up a Home*
 (a) Types of houses. Contact with local housing manager.
     Rent and rates.
 (b) Public Services: e.g. street lighting, cleaning, and repair; refuse collection; allotments. Contact with Borough Surveyor's Department.
 (c) Public Utility Services – gas, electricity.
     Filling in forms for supply.
     Demonstrations at gas and electricity showrooms.
     Arithmetic in connexion with running costs. Cost and care of apparatus.
 (d) Furnishing the home.
 (e) Mothercraft.
 (f) Floral decoration.

II. *Recreation*
The facilities for recreation in their town: e.g. parks and open spaces, baths, cinemas, theatres, concert halls, youth organizations, etc.

III. *The Health Services*
The sanitary inspector and his work. The health visitor, clinics,

doctors, National Health Insurance. Simple first-aid and home nursing.

IV. *Running our Town*
Our part – elections, rates, public property and our responsibilities. Visit to a council meeting (if possible). Contact with at least one councillor.

During their last year at school these children need specific help, at their own level, in preparation for work and leisure after they leave, and also for home life.

So often they either have no definite ideas on what work they want to do, or they are intent on following their friends into factory, laundry, etc., and even into work which is quite unsuited to their ability.

With the freedom from time-table pressure which is given by partial specialization, it is possible to make a survey of the types of work available in the area, and to arrange for the girls to visit those places where the work is suited to their abilities, to get some idea of qualifications necessary, hours, a typical day's work, rates of pay, opportunities for promotion, length of holidays, and to hear talks in school from personnel managers.

If contact is made with the Youth Employment Officer early in the fourth year, a talk can be given on the general state of the labour market which will provide the children with food for thought and discussion, and may possibly influence some of them to complete their fourth year at school.

They certainly need help in the use of leisure. The habit of relying on 'looking in', visits to the cinema, or hanging round undesirable cafés as the only way of using leisure seems all too prevalent. In my view, automation will bring as great a change in the way of life as did the Industrial Revolution, and the use of leisure time is likely to become a greater social problem than it is today.

Time could well be spent discussing leisure activities and local facilities for pursuing them, for which of us has not, at some time, heard the children say they don't like holidays because there is nothing to do? It is almost unbelievable that although the centre of our town is only about two miles from the Downs, one frequently comes across children who, at the age of 11, though born here, have never been on them.

The idea of cycling or rambling as a means of exploring the district might, with advantage, be put before many of them, while a study of cheap holiday facilities such as are provided by Holiday Fellowship, Youth Hostels Association, and camping in connexion with youth organizations might help to widen their outlooks in this respect.

Profitable subjects for discussion might be local cultural opportunities such as musical and dramatic societies, library facilities, theatre and concert halls with examples of productions, prices of admission, and a visit where possible. It is worth noting that even children who are really interested in drama, and show ability in that direction, will be found never to have been inside a live theatre. Yet, once introduce them to it, and you'll see them, from time to time, attending shows after they leave school.

Details of further education facilities likely to be of interest to them, e.g. dressmaking, cookery, and other handicrafts could be given.

In addition a survey might be made of local youth organizations, with name, aims, particulars of membership, place and frequency of meeting, type of activities, and the leader's name. If the children could also meet and talk with somebody keenly interested in the local youth movement, they might themselves become sufficiently interested to join their nearest club, as was the case when a councillor serving on the youth committee spoke to one of our fourth year groups.

If such work gives only a glimpse of creative leisure activities the time is well spent since it may help to break down the present habit of being spectators only. If, in addition, it leads to the use of more socially acceptable meeting places for adolescent girls and boys, then it will have made a real contribution towards solving a social problem.

In preparation for home life they will need to know where to go for various kinds of help, e.g. how to get a Home Help in emergency, where to go for financial help both for themselves in time of need or for aged relatives, how to set about getting an allotment, or what facilities there are for social life for old people. There is much value in arranging for them to have talks from social service workers, such as the leader of a Darby and Joan club, or the person in charge of the Council of Social Services.

It is invaluable for them also to meet the health visitor and come to know her so that the clinic where she works becomes synonymous with friendliness, a place to which they will not hesitate to go for help with their own children.

Every health visitor has received special training in the teaching of mothercraft, and is available to schools for these lessons which are an important part of fourth year work and form a valuable link with adult life.

If during the three previous years, some work has been done on hygiene and simple human biology, including reproduction, as part of the basic work, the children will know something of how their bodies work and be ready to learn how to care for the baby and toddler which will in all probability only too soon be their responsibility.

A typical syllabus is as follows:

> Value of parentcraft.
> Cot and bedding, layette.
> Dressing baby and putting on a napkin.
> Bathing a baby.
> Breast feeding.
> Bottle feeding.
> Daily routine.
> Weaning.
> Milestones.
> Daily routine for a 1-year-old.
> Feeding, rest and play for toddlers.

In addition to this our health visitor took a series of lessons on:

> The work of a health visitor.
> Clinics and how they help us.
> Prevention of ill health and promotion of good health.
> Infectious diseases and isolation.

Some of these lessons and those on biology and simple hygiene referred to above can be supplemented by films, examples of which are listed at the end of the chapter.

The knowledge gained and the practice the girls have in actually doing the job stand them in good stead and give them confidence when they are faced with preparation for, and care of, their own children.

Since they will all have a vote they should see themselves not only as members of a home but also as citizens.

In preparation for this it is possible to give a general idea of local government work even to slow children if it is done under such a guise as, 'How is our town run and in what way can we help?'

They learn a lot through meeting people, and there is much value in arranging for them to have talks from such officials as the housing manager, sanitary inspector, an officer from the Borough Surveyor's Department, etc.

If, also, the actual cost in a given year of some of the public services is made known to them (available at the public library), as well as the source of income to meet such costs, it will help to eradicate from the children's minds the picture of the local council as 'They' who have plenty of money and should always be doing more for us. It will also provide an opportunity for replacing it with a more accurate one which will include themselves as citizens with responsibilities as well as rights.

In arguing the pros and cons of specialization I said that a much greater emphasis on social training is necessary for slow children. An excellent opportunity for such training can be created by the introduction of 'family group' work, which will also help the children to feel that they 'belong' in a large school and that their work is of value to others. Some examples of this in operation, will help to clarify what I mean.

It involved the four special classes, one for each year, which were working on unified schemes.

A second year class was taking 'Flour' as a unit of work. A visit to a mixed farm in a village a few miles outside the town was arranged, in which a fourth year class joined.

The second years visited the farm, returning with specimen ears of wheat, oats, and barley, while the fourth years made a survey of the village in order to get some idea of what living in a rural district meant.

The visit was followed by an invitation to the second years to refreshments in the fourth years' room.

Wheat, oats, and barley were used to make scones, flapjacks, and lemon barley water, and the three kinds of cereal were on show, both as grown and in the form of wheat flour, rolled oats, and patent barley.

The fourth year girls had not only to work out the quantities required and their cost, and do the necessary cooking, table laying, and floral decoration, but each one had to receive one or more guests, including the visiting teacher, seat, and entertain them.

Later, the second years invited not only the fourth year girls, but the first and third year classes also, to a performance of the play which they had written around the story of Ruth and Naomi.

As well as providing a suitable audience for the slow children, it gave an opportunity for votes of thanks and appreciation of the hard work which the children had put into the production.

In connexion with speech work, we use the tape-recorder. The first year children are very nervous of it, so the fourth years invited them to their room and demonstrated its use, after which the first years tried it out.

In return the first years invited the fourths to their room for biscuits and cocoa. As they had no means of making the latter, the older girls did it for them, and were much entertained by the way the younger ones served it. In fact a good time was had by all. But again, there was much value in the training in pleasant manners and acceptance of responsibility which was involved.

Slipshod speech is not the prerogative of slow children but it enhances their difficulties; lazy tongue and lips, and untrained ear, are part of the reason for both their inability to write correct English and to express orally what they wish to say. They find great difficulty in merely pronouncing words which to the brighter children present no difficulty at all, as well as in such things as delivering a message accurately, speaking clearly over the phone, performing an introduction correctly and so on.

These are all covered in the speech work syllabus recently introduced for use with the four special classes. It is a modification of that which is used throughout the rest of the school. The aim of the work is clear, pleasant, correct speech, and a badge is available for those reaching the required standard. The work is well within the capacity of the majority of our slow learners, so that in this respect they are able to feel the same as all the others.

Great benefit is derived by the children from the emphasis on speech work throughout the four years, and integrated work such as I have suggested gives much opportunity for both realization of its value and for using what is learned.

What I have been trying to suggest is ways of meeting the needs of these somewhat handicapped children in the ordinary school, and of helping them to integrate their knowledge so that it can be applied to every day situations.

Much that is essential in their education remains outside such integrated work, which must be supplemented by literature, poetry, religious education, and by specialist teaching in art, craft, physical education, and music; although at times, as has been shown, these can also be naturally incorporated.

Perhaps the greatest value of such an approach is that it affords special opportunities for training in home membership. In *Purpose in the Curriculum* S. Nisbet defines this as, 'preparation for effective and satisfying membership, in whatever capacity, of the most fundamental and important social unit in the community – the home and family'.

The children we teach are the potential parents of the next generation, who will in fact create the home environment which exerts such a strong influence on the young. The acquisition of skills is certainly necessary for the efficient running of a home, but the development of good attitudes is even more important if that home is to provide a good environment for the children. Moral, social and citizenship training should therefore be an integral part of the teacher's work if it is to be effective in helping these slow children to become both good parents and good citizens.

Bibliography
CLEUGH, M. F., *The Slow Learner*, Methuen, 1957.
GLOVER, A. H. T., *New Teaching in a New Age*, Nelson, 1946.

TEACHING THE SLOW LEARNER IN THE SECONDARY SCHOOL

INGRAM, C. P., *Education of the Slow Learning Child*, Ronald, 1953.

KIRK, S. A. and JOHNSON, G. O., *Educating the Retarded Child*. Harrap, 1954.

NISBET, S., *Purpose in the Curriculum*, U.L.P., 1957.

Films

A Brother for Susan, free loan, Sound Services.
Growing Girls, free loan, Sound Services.
Jenny Comes Home, free loan, Sound Services.

J. M. COOPER

Index

adolescence 15 18 27 28 33 53 119 253
adults, see backward adults
approved schools 214-229
arithmetic, 4 5 60-82 127 146 149 170 171-172 176 200 217-219 221 222 234 243-248 251-252 253 257 259
  aims 62-3
  bibliography 82
  games 66-68
  mental 65-66 68
  methods 63-71
  organization 68-71
  practical 65 70-71 127 146 170 200 217-219 245
  records 60-61 208 209-210
  scheme 71-81
  testing 60-62 71-72 209 215
  textbooks 66 81-82
art 83-103 164 200
  aims 87-90
  and craft, see craft
  applied 99 101
  bibliography 103
  design 98-99 100 140-141
  display 102-103
  organization 88-90
  room 88 102
  scheme suggestions 98-102
  specialization 85-86 101-102
  teacher 84-86
  teaching 90-96
assembly 7 194 198
attitudes,
  children's 3 5 12 13 60 88 105 112 114 115 117 124 157 211 217 225 227-228 265, see also behaviour
  teacher's 2 3 4 5 6 12 13 14 16 19 28 84 85-86 89 115 159 162-163 167 216 231
aural discrimination—reading 51-52
aural perception—music 110
aural training—music 120

backward adults, teaching of 230-249
  arithmetic 232 243-248
  reading 232-242
backwardness, causes of 83 94 230-231, see also dull children
basketwork 139-140 224
Beagley, W. C. 58 65 189 192 254 259
behaviour 2 4 6 7 33 144-146 147 150 159-163 205 211-212 213 214 215 216 217 252, see also attitudes
Beinder, R. E. 142
Bienstock, S. F. 107
Binet, A. 110
Brien, W. 125
Burt, C. 108 167 215

cardboard modelling 137-138
Carpenter, M. 217
case histories 211-213 214-216, see also records
centre of interest, see projects
Chamberlain, M. 120
child guidance clinic 211
citizenship 30 263 265
classifying schools 214-215
clay modelling 138
Cleugh, M. F. 40
clubs 9 103 123 174 206 225 226-227
Coffman, A. R. 106
Collman, R. D. 254
confidence 3-4 6 9 23 24 35 41 132 137 142 146 153 163 164 169 205 216
Cooper, J. M. 65 154 167 170 266
co-operation,
  at home 15 16 136-137 144 256
  in school 136-137 138 149 168

Courtier, J. 110
craft 96-97 99 129 131-142 200 219 224 235
  bibliography 142
  display 140
  materials 135
  organization 133-136
  suggested activities 137-140 141
curriculum 63 166 170 199 250-266

dancing 9 18 24-25
Dearborn, F. 108
delinquency 2 214
Denisch, M. 126
Devereux, H. 65 165 255
diagnostic tests 60 208 209
discipline 19 90 115 133 159 229 230, see also attitudes
Diserens, C. M. 110
domestic science, see housecraft
drama 4 28 51 126-130 172 176 180 220 261 264
  bibliography 130
dull children, characteristics and needs 1-2 3 6 7 11 12 18-19 20 21-22 46 52 66 67 84 104-108 112 114-115 116 117 118 132 143-153 160-163 174 250-252 255-256

education—aims 1
Eng, H. 93
english 54-59 170 171 199 219-221 236 253 264, see also drama, letter-writing, reading speech
  bibliography 59
  composition 55-56
  grammar 30 56
environmental studies 65 166-189 192, see also projects, bibliography, 189-191

Fernald, G. 38 242
films 155 168 172 238 257 263 266
Fleming, M. K. 10
Furlong, A. 258
further education 261

Gagg, J. C. 233
gardening 139 169 221 223 235 247, see also nature study
Gates, A. I. 38
geography 14 28 129 167 170 256-258, 'see also environmental studies
Gibbs, E. 94
Glenn, M. 105 107 113 115
Golding, C. G. 130
grammar 30 56

handicrafts 131-142, see also craft
health education 11-26
  bibliography 26
health visitor 259 262
histograms 209-210
history 14 28 129 167 170 173 258-264, see also environmental studies
hobbies, 29 260-261, see also clubs
home environment 2 6 13 53 63 84 136 138 144 145 152 165 168 209 265
Hooper, C. 122
housecraft 14 65 97 143-165 169 170 254-264
  bibliography 165 254
  schemes of work 154-158 254-264
  standards 150-153 155 157 159

intelligence tests 36 41 60-61 209 215

Jacques, R. 120
Jersild, A. T. 107

Keir, G. 38-43
Keller, H. 38 242
kinaesthetic methods 38-39 242-243

leavers 8 65 102 152 158
letter-writing 56 170 171 198 199 203 220 239-240 251 257
library,
  public 58 199 203 220 261 263
  school 57 175 203 220

INDEX

Lombard, 110
Lyon, L. H. 32 57

McMahon, D. 120
Mainwaring, J. 122
McIntosh, E. L. 254
McKinder, M. 237
Mellalieu, W. N. 119
memory 144-146
Merrill, M. A. 36 61
metalwork 14 97 139
mime, 51 128
Monroe, M. 38
moral education 8-10 215-217 228 265
Morrow, H. 257
mothercraft 259 262
Mursell, J. L. 105 107 113 115 122
music 104-124 257 258
  ability 105-108
  and drama 127
  aural work 110 120
  bibliography 124-125
  changing voice 119
  corporate activies 123
  creative work 122
  environment 108-110
  instrumental 123
  singing, songs 107 111-114 116 119 200 257
  standards 113-116
  teaching methods 116-119
Myers, J. 103 140

Nameny, G. 106
nature study 16 173-174 199 221 223-224 226 227
needlework 9 97 101 138-139 163-165 254
Newlyn, D. 254
non-readers 33-35 39 41 42 43 44 46 48 50 53 116 219 231
Nisbet, S. 265

oral work, see speech and oral work

paper modelling 137-138
parents, see co-operation at home, also home environment
Phillips, D. H. J. 39 249

phonics 38 43 48 52 220 238 240-242
physical education 11-26 200 212 226
  aims 17
  bibliography 26
  organized games 22-23
  planning the programme 18-22
  remedial exercises 22
  suggested game-like exercises 25-26
Pichot, P. 106
poetry 9 100 265
project work 5 56 58 157 166-189 221-223 256-264
  bibliography 189-191 265-266
  examples of 177-188, 221-223 256-260
  study titles 188-189
public services 259 263
puppetry 97 129 220 236

radio programmes 7 30 56 168 171 172 236 238 248
Ralph, R. G. 57
Read, H. 126
readers 42-43 49 50 55 58 220 235
reading 4 33-59 128 129 146-149 170 171 199 219-220 232-243
  activities 40 43-52 54 219-220 232-243
  bibliography 59
  games 46-50
  records 37-38 208
  testing 36 37 38 41 42 209 215
records 207-213 216 217
  arithmetic 60-61 110 208
  confidential 202 208-213
  for class display 207-208
  reading 37-38 208
religious education 6-8 9 10 14 28 129 194 196 198 228 253 264 265
Richards, M. E. 82
Rothney 108

Say, E. A. 26
Schonell, F. J. 37 38 61 215

school journeys 192-206
  educational programme 197-201
  follow up 206
  preparation for 192-196 201-204
  social value of 205-206
school meals 13-14
Scottish Education Department 107 112 122
sex education 15-16 262
singing, see music
Sleight, G. F. 61
Smith, M. 213
social education 1-10 17 23 30-31 97 116 126 137 170 205-206 215 225 227-229 252-257 259 260 263-264 265
social services 172 178 251 258 259 260 261-262 263
social studies, see environmental studies
special classes 39-40 143 212 213 254 263 265
special schools 40 106 143 231
specialization 12 85-86 101-102 131 166 167 250-253 263 265
speech and oral work 27-32 57 114 128-129 172 176 219 236 251 257 264-265
spelling 56 158 176 209 239
Sterry, E. G. W. 173 206
Stopa, J. 59 242
stories 7 55 58 100 129 219 243
swimming 18 23-24

tape recorder 27 129 236 264

Taylor, R. S. 229 254
Terman, L. W. 36 61
tests,
  arithmetic 60-62 71-72 209 215
  attainment 209 215
  diagnostic 60 208 209
  intelligence 36 41 60-61 209 215
  music 104 107
  reading 36 37 38 41 42 209 215
  spelling 209
topics, see project work

Valentine, C. W. 106
visits, educational 10 56 58 96 102 123 155 157 167 171 172 173 195 196 198 219 227 256 257 260 263
visual discrimination 38 51-52
vocational guidance 32 171 177 179 228 259 260
vocational training 32 87 155 215 224-225
voice, change of 119

Wing, H. D. 104 106 107 108 122
Winn, C. 107
Witty, P. 55
woodwork 14 97 134-136 140 141 169 220 235

youth employment office 155 228 260
youth organizations 227 259 261

For Product Safety Concerns and Information please contact our EU
representative GPSR@taylorandfrancis.com
Taylor & Francis Verlag GmbH, Kaufingerstraße 24, 80331 München, Germany

www.ingramcontent.com/pod-product-compliance
Lightning Source LLC
Chambersburg PA
CBHW052218300426
44115CB00011B/1745